We Can't For

PART TWO
More Memories of World War II Veterans

Doris Eggleston

Roll of Honor, Sidney, Ohio—courtesy William Zorn

CHICAGO SPECTRUM PRESS
4824 Brownsboro Center
Louisville, Kentucky 40207
800-594-5190

Printed in the U.S.A.

10 9 8 7 6 5 4 3 2 1

Books can be ordered directly from:
Evanston Publishing
4824 Brownsboro Center
Louisville, Kentucky 40207
800-594-5190

ISBN: 1-886094-91-8

THIS BOOK IS DEDICATED TO ALL THOSE WHO HAVE RISKED THEIR LIVES FOR THEIR COUNTRY AND TO THOSE WHO GAVE THE NECESSARY SUPPORT TO MAKE IT ALL POSSIBLE.

Thanks to all the veterans who have taken time to write out their memories and send them to me; to Dr. Milo B. Tesar for writing the Introduction; to the librarians at Amos Memorial Public Library, Sidney, Ohio, and to those at Petersburg, Alaska, who have been so helpful in my research; to Betty McCasland for reading the manuscript and always being interested in my progress; to my husband for his endless assistance and encouragement; and to our daughters and their families who have given moral support.

Troy, Ohio

TABLE OF CONTENTS

INTRODUCTION
Milo B. Tesar, Major, Field Artillery, WW II
Professor Emeritus, Michigan State University

FORWARD

PERSONAL EXPERIENCES (in own words)

EFFECTS OF THE ATOMIC BOMB, Nagasaki, Japan

PERSONAL EXPERIENCES (in own words)

INTRODUCTION

Pearl Harbor, December 7, 1941: The unprovoked aerial bombing of our ships by Japan, without a declaration of war, with over one thousand men entombed in the USS Arizona and many soldiers killed or wounded on land, started World War II for the United States. President Roosevelt called the bombing "a date which will live in infamy" in his December 8 address to Congress, which immediately declared war against Japan and Germany.

"Remember Pearl Harbor" galvanized America's will to defeat Imperial Japan and Nazi Germany in World War II in 1945, after 3½ years of conflict.

Sixteen million Americans, young and some older, responded to the call to defend their country. The experiences of some of the 15½ million air, land and sea survivors in Europe and the Pacific are presented in this book.

In 1985 my wife and I visted Hiroshima, completely rebuilt in brick after the 1945 atom bomb. (I saw that destruction while in the army of occupation in September, 1945; only a few brick chimneys were left standing; wooden buildings were incinerated.) We visited the Peace Museum, which had been built near the epicenter of the bomb. It depicted the bomb's effects on mannequins, showing how strips of skin were falling from the victims who survived the explosion. There were many photos of those killed by the atom bomb. Japanese tourists found it a prime attraction. Photos of the bomb cloud and Hiroshima's destruction by the U.S. atom bomb were most evident. Cameras were flashing everywhere.

There was no explanation in the Peace Museum that the U.S. declared war on Japan *only* after the Japanese bombed our ships in Pearl Harbor—without a declaration of war. There were *no* photos of their destruction of part of our navy at Pearl Harbor. And there were *no* photos or description of the USS Arizona where a thousand U.S. sailors, killed by Japan at Pearl Harbor, are entombed—and that another thousand military personnel and civilians were killed in that unprovoked attack on December 7, 1941.

The world knows today that atom bombs on Hiroshima and Nagasaki ended World War II, with Japan's unconditional surrender on V-J Day August 15, 1945. Some historian revisionists, however, contend that the bombs were not necessary, that Japan was ready to surrender. The Emperor was ready but the controlling Japanese army was not. The army refused to "surrender unconditionally" as demanded by the Potsdam Proclamation of the U.S., England, and Russia in late July. The U.S. dropped the bombs to get Japan to surrender unconditionally—and to end World War II without the loss of any more lives on both sides.

The loss of 95,155 Japanese civilians in the two bomb blasts is most regrettable. But it is likely a much lower loss than the estimated total loss of possibly a million Japanese military and American civilians if the U.S. and allies had invaded Japan in late 1945. Many in this book, and in the rest of our forces, would have made the supreme sacrifice in those invasions starting in November 1995.

Dr. Milo B. Tesar
Major, Field Artillery, WW II
Prof. Emeritus, Michigan State University

Altar of the Nation, recognized in 1957 by Congress as
"the first memorial to all men and women who have given their
lives in service to this country." Courtesy Jed Brummer,
Cathedral of the Pines, Rindge, NH.

FORWARD

A brief summary of World War II, as well as for Korea, Vietnam, and Desert Storm, was included in *We Can't Forget! Memories of World War II, Korea, Vietnam, and Desert Storm, in War Zones and on the Homefront.*

However, the account of the U.S. during World War II would not be complete without an acknowledgment of the part the Aleutian Islands played. Their strategic position made them a steppingstone to the U.S. for the Japanese. The importance of the expulsion of the Japanese from the Aleutians cannot be minimized. Because of this, "American Land Bombed and Invaded!" is included in this Part Two of *We Can't Forget!*

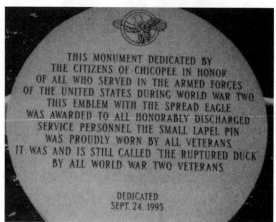

WWII monument, Chicopee, MA. Courtesy Delfo Barabani

PRISONERS OF WAR

Parade, Ft. Loramie, OH, 6/29/97. Courtesy Robert, Trevor and John Huston

Rockport, TX

RAYMOND F. HALLORAN

MENLO PARK, CALIFORNIA

Air Corps, 878th Bomb Squad, 499th Bomb Group, 73rd Bomb Wing
Navigator, B-29, 1st Lt., 1942-46
Duty in Pacific. P.O.W.

On their fourth mission they had taken off on January 27, 1945, from Saipan at about 7 a.m. aboard V-Square 27. They were enroute to a strike against the toughest target of them all...the Nakajima Aircraft Engine Plant at Musashino, Tokyo, Japan....

Sixty-two B-29s were met by 984 fighter attacks, beginning before landfall until after coast-out. It was a wild air battle, Japan's most vigorous defense against our B-29 forces. Target 357 was the best defended target in the Tokyo area. U.S. B-29s visited this target 12 times during the air assault against Japan....

Our 499th Bomb Group lost three B-29s that day....For Hap and his crew it was also a fateful day....They were attacked by Japanese fighter planes after passing Mt. Fuji, well down their bomb run. While still slightly west of their target, at about 32,000 feet of altitude, in one quick pass a twin-engine Nick fighter came in from one-o'clock high. Firing its 20 mm. cannon, the Nick blew out the greenhouse nose of their B-29. The Nick also disabled the electrical system; the instruments were shot out; and the B-29 caught fire. Above all, the pilot could no longer control his airplane. He used the interphone and the alarm bell to order the crew to bail out.

Somewhere between 30,000 feet and 27,000 feet the B-29 made a long lingering descent. Hap could only estimate their altitude since the instruments had been badly damaged. He had time to consider several things....First, it looked like it would be a long time before he might have a decent meal again. He took a few moments to gulp down the turkey sandwiches and chocolate custard he had brought with him on the mission. Then he quickly tightened the leg straps on his parachute harness. This was an important standard practice. Finally, he snapped on his chest pack parachute. The crew was thwarted in its attempt to get out of the B-29. The exit ordinarily would have been through the nose landing gear hatch, with the nose gear extended. With the electrical system disabled, however, the nose gear would not extend normally. That left the manual system, but it was jammed and would not work either. The only way out would have to be through the forward bomb bay. However, the bomb bay was still full of the high explosive bombs meant for their target. The bomb bay doors were about 70 percent open. Hap did not explain to me why the bombs were not salvoed manually....The crew members found that there was just enough room for them to slide under the bombs and fall free from the bomb bay.

Raymond F. Halloran

....Hap estimates that he got out of the B-29 at about 27,000 feet. He suddenly encountered a severe temperature shock. From the nominally 70 degrees cabin temperature he dropped into roughly minus 58 degrees, a 128 degree drop....

Hap was able to free fall until he reached somewhere between 7,000 feet and 4,000 feet. When his chute opened he had another sudden moment of stress, when he lost one of his fur-lined boots. For a brief wild moment he thought he had lost part of his leg and foot. Then two other things hit him: first, the extreme quiet of his noiseless descent, and then, he says, severe fright set in for the first time, as he contemplated his unknown future. Below him he could see people following his chute. A crowd was gathering. What a situation he was in. He was still a very young man, one week short of his 23rd birthday. Their tail gunner was evidently dead in the airplane, but 10 of his crew had bailed out. Hap had no idea of the status of any of the others.

B-29 bombers in World War II passing Mt. Fujiyama enroute Tokyo target, January 1945. FLAK and Japanese fighter planes just ahead.

Hap landed in a northeast suburb of Tokyo, to be greeted by a crowd of at least 2,000 Japanese citizens, who beat him, kicked him, and stoned him. He remembered that he left his .45 caliber Colt automatic back on the airplane. He concluded that this was probably the smartest thing he did. He undoubtedly would have died right then and there if a Japanese army truck had not driven up, with orders to bring him back alive for interrogation. He had been in critical condition from those beatings before the MPs arrived. They had to take him forcefully from the crowd. They blindfolded him, tied him up and gagged him with pieces from his own parachute. He was thrown into the truck. A Luger-type pistol was put to his head. Hap told me that this happened over and over again. He told me it was the beginning of an ordeal that was to include 67 days of solitary confinement, then two days locked in an animal cage at Tokyo's Ueno Zoo, when he was put on public display. He was then confined for several months at a concentration camp at Omori, with 43 barracks mates, mostly B-29 crew members....

Hap told me that there was not a day during his initial confinement when he was not beaten and that it was invariably administered with a steel rifle butt. His beatings included his head and all body parts, front and back, down to his feet. He said there was not a day that he did not feel was his last. The threat of death as a war criminal was kept hanging over him throughout his captivity....

Although he was blindfolded at all times, he came to realize that he had at first been placed in a special prison. It was a torture prison built originally to house Japanese citizens in solitary confinement. It was called "Kempai Tai." He was taken from his cell daily for interrogation. The Japanese were trying to force him to tell them about the B-29 airplane and his organization back on Saipan. He was usually unable to walk due to his daily beatings, so his captors dragged him across the courtyard to the interrogation room. Snow often covered the ground so he would be dragged through the snow. His blindfold was removed when these sessions began, but the beatings never stopped. There was always the threat of immediate death. His diet was meager, sometimes only one small rice ball daily, or two, or maybe three.

One day...he saw a full-blown blueprint of the B-29 mounted on a wall. The blueprint was displayed when his captors opened a curtain on the wall. He said it seemed like it must have been at least 10 or 12 feet long. The drawing showed a cutaway view of the B-29 and it showed every possible detail....He immediately had the strong belief that if they had that print they surely must have had every other B-29 blueprint....

Hap was eventually moved to a new location, into what had been a horse stable. He was to learn later that it was right next to the moat around the Royal Palace and that the stables had undoubtedly housed the horses used by the Royal family. He was still kept blindfolded at least a portion of the time he was in his cell, and he was always blindfolded when taken out of his cell for whatever reason. The food did not improve. Worst of all, next to the beatings, was that he could not bathe. He became covered with sores. He had bugs of all kinds, and he knew he was filthy. Life was at a terribly low ebb.

I asked Hap about his awareness of our radical change in tactics when we started the fire blitz early on the morning of March 10, 1945. ....Some 16.8 square miles of the big city burned to the ground. It proved to be one of the largest fires in the history of mankind. He was very much aware of what was taking place, as he pieced it all together later. He was not blindfolded that night, but it was so dark in his cell that he might as well have been. He could still hear and feel, even though his hands and feet were bound to his horse stall cell.

The first thing he noticed was the great noise and vibrations of many powerful engines. He thought, "Where would the Japanese have possibly come up with so many airplanes?" The B-29s roared over the city at between 6,000 feet and 8,000 feet above sea level, at about 2A.M. or 3A.M. Then he began to feel the heat of the fire and see flickering light from a small window high in his cell. His place of confinement was on the edge of the area which was burned that night. His cell became very hot and quite bright. The roof of the horse stable prison caught fire. His captors, however, managed to put out the roof fire with sand and so Hap was spared again.

He heard many citizens of the city outside the horse stable prison running to avoid the fire, then jumping into the nearby moat at the north edge of the Emperor's Palace. He could also hear the roar of the winds associated with the firestorm. It was frightening....By then he knew those engines he had heard were our B-29s.

...one of the guards, a kindly person, came in late that next morning for his shift of duty. He told of seeing bodies of dead civilians stacked on top of one another in great heaps. He also told Hap that his captors were discussing and planning to kill all the B-29 prisoners that morning. He then reached through the little access slot in the cell door and shook Hap's hand and wished him well.

Then came the Ueno Zoo experience. He was taken to an empty animal cell. All animals had by then been removed from the zoo. His blindfold was removed, and he was stripped of all of his clothes. For two very long days the citizens of Tokyo streamed by his cell to see this bedraggled B-29 crew member. There may not have been any animals left in the zoo, but the Japanese had put on display a new kind of animal. It was associated with the dreaded B-29....

From the horse stable Hap was finally moved to Omori on April 2. The daily beatings were reduced considerably, but the food was just as limited. At last he was thrown in with a large group of Americans, mostly airmen. It was in fact his first look at another American. He was astonished when the man standing right next to him at his first roll call answered to the name of his aircraft commander, 1st Lt. E. G. Smith. Both men looked so miserable and disreputable that neither recognized the other. It was quite a reunion. Five of the "Rover Boys' Express" had survived their bailout from V-Square 27. They were now located in the same P.O.W. camp at Omori.

The most famous prisoner in the Omori camp was Colonel Gregory "Pappy" Boyington, a Marine Corps pilot with the famed Black Sheep Squadron VMA-214. Not only had Boyington shot down 28 enemy aircraft, but his squadron had accounted for 197 airplanes brought down....It was here that Hap and Boyington became friends. Halloran was the first to inform Boyington of his award of the Congressional Medal of Honor by President Roosevelt posthumously. Everyone in the Navy and the USA believed he was dead. President Truman presented the actual medal to Boyington at the White House after he was repatriated following the War.

Greg "Pappy" Boyington's Black Sheep Squadron taken on Vaella Lavella Island November 1943, two months before Boyington was shot down off Rabaul in Southwest Pacific, WWII — courtesy Hap Halloran

Hap's confinement at Omori was far different than what had gone on before. There were about 500 American prisoners of war in the Omori camp, which seemed to be a sort of headquarters P.O.W. camp. As one of the many so-called federal or special prisoners, Hap was still under 24-hour guard. He could not associate with or talk to prisoners from Corregidor or Bataan....He was to find out later that his special status as being alive and a prisoner of war of the Japanese meant that his captors did not recognize his existence. Their obligation was to report his status to the International Red Cross. No one in America knew that these special prisoners were still alive. That included Boyington. Some of his flying mates had seen his airplane explode just before it hit the water in the South Pacific. They believed it would have been impossible for him to survive, but he did. He had then been plucked from the ocean by a Japanese submarine. He was eventually brought to Japan.

Hap was one of 43 prisoners kept in a Butler-type building day and night, except when they were taken out under guard in work parties. At first they cleaned up the rubble which remained from our fire bombing missions. Later, toward the close of the war, they were put to work digging caves back into the sides of nearby hills....there were 24 B-29 crew members at Omori. In addition, there was a B-24 pilot along with two Marines and the survivors of a Navy submarine crew which had been captured that he knew of.

Hap told us that some of the wildest moments in his captivity were when our P-51 Mustangs and U.S. Navy fighter aircraft came over at about mast height, strafing with their machine guns. If they were not out on a work party, the prisoners were invariably locked up in their confinement building, unable to get out and into slit trenches. They would just have to stay put and take whatever came. Hap said that the only way you could get out except on a work party was to be given a special ticket to use the latrine. When such an attack came the guards would not issue any tickets.

...on one occasion Pappy Boyington was out on a ticket when an attack began. He was headed back to the barracks when the bullets started to fly. Boyington was just passing a special air raid shelter used by the top Japanese officers of the camp. It had old-fashioned storm cellar double doors on it. It was off limits for any prisoner to use this facility. Pappy Boyington, with .50 caliber bullets flying all around him, made a dive for the cellar doors, off limits or not. He was down in the old cellar air raid shelter for the better part of two hours. Finally the raid was over. Hap and his fellow prisoners had about given up on Pappy. "Poor old Pappy," they said to themselves,

"He's gone and done it this time." Suddenly the double doors opened and out came Pappy Boyington. He was laughing all the way. It appeared that Pappy had been the guest of the prison commandant and his staff over a bottle of sake. He was accompanied by a couple of guards armed with big rifles, with their bayonets fixed, who prodded him in the posterior all the way back to the entrance of his barracks. Hap and the others were certain that no one in the whole camp could have gotten away with that except Pappy Boyington....

Through it all, there was the daily fear for his life...he had absolutely no certainty that he would live through any given day. There were still those occasional beatings, always with rifle butts. The rifles always had fixed bayonets. Those beatings were later to become the basis of many a nightmare.

I finally asked Hap about the P.O.W. supply drop missions we had flown with our B-29s. Had he gotten in on any of them? Yes, indeed. "It was beautiful," he said. What a sight it was for all of them in their enclosure. A friendly guard had already told them of the surrender, and as a matter of fact conditions began to improve. They began to receive more food. The beatings suddenly stopped. There was a complete changeover in the attitude of their captors. When the supply drops began, there was one very serious problem....The cargo chutes would sometimes part company with the double-drum arrangement, and their loads suddenly became missiles. Then it would get highly dangerous in their compound. The clothing, the medicine, and especially the food were enthusiastically received. It was definite confirmation that the War was over. Hap said, "We loved those B-29 guys who came to help us."

Hap's food had usually consisted of two or three rice balls daily. He weighed 215 pounds when he was captured and 112 pounds as he stood on the hospital ship on September 2, the day the Instruments of Surrender were signed on the deck of USS Missouri. The ceremony also included the overflight of 464 B-29s that day, which gave him a very special thrill. He told us, "I stood on the deck and cried when the B-29s flew over. What a great day. For me, it was as if the B-29 guys were coming back to take care of their own."

What about after the War? Hap told us that several things happened. First, he was repatriated to the USA, and he began to fit into civilian life. It was not easy....

Undoubtedly his worst concern was the recurring night-mares he suffered over 30 years. He simply could not forget his terrifying experiences while in captivity. He told me that his nightmares fell into three categories: (1) falling through space; (2) fire and flames; and (3) the beatings. During some of these nightmares he would climb into closets to avoid the beatings. He would sometimes even tear closet doors off their hinges. There would be times when he would cry out so loudly that persons in adjoining hotel rooms would call the management to report that their next door neighbor was being attacked....He was only experiencing nightmares and screaming for help.

Hap finally decided there could be only one way to bring himself out of this state, to return to Tokyo and the place where he had been confined. He needed to make the return trip to Saipan, the part of his January 27, 1945, mission which he was not able to complete. This preferably needed to be done on the anniversary of that mission. He then started to plan just how he could accomplish all of this.

It was in May, 1984, that Hap finally made it back to Tokyo. He was able to arrange his itinerary with the help of the U.S. Embassy and U.S. Ambassador Mike Mansfield. He toured most of the major cities of Japan. He visited the Emperor's Palace. There were two other events, however, which were to become unforgettable. First, he had communicated with and arranged to meet one of his captors in the Omori P.O.W. camp, Kaneyuki Kobayashi, the one guard who had befriended him and who had shared a few bites of chocolate and who gave him encouragement. The P.O.W.s called him Johnny. Johnny was there at the Tokyo International Airport to meet him. He served as his host and tour guide during a portion of his 1984 visit.

Johnny had been an Imperial Naval Intelligence cadet. He had quietly informed the prisoners of all the destruction which was taking place throughout his country. He evidently had no delusions about the War being lost. Later, Hap was to vouch for Kobayashi's entry into the USA to attend the University of Illinois. This 1984 meeting with Johnny, however, was a key event.

The second important stop Hap made with Johnny was at the site of the old Omori P.O.W. camp. There were two check-points which both Hap and Johnny were able to locate, which confirmed that they were in the right place. Much of Tokyo had been rebuilt. There had been an old Shell gas station and a "meshi" house which the prisoners would see from their camp. The old Shell sign was one of their few ties back to the USA. As for the meshi house, it had been a place where just one woman had worked, making rice cakes for use in other parts of the community. The prisoners could smell that operation, and Hap said they would give most anything for some of that rice cake. Both the Shell station and the meshi house were still standing....A real flood of memories came over Hap as he stood there with Johnny and recalled the difficult months of his captivity.

Hap repeated...how pleased he had been with the cooperation of the U.S. Embassy staff....They were able to arrange for Hap to meet and visit with the leading living Japanese fighter ace of the war, Saburo Sakai....Hap's crew knew it had been shot down by a Nick. Hap's idea was to track down the actual pilot who had shot them down if at all possible. He asked Saburo Sakai to help him with this search.

During the time he spent in Tokyo....he was introduced to a well-past-70-year-old ricksha driver, Takuii Inaii. Mr. Inaii told him through Johnny about the first days under General MacArthur as Allied Supreme Commander. He described how the crowds would gather to bow to him as he arrived each day at the Dai Ichi building. He also told Hap that his wife and daughter had died in the March 9-10 fire, which Hap had heard and felt on that fateful night. Hap reached for the old man's hand and said, "I'm sorry, sorry." "War is over," said the old man. Finally, for Hap, the War was over indeed.

That is not all of the story. Saburo Sakai began to check out Hap's account of their being shot down, and the pilot of the Nick was finally identified....In July, 1984 Hap wrote a letter to the Nick pilot. His name was Isamu Kashiide. The letter said, among other things, "Obviously, I have mixed feelings, but after 40 years, the passing of time has healed the memories of war. We were both doing what we were trained and directed to do when our paths crossed at high altitude over Tokyo that fateful day long ago."

....On September 17, 1985, Mr. Kashiide along with Mr. Sakai greeted Hap at his hotel in Tokyo. They enjoyed an at-first shy, gentle conversation with sometimes a humorous vein. Finally, the three of them drank a champagne toast to friendship and understanding. He also encouraged the pilot to come to

America. "I think the visit meant as much to him as it did to me," Hap said. "We spent two days together, during which we enjoyed a formal dinner at the home of a colonel located in the Embassy compound."

What was the upshot of all this? Hap's nightmares completely stopped. These visits and these new associations had done it. Hap was altogether free, at long last.

On January 11, 1988, Pappy Boyington, Hap's friend from his Omori P.O.W. days, died. Hap was asked to write and give the eulogy at Arlington National Cemetery on January 15....

On January 27, 1989, he (Hap) boarded a Continental Airlines DC-10 at Tokyo and made the return trip he had been unable to make back in 1945....He told me there were 220 Japanese tourists on that airplane and...the pilot told them who their special passenger was. He rode the jump seat between the two pilots. They made a complete circle of the Island of Saipan before they landed, so Hap could get an excellent view of his former home base. He told me his big thrill was coming down the final approach for a landing at Isley Field, now Saipan International Airport. It simply brought back a flood of memories of the very approach they were used to making in the B-29 in early 1945, 44 years before. As he got off the DC-10 he knelt down and touched the ground.

During his stay on Saipan, Hap visited the 73rd Bomb Wing monument three times. It was simple and small, and there had been some damage by vandals. Another idea crossed Hap's mind. A suitable memorial should be provided, to include all of the different units which had a part in the taking of Saipan. The 73rd Bomb Wing, which engaged in the air assault against Japan with their B-29s back in 1944 and 1945 would also be represented.

Hap arranged to testify before the U.S. House of Representatives Subcommittee on National Parks and Public Lands on June 13, 1989, along with the chief historian of the National Park Service....

Nine days after Hap Halloran testified in Washington about the American Memorial Parks in the Marianas, he appeared at Yuma Marine Corps Air Station at Yuma, Arizona, on June 22, 1989. He was there to honor the achievements of his friend, Pappy Boyington. A life-size bust of Boyington was dedicated there in ceremonies put on by the Marines of VMA-214, the

Black Sheep Squadron of World War II fame....

Hap Halloran was far from done. Following his testimony before the Department of the Interior, action began to authorize funds for and build an "American World War II Memorial" in the United States Commonwealth of the Northern Mariana Islands, Saipan. A large Court of Honor, a Flag Circle, and a Memorial Wall were all located on a prominent spot on the Island of Saipan. Construction was finally completed just in time for its dedication on June 15, 1994, the 50th Anniversary of the beginning of the assault on Saipan in 1944.

Halloran was not only present for the dedication, he was selected to give the keynote speech. He told me he stood at the foot of the five flagpoles there. The tallest in the center flew the U.S. flag. It was surrounded by two flagpoles on each side bearing the flags of the armed services which were involved in the taking and the using of Saipan in World War II. The encircling Memorial Wall shows the names inscribed of those killed or missing in those decisive and historic battles.

The Memorial is impressive....One of its distinctions is that this is the only U.S. Memorial which flies the Service Flags along with our National Colors. They now fly day and night for all to see from every direction.

"A wrong has been righted," wrote Haydn Williams, President Emeritus of the Asia Foundation. "For years the only real memorials on Saipan were erected by the Japanese to their war dead. Numerous Japanese memorials and shrines dotted the island....Now the new U.S. Memorial is a visible reminder of the debt owed to those who gave their lives in the cause of freedom."

Summarizing, for Hap Halloran grim recollection had come all too easily. He said, "Obviously, the first week that I was out of prison I had no thought except of contempt. But time heals everything, sort of....I think the real thing is, I wanted to end up purging the negative things I remembered. I just wanted to get things in order. I simply thought I'd come back and view it all from a positive standpoint."

That is just what Hap Halloran has done.

Reprint of Chap. 14, *Rain of Fire: B-29s Over Japan, 1945*, with permission of Charles L. Phillips, Jr., Colonel U.S. Air Force (Ret.), author. In 2nd Ed., 1996, he has recounted personalized history of B-29 air assault against Japan as an aircraft commander, as well as squadron operations officer, flying 31 combat missions over Japan. For a copy call 909-242-1436, or send $19.95 plus $3 S&H and $1.55 CA tax, if applicable, to: B-Nijuku Publishing, 11875 Pigeon Pass Rd., B-14-357, Moreno Valley, CA 92557.[1]

Eulogy for Colonel Gregory Boyington

Arlington National Cemetery • January 15, 1988

Today, Colonel Gregory Boyington, U.S. Marine Corps, joins others in this hallowed ground at Arlington National Cemetery. He will be with those who, like 'Pappy', contributed so much to the good of our country.

I know that Pappy would like us to recognize his wife of 13 years, Jo, and members of her family. Also, his son, Gregory Boyington, Jr., and his family. They are gathered here today with a deep sense of pride. I'm sure that Pappy would want to express a special thanks to the Corps for their all out efforts to recognize one of their own.

My feeling after discussions with many Marines is that they consider Pappy as one of their very best - The Original Top Gun - A Hero - A Legend in His Own Time - An Inspiration.

I first met Pappy in a prisoner of war camp in early 1945 at Omori on the southern edge of Tokyo. He was already a hero to me with his 28 aerial victories long before our B-29 was shot down over Tokyo. He obviously had lost much weight, like the rest of us on our meager rice diet. However, he maintained the sparkle in his eyes, the built in look and mannerisms of a natural leader.

He instilled confidence in us in a quiet way. I know I felt I would be OK as long as Pappy was there. He took things in stride and did not complain. He set the pace. He was extremely solicitous for fellow P.O.W.'s in our special barracks at Omori - especially the very young fellows. He spent many evening hours tending to them, talking to them and exhorting them to hang in there and to perpetuate their desire to survive.

I sensed that when US carrier planes and B-29's strafed and bombed our immediate area, that he craved to be free of his confinement and to join them in their exciting missions on the road to victory. He always wanted to be in the thick of the action, a fearless warrior, and yet a gentle, caring and considerate person.

He inspired us not only by reputation, but also by actual performance. His exploits with the Black Sheep Squadron are legendary. These were professional, skilled flyers, a tough fighting group that, under Pappy's leadership and training, scourged the enemy in combat. Two of the original Black Sheep visited Pappy at the hospital in Fresno shortly before his death. Their clear message was "Pappy led us, taught us and always took care of all of his boys".

After the war years and a variety of ventures, he eventually settled into the more stereotyped role of family man and homebody. He loved his grandchildren, and was hooked on late night movies. He loved golf and lived alongside the course in Fresno. He attacked the game with the same intense vigor of his days of aerial combat.

written aboard Marine plane carrying Pappy's casket Fresno, Ca to Arlington Natl Cemetery 1/1-13 88.
& read in Arlington Natl Chapel 1-15-88 —
R F Halloran

14

I can recall vividly, caddying for Pappy when he played in the Bing Crosby Pebble Beach Pro Am 8 or 9 years ago. After 4 days of pressure packed golf, his group was on the 16th green at Pebble Beach. A massive crowd surrounded the green. Pappy had a 40-foot, downhill, sharply breaking putt. He cooly knocked it in for a crucial birdie. He enjoyed it - he smiled - another victory. He always performed well under maximum pressure.

His days at the air shows were special, happy days over the years - at places like Reno and Chino and Phoenix and Oshkosh and Yakima. Jo worked these shows with him. He loved to meet his friends and admirers, to pose for photos with the kids and grownups of all ages and to autograph his books and color prints. Sheer joy - "fulfilling days" is how he described them.

On Tuesday and Wednesday of this week, there was a constant line of people all day long at the mortuary in Fresno to pay their final respects to Pappy Boyington. Some had driven hundreds of miles for a final good-bye to him. I talked with some of these people.

Some of their comments were:

"Never met him, but I admired him and just wanted to say thanks to him for all that he did for my country and for me."

A husband and wife:

"He was always so nice to our children at air shows over the years. We just had to stop by to say 'thanks and good-bye'."

An elderly gentleman:

"Pappy always was and always will be a hero to me. I'll miss him, the country will miss him."

And later:

The Marine Corp Honor Guard at the mortuary and the Marine Fly By Pilots of the present day Black Sheep Squadron from Yuma, Arizona, commented almost in unison:

"We are proud to have been selected to participate in these ceremonies. Pappy Boyington is a great Marine, a true hero and inspiration to us. A Great Marine!

Pappy, we all share the hope and conviction that our memories of you and your spirit and inspiration will remain with us over future years.

We need people like Marine Corps Colonel Gregory 'Pappy' Boyington to keep our country strong. We'll miss you Pappy.

Delivered at the Arlington National Cemetery Chapel

Hop Halloran

JAMES T. HUXTABLE

DEMING, NEW MEXICO

Army, M/Sgt., 200th Coast Artillery, Anti-Aircraft, 1941-45
Basic Training: Ft. Bliss, Texas
Duty in Philippines. **P.O.W.**

In the latter half of 1940 the world was in a turmoil with Germany and Great Britain at war. The President called up the National Guard units; the New Mexico Guard was one of the first, and I had joined the unit in 1938.

Ft. Stotsenberg in the Philippines became our permanent camp. It was right next to Clark Field, for which we were to provide anti-aircraft protection.

On our arrival the fellows that had been on the advance detail came out proudly holding a 16-ft. python which they had just caught under our barracks. We didn't sleep too well that night, but I never saw another python there.

We were immediately under alert, had to carry our arms; our guns were dug in; we were ready.

On December 8, (we were across the International Dateline) about 12:15, while we were all in the mess hall eating, we heard heavy planes coming but assumed they were our own until suddenly the bombs started hitting. My mess kit flew off the table when the first bomb hit, and we all started bailing out. I crawled under the barracks and think being under there made me more scared than if I had been out where I could see what was happening. Also, I was lying in an ant bed and they have huge red ants!

Clark Field and Ft. Stotsenberg were hit by 54 heavy Japanese bombers, and after they left, 21 fighters came and strafed the heck out of everything. The only ditch we had was where a pipeline was being put through the barracks for water to the showers. We hadn't been smart enough to dig a foxhole until then, so we were all in the water ditch. Before dark, though, there were foxholes all over that place. In fact, you didn't dare go to the shower, maybe 25 yards from the barracks, without a flashlight cause you'd fall in one of those foxholes.

We stayed at Stotsenberg trying to shoot down the planes that came daily to bomb. On Christmas Eve, 1941, we evacu-

16

ated to Bataan. Just as our rear echelon was leaving one side of Clark Field, Japanese advance units were coming in on the other side. It was a race to Bataan, blowing up bridges behind us.

James T. Huxtable

Manila Bay was a horseshoe shape, with Manila at the back of it, and right at the mouth was the rock called Corregidor. Bataan was a peninsula that came down on the north side of Corregidor. The plan was to use the narrow neck of the Bataan peninsula as a battle line. We had maybe 15,000 ground troops and the Japanese had 150,000, so we were fighting a losing battle and knew it. By holding Corregidor and Bataan, it was giving the rest of the U.S. forces a chance to assemble in strength so that they could start action in the South Pacific and work north. General MacArthur gave us credit for having held the site long enough that the Japanese were unable to take Australia.

Japanese intelligence wasn't too good because some of the surrendering American high-ranking officers were slapped around quite a bit by the Japanese wanting to know where the rest of the men were. They were convinced that we had maybe ten times the troops that we did.

On April 9 Bataan was surrendered by the American commanding general to the Japanese forces. The Japanese wanted to get the prisoners out of Bataan as fast as they could so they could move the heavy artillery in and start shelling Corregidor. They wanted to use Manila Bay, and as long as the Rock, setting right at the entrance of the Bay, was held by the Americans, their shipping couldn't get in. That was the beginning of the infamous Death March. In their haste to get us out, they marched us day and night and anybody that couldn't keep up, fell out, was bayoneted and shot right beside the road. I got pretty tired a couple of times, got close to the rear and found out what was happening to those that fell out, and that gave me a whale of an incentive to keep going.

On our Death March of over a hundred miles to San Fernando, many of our comrades did not make the destination. The last couple of months that we were on Bataan we were practically on a starvation diet. We had hardly any food and many of the guys had dysentery, so when the surrender came, most of us were weak. That primarily accounted for most of the guys that fell out and were killed.

Our first prison camp was Camp O'Donnell. They had brought many of the Philippine scouts who were really excellent soldiers. They put them on one side of the camp and the Americans on the other. At one time the daily death toll reached 500. At that rate, knowing how many were in camp, we could almost figure how many days it was going to be before it was our turn.

After about a month, they transferred us to another camp, Cabanatuan, which was the largest Japanese prison camp in the Philippines. Things began to look up. The Catholic Church was able to convince the Japanese that they should let the church donate some carabao, which would provide us with some fresh meat. We also started getting some Red Cross boxes, and the death toll dropped to almost nothing right away. Then they started putting us all to work.

In Cabanatuan there was probably about an average of 10,000 Americans, and the Japanese decided that we, the prisoners, would build a farm. They had us cut down the 120 acres of high buffalo grass and build a farm to grow vegetables, not only for ourselves but for the Japanese army.

At one time many years ago this whole area had been a rice paddy, so there were dikes, and termites had built huge mounds, some as high as the ceiling. They were in our way for this farm, and we had to knock them down. All we had to wear was shorts; our shoes were long gone. When buffalo grass is cut down it leaves stubble, which is hard on the feet.

When tearing down the first termite mound, which was like concrete, I had a pick and mattock; I'd stick the pick in a hole and bear back on it and flip it out. As I looked down, there was a cobra sticking its head right through my bare feet. The pick went one way and I went another! The Japs grabbed me, not knowing why I was running. When they found out what it was, they wanted us to capture it so they could eat it. But it had to be captured alive! We all became quite proficient in capturing cobra as about every fifth mound would have one in it. Catching one alive and giving it to the Japanese meant getting a half day off and a pack of cigarettes. That was quite an incentive to become a cobra catcher!

Cooking rice for 10,000 men took a lot of wood, and I got on the wood detail, which consisted of 100 men. We'd go out into the jungles every day on trucks and chop wood for three days; then for a day we'd carry all the chopped wood to where the trucks could get it, load and then unload them. During rainy season we couldn't get off the road, so we had to chop enough during dry season to carry us over during the rainy season.

I was fortunate to have a partner from Georgia who was an excellent chopper; I had never done this before. He carried me for about the first three weeks while I was letting blisters heal. We started out with old fire axes, weighing about seven pounds. We had to make our own axe handles for them; and they weren't too sharp. They finally found some guys that were adept at making axe handles, so we had a 10-man axe handle crew. We found whetstones in the creek, and would sharpen those axes until you could shave the hair off your leg. The sharper your axe was, the easier it was to cut wood.

The first summer we were at Cabanatuan some of the guys planted a garden, and we thought that was pretty stupid. We weren't going to be there long enough for them to harvest the crop! Next summer we planted a garden and we harvested the crops—okra, corn, papaya (they grow like wild).

In February, 1944, I was selected for one of the details being transferred to Japan, most of which had 3,000 men. Those must have been horrible, because with the 500 that I was with, we were really packed in the hole of the Japanese ship. The ship was unmarked. The whole deck was covered with military vehicles, ours, that they were taking back to Japan, and logs. The Number One forward hole was full of logs that they had picked up.

One night while on the way to Formosa, in the North China Sea, we hit a typhoon and the waves practically stood the ship on end. And when they'd come down, the next wave would come completely over it. In the process all these big heavy logs became unleashed and started sliding back and forth. We were in Number Two hole with just a little steel plate separating Number One and Two. Every time we'd start uphill, those logs would come back and hit that thing and it would buckle. We would think we were going to get crushed. But I'll give those Japs the benefit of the doubt—they had courage. They went down in that dark hole with those moss-covered logs and relashed them. Actually, they probably would have sunk the ship.

The next morning when everything was calm, we couldn't see any of the ships that had been in the convoy. There was nothing left on deck; all the trucks, the logs that had been there, everything was gone. It was a horrible experience, and we are thankful that we lived through it.

Since the ships were unmarked, our submarines patrolling the area would identify them as Japanese ships and torpedo them. Many of our comrades were sunk in those ships that were torpedoed by our submarines. Fortunately, mine wasn't, and I lived to get to Japan. We left in February and didn't get to Japan until April; spent about a month in Formosa. The day before we landed at Osaka they brought out a bunch of U.S. navy uniforms and made us put them on. When we got off the ship the next day they marched us down to the town square and put ropes around us. Citizens came and looked at us dog-faced soldiers sitting there with navy uniforms on. I'm sure the citizens were told that we were the remnants of the American navy.

The next day they put us on a train and issued us box lunches with rice and pickles. We travelled all day and night, with the blinds pulled, and didn't even know which direction we were going in. We arrived at a copper mining camp, and to this day I have never found it in any atlas. I don't know where I was. This mine was 120 years old and had never been retimbered in many places since they dug it. As short as I am, I almost banged my brains out on the overhead timbers before I learned to duck.

It was a pretty nice camp, setting up on the crest of a hill; we had to walk on a zigzag trail about a half mile down to the bottom of the valley floor. We went into the entrance of the mine and back about a half mile into the mountain. The level I worked on was 754 steps down, and we climbed them up and down. It was hotter than blue blazes down there.

I didn't know any Japanese, but they have a way of giving you an incentive to learn. Over in the corner was a bunch of mining tools and they'd tell you to go get whatever. If you brought the wrong thing, they'd *tap* you on the head *gently* and send you back after the other one; we soon learned which was which. We worked in that mine probably from April to August and then were transferred again.

The second one was the largest copper smelter in Japan. I found it on the map and it's around Honshu, back in a bunch of barren, steep hills. The smoke from the copper smelter had killed all vegetation, and they had made rock terraces from the bottom to the top of every mountain to keep the soil erosion down. We lived around the corner and back up another canyon that had some vegetation. It was about three miles from our camp to the smelter. We'd go through a small town and the little Japanese kids were standing there pulling their eyes down to look like a Yankee, just as we used to make ourselves look like Orientals.

Things went along pretty well at the copper smelter. We'd work ten hours a day, seven days a week, getting one day a month off to wash our clothes. When winter came it got so cold and the snow was too deep for the trucks to go, so we walked three miles through the snow. Then after working ten hours, we walked three miles home, only to have a bowl of maize to eat.

One time the Japanese that I was working with said, "What's that you're eating?" "Maize. In America we feed that to the chickens." He said, "Oh, yeah, yeah. We used to feed it to the chickens, too. Now we've got so many American prisoners we have to feed it to them and we don't get any eggs." I thought it was time to change the subject. We didn't eat too well in Japan, but they weren't eating too well, either. This was about the last year of the war. At night we could hear the B-29 bombers coming over. They made us turn out every light when there was an air raid warning so that the bombers couldn't locate us.

On August 9, when the first atomic bomb was dropped on Hiroshima, our interpreter disappeared for awhile. After the second one was dropped on Nagasaki, he came back and was telling us that the war was going to be over soon. He said, "Americans dropped one bomb and destroyed the whole city." We thought he had been drinking too much saki because there wasn't anything in existence that powerful. But he assured us that it was true. He told us to go out and get rocks and make a big PW in the middle of our compound. We made the big PW and then one day we heard airplanes and ran out to look. We saw three navy F4Us, Corsairs with the gull-shaped wings like Pappy Boyington flew, and they went right over us. We thought they didn't see us and were terribly disappointed. A little later we heard them again. They had seen our PW and had gone up to the head of the canyon, and here they came! We could have flipped a rock up and hit them, one right behind the other with their flaps down, going just as slow as they could. They slid the cockpit canopy back and each one dropped a carton of cigarettes tied to a string. We cut them right down to a third of a cigarette and distributed them to each man.

The next day we heard more planes, same thing. They came over, disappeared, then came from the head of the canyon. This time they were torpedo bombers. We were all standing there waiting for cigarettes to come out the top, and the bomb bay opened and a big seabag tied to a flare chute came sliding out. The first one hit and tangled three guys up in the chute, dragging them through the compound, hitting the fence on the other side. It hurt them pretty badly. We watched the rest of the seabag drops while peeking around from behind the barracks. We got medicine, more cigarettes, K-rations, and divided it all up equally.

The next day they bombed us with twice as much, and soon we quit dividing it up; everybody just took what they wanted. Finally after about ten days of bombardment with blankets, chow, medicine, and cigarettes, a B-29 came over. He didn't come down the canyon, was up above it. Both big bomb bays started opening up and stuff started falling out. It looked like No. 10 cans of tomatoes, and the closer they got, the bigger they looked. They were tied to chutes, too, but were 55-gallon drums full of everything. They strung them all up and down the canyon. Some of them went through Japanese houses, but everything that fell, the Japanese brought back to the camp.

The Japanese soon told us they would be taking us to the train the next day. It would take us to Tokyo to be returned to American control. We carried all the goodies we could but had to leave some for them. At the time it broke our hearts cause we didn't think they deserved all that good stuff.

We boarded the train; the guards still had the guns, but when we pulled into Tokyo, they surrendered their guns and turned us over to the Americans. We were delighted!

The first thing the Americans did was delouse us and issue us new clothes. Then we were late getting to the dock because the driver got lost in Tokyo. All the American hospital ships were already full, so we were put aboard a British hospital ship. It was nice, but instead of having turkey and cranberry sauce like the guys on the American ships, we had tea and soup. They gave us nice beds, but they were so soft that none of us could sleep in them, so we all wound up sleeping on the floor. The next day they took us to the airport and put us on planes, and we headed back to the Philippines.

In the Philippines we were taken to a reception camp, where we had all the beer we could drink, all the cigars and cigarettes we could smoke. I didn't smoke and didn't drink beer, so I decided to give my beer ration and cigars to the mess sergeant. He got my daily ration of beer and cigars and I could go in the mess hall any time of the day or night and get a steak.

Four years, two months, and eleven days later, and having covered 25,000 miles, I was back in the United States. I was tickled to death to be alive, and I think the experience has made me appreciative of everything in life since then. While I wouldn't want to go through it again, I think the experience was excellent for me, and I hold no malice toward the Japanese race. I have quite a high regard for them, and it's just made life in general real wonderful for me.

James T. Huxtable (left) and Donald Marksbury.
Courtesy Betty Huxtable.

GEORGE F. KING (Tony)

ARTESIA, NEW MEXICO

Military Band, 200th Coast Artillery, Anti-Aircraft Artillery
Army, Sergeant, 1941-46
Basic Training: Ft. Bliss, Texas
Duty in Pacific. **P.O.W.**

We were stationed in the Philippines at Fort Stotsenburg, located at Clark Field, on the island of Luzon. Band members were armed and qualified with 45 automatic pistols, while other batteries of our regiment were armed with rifles, 37 mm, 50 mm and 75 mm guns.

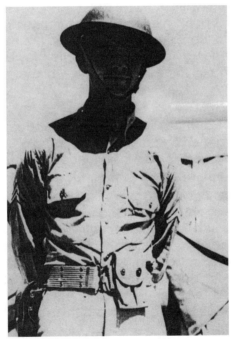
George F. King

December 8, 1941, was just like any other day except we had been placed on war alert (we were across the International Date Line—it was December 7 at Pearl Harbor and in the U.S.). Our P-40 fighter planes had been up all morning patrolling and at noon they landed and came in for lunch.

We had just finished lunch and were standing in line waiting to wash our Mess Kits when we noticed a large flight of planes coming in from the North. Some of our guys remarked, "They sure do look pretty," assuming they were our Navy.

About that time, bombs started exploding all around us and all over the air field. Our air force was literally caught on the ground, just like it happened at Pearl Harbor.

Nichols Field and Manila were being bombed about the same time and a little while after the bombing of Clark Field and Ft. Stotsenburg. The bombings during the month of December were devastating, and about the middle of December the Japanese landed large forces on the northern coast of Luzon and southern coast at Legaspi.

Due to overwhelming odds, American and Philippine forces were forced to retreat. Strategy for the defense of the Philippines had been planned years back that armed forces would retreat to the Bataan Peninsula and hold this stronghold until reenforcements would arrive. Thus, the day after Christmas we were moving all forces and what few planes we had left, to Bataan.

Reenforcements were never sent to the Philippines since the U.S. had its hands full with the war in Europe and defending Australia. Our armed forces managed to hold Bataan for four months and we were forced to surrender on April 9, 1942.

During that four months our unit shot down 117 Japanese planes. Armed forces on Corregidor Island in Manila Bay surrendered on May 6, 1942. We band members had put away our band instruments and were performing details such as moving large quantities of ammunition to the different batteries and were issued rifles, in addition to our 45 automatic pistols, and performed guard duty around battalion headquarters. Upon receiving orders to surrender, we immediately dismantled our weapons, scattered and buried parts thereof, so they were useless to the enemy.

The Death March out of Bataan took the lives of hundreds of American and Philippine soldiers. During the next six months, thousands of American and Philippine soldiers died from malnutrition, malaria, dysentery, and starvation. We were beaten and forced to do work that our weak and broken bodies could not stand.

About September, 1942, the Japanese started shipping POWs to Manchuria and the Japanese mainland on unmarked ships. Some of these were torpedoed by U.S. submarines and thousands of prisoners died, lost at sea. I was on the Japanese ship Totori Maru with about 1500 other prisoners; we survived a torpedo attack and barely missed hitting a mine. We left the Philippines about October 5, 1942, and arrived at Yokohama, Japan, about November 12, 1942. Thirty-six POWs died enroute and were buried at sea.

The POW camp in Yokohama was an old baseball stadium that had been converted to a POW camp. In the barracks here, each man was limited to a bed space only two feet wide. During the cold winter only one stove was erected for approximately one hundred men and it could only be lit for two hours each night. Each man was issued one pillow and two Japanese blankets. As needed, we were issued one pair of Japanese shoes. Also, we were issued British Army clothing that had been confiscated from British islands and possessions that had been over-run by Japanese forces.

Most of us were still suffering from malnutrition. During my stay in the Philippines, I suffered from wet Beriberi (Edema), which is the swelling of the extremities. Those POWs that did not survive this condition literally drowned in their own body fluid. I had managed to survive this and now had the resulting Dry Beriberi. With it I had much fever in the feet, which we called "hot feet." In the wintertime I slept with my feet out from under the cover and many of the guys would soak their feet in fire barrels (barrels filled with water to fight fires). During the summer, my feet would perspire continuously, my socks wet with sweat.

As our bodies became stronger, we were forced to work in Japanese factories and industries. One workplace was the Asano Dockyard, shipbuilding yard, where we were forced to move flat steel and steel girders. Would you believe! Most of it came from Bethlehem and American steel factories in the USA! Japan had been stockpiling this steel for years prior to the war.

Another workplace was an oil factory which processed and made oil from soybeans, copra, peanuts and castor beans. Another place was a brickyard where they manufactured fire bricks. We carried trays of six wet bricks into kilns for heat processing and drying. Then another detail was unloading ships, carrying sacks of beans, rice and copra on our backs, the sacks weighing 80-100 pounds.

All of this was hard work, which we had to do on two meals a day of a bowl of rice and some fish soup (made from fish-heads) or thin vegetable soup. Our average weight was about 120 pounds. During the latter part of 1943 the Japanese started paying us ten Sen a day, which we estimated to be about one cent a day in American money. One month's pay would buy one package of cigarettes, if they were available.

By the early part of 1944 we had become rather familiar with the Japanese language. Many of the Japanese civilians we worked with were good to us, gave us cigarettes, and kept us informed on how the war was going. They also brought us newspapers and some of us became quite proficient in reading and translating the Japanese characters.

Also, we started seeing daily, high-flying B-Ni-Ju-Ku's (American B-29s). Silent prayers were on the lips of all of us, praying that the war would soon come to an end. We knew that with flights of American planes over Japan, American forces were moving closer to the Japanese mainland.

Practically all the news we received was Pro-Japan, but we were able to, more or less, read between the lines and follow the American landings at Saipan, Tinian, Leyte in the Philippines, Iwo Jima, and Okinawa. During November and December of 1944, B-29s started night bombings of military installations in Yokohama and Tokyo. Many nights we would lie awake in our bunks and listen to the explosions and the rumbling of the bombs in the distance. We would start cheering during all this, only to be quieted down by shouting Japanese guards.

By the spring of 1945 American forces had taken Iwo Jima, which gave us another air base within about 600 miles from Japan. Along about the first of May, 1945, we were working at a brickyard on the outskirts of Yokohama. About 11:00 A.M. we began to hear the drone of a large flight of planes. Soon the sky was full of American P-51 fighter planes, which promptly shot down and cleared the sky of all Japanese aircraft.

This is when the fire bombing of Yokohama and Tokyo began. We all sat down at our workplace and watched flight after flight of B-29s come over at about 12,000 feet. We could even see the bombs coming out of the planes and dropping to about 100 feet above ground, and then they literally exploded into small fire bombs, hitting the ground and burning everything in sight. It was awesome! The planes were pattern-bombing the whole city. This went on for two or three hours and the whole city was afire. We saw one B-29 go down, probably hit by anti-aircraft fire. We lost count but estimated about 700 or 800 B-29s had flown over and hundreds of P-51 fighters. The whole city was burning! The Japanese guards took us back to our barracks and we just waited to see what would happen next. Would there be retaliation against POWs?

The next day we were told to pack up all our gear and were loaded on to a train. We were moved to the northwestern coast of Japan to Niigata. Here we worked the next three months unloading ships, carrying sacks of grain into warehouses. B-29s and Navy planes were bombing this area, also. They flew over at night, dropping mines in the Bay by parachute. These mines took their toll of Japanese shipping during the following days.

On the morning of August 6 we were at work carrying sacks of grain when the Japanese civilians told us the Americans had dropped an "oki bombu," a large bomb, on the city of Hiroshima, which was several hundred miles from us. Then a couple of days later, we heard they had dropped another on Nagasaki.

About August 16 most of our guards had left and we had not been sent out to work for days. We saw an American plane land at a nearby airfield and soon an American officer was escorted to our camp in a Japanese military vehicle. He told us the war was over and to "sit tight" and not leave the camp. They would arrange transportation for us soon.

On September 2, 1945, we boarded a train at Niigata and on September 5 we arrived at the war-torn city of Tokyo. We were greeted by numerous American military personnel and American Red Cross people and were able to send messages home. **What a feeling! We were free!**

Thanks to the Atom Bomb, we were alive. We later learned that all prisoners of war would have been executed in the event American forces invaded the mainland of Japan. If an invasion had come, I think of all the millions of American and Japanese lives that would have been lost, besides our own.

• • •

CHARLES L. PRUITT

SWEETWATER, TENNESSEE

U.S. Navy, Carpenter's Mate & Mine Technician, 1940-60
Basic Training: Norfolk, Virginia
Duty in Philippines; **P.O.W.**

December 10, 1941, began as a normal workday for me. I was stationed at the Naval Ammunition Depot, Cavite Navy Yard, in the Philippines on the Island of Luzon. My duty station, as well as my work station, was in the mine section of the Ammunition Depot.   For several days the Ammunition Depot was a beehive of activity, and December 10 started out the same way. We were busy rigging mines, Mark 6, to be planted in Manila Bay, Subic Bay, and other selected areas. Also, bombs, torpedoes, and ammunition for ships of the Asiatic fleet were being made ready and loaded aboard barges to be taken to and loaded aboard the ships.

Around 12:00 the air raid siren sounded. All personnel went, double time, to general quarters station. Some were assigned to man machine guns mounted on top of the casements, others to security stations inside the casements. On hearing the air raid warning, I proceeded to the magazine area, No. 25.

The casements, which numbered around 30, were built by the Spanish. They were stone, with outer walls about eight feet thick at the base, and appeared to be several feet thick at the thinnest part on the top. The ceilings were domed; the doors of passages connecting the casements and windows on the side facing the bay were arched. There were no other openings.

At approximately 12:20P.M. the bombs began falling. I, being in the depot casements, could not see what was happening; however, I could hear bombs, many, many bombs exploding. They sounded like large bombs; the mines in casement 25 were bouncing around due to vibration of the earth. It sounded like the bombs were on the parade ground side of the ammunition depot. The machine guns on top of the casements were firing at such a rate I was sure the barrels would melt. Then it was over....but only for a few minutes. Since secure from G.Q. had not been sounded, I thought the bombers would be back for another run, which happened very shortly.

Charles L. Pruitt, Prisoner of War ID at Omine Machi coal mine, Japan

I was at the barred window, which afforded a view of the bay between Cavite and Sangley Point, and I could hear the bombers coming back on their second run. Since I had not heard them on their first run, I felt sure they were on a different approach. This time I could hear the whistle of the bombs. One string of bombs fell in the bay parallel to the depot, others fell on Sangley Point. I saw one of the radio towers fall, just like a tree, but was unable to observe any other structures destroyed by the bombing.

Secure from G.Q. was sounded, or rather the word was passed. We had no power to signal with, nor any device with which to signal, except boatswain's pipe.

After word was passed to secure from G.Q., I went to the entrance to the depot which faced the parade ground. The parade ground was full of bomb craters, one row of which was not more than a hundred feet from, and parallel to, the ammunition depot. The entire Cavite Navy Yard was totally demolished with the exception of the ammunition depot and a few other buildings.

Bodies were everywhere; some were apparently dead; others wounded. I noticed the station wagon assigned to NAD parked by the depot which appeared to be undamaged. I was one of the few men who knew how to drive and possessed a driving permit. (Prior to WWII, not many service personnel could drive.) Chief Taylor did not see Roebuck, the driver, and was not sure whether he was dead or alive. He ordered me to take the station wagon and haul the wounded to the Naval Hospital at Canaco. Other personnel were assigned to help load the wounded men. Everyone was pressed into service to fight fires, care for the wounded, or shoot saboteurs, no questions asked; things were in total chaos!

I took the station wagon and proceeded to load wounded men to be transported to the hospital. We filled the wagon with as many as we could pile in; one who was wounded in the buttocks had to be tied to the back of the wagon with his feet on the bumper and his arms lashed to the cargo rack on top. We applied tourniquets, bandaged with handkerchiefs, cut off shirt sleeves to use as compresses. One man's leg was blown almost completely off, so I amputated it with my jackknife and proceeded to the hospital.

We had to go through the towns of Cavite, Caradad and Canaco. The town of Cavite was a disaster, dead and wounded bodies everywhere; all civilians were begging for assistance. There was nothing we could do except try not to run over them. By the time we arrived at the hospital, they were already overburdened with wounded. The doctors, apparently thinking I was a medic, put me to work in the hospital assisting surgeons. When I advised them that I was not a medic, they said I did a good job thus far and they needed help. I departed, returning to Cavite for another load of wounded men.

After all the wounded had been removed from the Navy Yard, which was about dark, we were instructed to abandon the Navy Yard to a nearby village and to return to NAD the following day.

The next day we returned to the Navy Yard to await orders. In the bombing raid NAD did not lose any personnel, probably the only activity without any loss of personnel. While we were awaiting orders, we simply roamed around the Navy Yard assessing damage, checking and noting locations and conditions of equipment, searching for bodies, etc. No smell is more repulsive than that of a burned human body, and there were plenty of them.

While awaiting orders I was assigned to security of the armory. No specific instructions were given to me, and there were a lot of requests for rifles, 45s and Thompson machine guns. Generally the person requesting a piece (weapon) would have a requisition approved by an officer. A weapon and ammunition was issued on this basis and the person receiving the piece signed a receipt and a log book indicating proper authorization. A printer from the yard print shop wanted two 45 caliber automatic service weapons, supposedly to guard the nurses (I think he assigned himself). I had him sign the receipt book, but did not enter it in the log book, just placed it in file 13, the trash can. The next time I saw him was at the reunion of the Defenders of Bataan and Corregidor at Fontana Village, North Carolina, in August, 1983, almost 42 years later. He said some officers took his two 45s.

December 12, 1941: Dogs are going wild! There are so many dead humans in Cavite and adjacent areas; dogs seem to appear in unbelievable numbers, feeding on the carcasses. A Chief Gunner's Mate is issued a shotgun from the armory with an unlimited or open draw of ammunition and is instructed to patrol Cavite looking for and shooting any and all dogs and any other carnivorous animals. Medical authorities feared that the animals would spread diseases, and they did not need a health epidemic on top of everything else. The Chief must have killed hundreds of animals. Work details gathered up the dead animals. I don't know what disposition was made of them. Work details also recovered the human carcasses. There was so much destruction, disorganization and confusion. We were in shock!

December 12, 1941: We loaded a dump truck with twelve men and necessary equipment and proceeded to Olongapo to mine Subic Bay. The road over Olongapo Mountain was very crooked and at some of the curves it was necessary to back the truck to negotiate the curves. We arrived about 4:00 P.M., prepared the mines for planting after dark, and acquired a tugboat. My assignment was to stay with the truck, get some sleep, and be prepared for a fast exit. I removed the distributor rotor, locked the doors, and laid down nearby. I slept some, but the mosquitoes did not.

The crew completed their mission and were ready to return to Cavite on December 13. They piled in the truck and on our way out of Olongapo we were spotted by the Japs. As I recall, a single Zero was dispatched to "take care" of us. In his strafing passes he bounced a few bullets off the steel plate of the dump bed, which extended over the cab of the truck. The Zero gave up the chase in the mountains, however; we made the tight curves at a high rate of speed by skillfully skidding the truck around them. Learning to drive on similar roads in the hills of East Tennessee helped prepare me for this trip.

A few days later I was to return to Olongapo, accompanied by a cook from one of the Navy squadrons, and transport supplies to Laguna DeBay (not sure of the accuracy of the name) which was to be the new location of the squadrons. A LTCDR from the squadron was to travel with us, driving his personal '37 Ford. After delivering the supplies, I spent the night there sleeping on the ground, using a blanket and a Kapoc life preserver as bedding. The next morning when I awoke I discovered that my truck was missing. Someone had "borrowed" it after it was unloaded. The LTCDR was there by now and verified my verbal orders, so my truck was returned to me.

During my short stay at Laguna DeBay, an airdale (a flyboy) had left his Mae West near where I was lounging while awaiting the return of my truck. I had never seen one of these things before and decided to inspect it. My inspection revealed a lever arrangement attached to a CO_2 cartridge and instantly the Mae West inflated. It can't be turned off once activated. Did I ever get reamed out by a pilot! This was grounds for a court martial according to the airplane jockey. I was glad to get back to Cavite.

Orders to evacuate NAD explosives to Sunset Beach had been received, and they needed a crane operator for off-loading the ammo. Never having been on a crane, I said that I could handle it. This was a Bay City mounted on a tandem Ford chassis, a new rig which had only recently arrived in the Philippines. The rig was undamaged and stood fully serviced. By the time I got the rig to Sunset Beach, trucks loaded with mines, bombs, and other explosives, were already there awaiting arrival of the crane. I parked the rig, got the outriggers in place, entered the cab of the crane, fired the engine, unhooked and raised the boom. The levers and pedals were not labeled, so my next move was to find which lever did what and likewise on the pedals. By now I was being told to get the lead out and the trucks unloaded. I tried to reason with him, but a Seaman doesn't question an officer and, except for my already proven ability with machines, I would have been relieved of my job, and I liked being an equipment operator. I swung the boom over the truck and lowered the hook; the man on the truck hooked on 3 MK 6s, each containing 300 pounds of high explosives. I raised the hook, swung the boom and lowered the mines in the spot indicated. Everything went smoothly except that when I clutched to lower the load, I felt the cable and the hook free fall, but luck was with me. I caught the load just in time. When the brake was applied, the boom came down slightly as a result of the sudden application of the brake on the cable drum. The mines made a slight depression in the sand. While this was happening, everyone but the officer had taken off for the boondocks. I yelled that there was no point in running, the mines were unarmed and the likelihood of an explosion was remote; besides, if they were to explode, it was already too late to run. The only safe and sensible thing to do was hit the deck. Since an explosion takes the course of least resistance, the force would have been up away from point of impact. The officer apparently thought I was clowning, after all I was a mine and explosive technician! Again, another threat of a court martial! The crew returned and we continued our operation.

We departed Cavite on December 26 in truck convoys to Mariveles and were assigned to the newly formed Navy Infantry Battalion. The Navy Battalion was assigned an area of Bataan to defend as infantry men. We had no training in this type of warfare. The Navy Battallion was surrounded by the enemy for three days. We had one canteen of water and one meal during this period. We were unable to fight our way out of this mess; so the Philippine Scouts, the best soldiers in the world, came to our rescue. Nearly 300 Japanese were killed in this skirmish. One member of the Navy Battallion was wounded and perhaps less than one hundred Philippine Scouts killed or wounded.

Too bad we had a commander, General Douglas MacArthur, who never recognized the Navy in the defense of the Philippines to his dying day.

The Navy personnel were then transferred to Corregidor

and assigned to the 4th Marines beach defense. We were in Bataan for about two months. We were captured on May 6, 1942, when General Wainwright surrendered the Philippines.

I was transferred to Bilibid Prison in Manila, where I spent twelve days in the dungeon for refusing to tell the Japs what I knew about the exploder mechanism of our mines.

I was loaded on a boxcar, along with a hundred other men; the doors were then closed and we were on our way to Cabanatuan. These boxcars were like furnaces, and many men died during this eight- or ten-hour ordeal. We spent the night in a metal warehouse, so packed with men we were unable to sit or lie down. The next day we marched to the camp where I stayed for three months.

From Cabanatuan I was sent to: Fort Wm. McKiney; Zabalin Field; Nielson Field. In August, 1944, I was sent to Japan on a hell ship, the Noto Maru, where many men died. In Japan I worked in the Omine Machi coal mine eight hours a day. The workday started after we were at our assigned work area. We were away from camp from twelve to fourteen hours. During this time we would go for weeks and not see daylight.

I was liberated in October, 1945.

For 37 years I never discussed my experiences as a POW, not even with my family or friends. Co-workers of 18 years never knew that I was a former POW until the State of Tennessee authorized a special auto license plate for former POWs.

I felt disgraced, as though I had dishonored my country, had let my fellow Americans down. It was an experience I wished to put behind me, to put it out of my mind.

How does one become a POW? Through a set of unfortunate circumstances, even by accident. First, one must engage the enemy in some manner. Flyers are shot down over enemy territory. Sailors are survivors of ships sunk during battle. Marines and infantrymen are overwhelmed by the enemy. Tank men have their machine destroyed. In some cases, through surrender by higher command. I know of no cases where individuals have taken it upon themselves to surrender. In many cases the military man or woman is wounded in the process and in need of medical attention, which is seldom forthcoming. In World War II, Korea, and Vietnam, those unfortunate to become POWs of the Orientals were not only denied medical attention but were also subjected to physical and mental torture and humiliation. They were given food that was foreign to them, often no more than 800-1,000 calories daily, not even enough for body maintenance. Many would lose as much as 30 to 50 percent body weight.

For years I experienced nightmares. Many times my wife would awaken me and sometimes I would have her pinned down; at times she would have bruises on her neck where I had been choking her, telling her, she reports, that if she so much as moved a muscle, I would kill her. She was always the enemy in my nightmares.

I did not maintain contact with any of my comrades of that unfortunate period. In August, 1982, I suddenly decided to attend a reunion of ADBC (American Defenders of Bataan and Corregidor). I did not make reservations for lodging, just drove up for the day to check things out.

Acquaintances were renewed with many people with whom I had been a POW, including two of my closest buddies of the POW days. This was a very emotional experience for each of us as we had been through so much together. We had supported each other, rendered aid and comfort when needed. When one became despondent we tried to boost his morale. No blood brothers could have been closer together.

I stayed for the entire week and made plans for attending succeeding reunions.

How does a person survive such an experience? Mental attitude, faith in God, country, self, and with the help of one's fellow POWs.

· · ·

ROBERT ZEDEKER

SIDNEY, OHIO

Air Corps, 458th Bomb Group, 753rd Bomb Squad.
2nd Lt., Co-Pilot, B-24 Liberator, 1942-45
Basic Training: Keesler Field
Duty in Europe. **P.O.W.**

On Saturday, April 22, 1944, we were called out twice, but the missions were aborted. Later in the day we got the green light. Our primary target was Hamm, Germany, a huge marshaling yard. At approximately 1936 hours, at 20,500 ft., we started the bomb run to the target. Less than two minutes later, before release of the bombs, we were to wish our ship bore a name other than "Flak Magnet."

There were three bursts of flak, one low and to the right of us; one directly ahead of us; another just to the left; and then a big jolt. The fourth one hit us dead center in the front bomb bay, came up through the plane and into the center wing section, putting a large hole in the two main fuel tanks. The 88 mm shell did not explode on impact (lucky for us) as it should have, but continued on out of the plane. In two or three minutes we lost about 550 gallons of fuel, going all through the plane, soaking all the crew except for Lt. Spaven, myself, and Lt. Kowal. They didn't wait for the bail-out order, but left the plane, thinking it would explode or catch on fire.

We left the formation to get away from the other planes. Our plane seemed to fly okay, and we had fuel left in the outer wing tanks. Spaven had Kowal give us a heading back to England, since we were not too far into Germany. While he was doing this, we got hit again; at first we thought it was more flak. But at the same time a German fighter FW190 came across the top of us and peeled to the right. He circled ahead and came around lined up on us, for a frontal attack. I said to Spaven, "Time to go!" He agreed and motioned to get going.

I went on the flight deck, turned to see if Spaven was behind me. Before he got up, all hell broke loose, everything started flying, instrument panel, windshield. Spaven was hit several times and killed. We were a sitting duck at this point with no guns in operation. I dropped off the flight deck out the bomb bay. Kowal went out the nose wheel door. Just as our chutes opened, the plane exploded. The FW190 circled once more, came close by. As he passed us he dipped his wings three times and kept going.

Two years ago we learned this German pilot was Major Hines Barr. By the end of the war he had 220 Allied planes to his credit. He had easy picking with us. We have a photostatic copy of the claim he turned in to his outfit. Two or three years after the war he was killed in a small plane mishap.

We came down in a farm field and people were waiting for us. They were not hostile, more or less friendly. A lady wanted to know if I was injured. In just a few minutes a German soldier came, put us in an Opal car and took us to the Mayor's house. They put us in separate rooms where we couldn't talk. With all the pictures of Hitler hanging around, we realized we were in trouble.

About two hours later a German army truck came and they put us in it, up towards the front. They sat at the rear, shining their flashlights on us every little bit. At Muenster they put us in a jail, still keeping us apart, no talking.

On Monday, they put us on a train, with two German soldiers in charge. They were pleasant to us; one spoke English. We changed trains in one town. Here they took us to eat in a place like a Red Cross for their troops. There were two or three hundred of them sitting at long tables and they sat us down in the middle of them. They didn't hassle us or make any comments.

Then on to Frankfort, which was really bombed out; not much left of the rail station; all the buildings in piles of rubble. They walked us up the street to find a bus or transportation of some kind out to the Interrogation Center. A hostile crowd, with ropes, gathered quickly, and came across the street toward us, wanting to hang us. Our two guards pulled their guns and backed them away.

In all this time we had food only once. They finally got us on a beat-up bus and to the Center, where there were one- or two-hundred POWs who had been captured in the last few days.

After being interrogated, about fifty of us were put on a train headed to Stalag III, Sagan, Germany, 60 miles southeast of Berlin. This was an officers' camp. When we arrived we were given clothing: a pair of GI shoes, pants, shirts, overcoat, one Army blanket, and one German Army blanket.

The barracks wasn't too bad. The rooms were about 10 x 12 with four double bunk beds, eight men to a room. We had a stove, but not much to burn in it. Every few days we'd get a few brickettes. There was a place to cook, and a washroom. We were given a potato and a couple slices of black bread each day. Each man received one Red Cross parcel per week containing two cans of meat, Spam or corned beef; can of oleo; can of powdered milk; chocolate bar; and five packs of smokes. We pooled our food in our room, and I was made cook, supposedly for one week, but I never got out of it 'til we left.

There were three compounds in this camp, separated by high barbed wire fences. Lt. Lieudell Bauer, who I ran around with until going into the service, was a navigator on another crew, and became a POW about two months before I did. He was in the compound next to mine, within hollering distance, but we didn't know that.

For a POW camp, life wasn't too bad here, as good as could be expected. We could hear cannon fire at night. The Russians were coming, not too far to the east of us, and we thought we'd get up some morning and the Germans would be gone, leaving us to the Russians. But we found out that we were better off with that not happening. Some Americans who the Russians liberated never got back home.

About 1:00 A.M., January 28, with snow four or five inches deep, and with 6 degrees below zero, SS troopers came into camp and told us to prepare to move out. We walked all that night and on to February 2, 1945, when we were put in boxcars of a freight train. They were so crowded that we had to stand up all the time. We were on this unmarked train 'til we arrived at Nuremburg Camp, Stalag XIIID. Conditions were bad: dirty barracks; bunks had burlap bags filled with chopped-up newspapers; food was one-half cup of dehydrated cabbage, full of little black bugs—that was all the meat we had. Water was turned on for about one hour each day just for drinking, no washing, couldn't clean up. We were close to the railroad marshaling yards and they were bombed two days in a row by our 8th Air Force. We had to lay on the floor while that was going on; otherwise, we'd have been shot.

The American 3rd Army was moving in our direction and getting closer, so the Germans marched us south on April 4,

1945. Weather was a lot better now. After about two or three hours on the road, we came near a railroad siding. About a dozen P-47s circled a couple of times, peeled off, and came down shooting or strafing these boxcars. Two of our POWs got hit. We tried to run out in the open to form a PW. They must have realized who we were then because they stopped shooting and pulled back up, circled, and left. After that, two P-51s would come in the forenoon and afternoon and buzz us.

During this 19-day march, farmers shared food with us, even let groups of three or four POWs come in and cook on their stoves. The farmers knew the war was about over, and we could see the light at the end of the tunnel. We ended this march May 25, 1945, at Mooseberg Stalag VIIA, and were there only four days before being liberated.

Early morning, May 29, 1945, we noticed different guards in the guard towers. We knew the American Army was closeby because the day before we could hear gunfire. Kowal and I were heating water for our instant coffee when two of our P-51s came down over the camp very low, pulled up, came down again, buzzed us, pulled up and away. This was 0900. At the same time, gunfire cut loose everywhere, bullets whizzing around. Kowal and I jumped in a hole nearby, keeping our heads down. This went on 'til 10:30 and then began to drop off sharply. It wasn't long 'til an American tank came in through the barbed wire, General Patton standing on it. This was a great time in our life that we hadn't been sure we would live to see.

We learned later that the German Army Commander met with the Americans earlier that morning and wanted to make a deal, declare Mooseberg and the POW camp an open area, and arrange for the disposition of the POWs. The Americans said, "No deal; only complete surrender by 0900 or fight." There were several thousand SS Troops and regular troops around the area, but after 10:30, most of these SS were dead.

That forenoon I ran into my friend, Lefty Bauer, and Chris Kelly from Sidney. Kowal and I were flown out, among the first to Lehavre, France. Two days later we were on a ship to the U.S., Boston.

I didn't mention in the beginning that our second mission was Berlin. We got hit with flak pretty bad. On the way back to England we were losing fuel. By the time we got to Holland on the coast, we were really getting low on gas. We had the crew throw out flak vests, ammunition, everything we could to lighten the load. We didn't think we would make it across the North Sea, but after what seemed like forever, we saw the English Coast. When we got over the coast, there was an RAF field dead ahead; we let down and headed for it. Before we got to the runway, the three engines began to splutter and cut out. We just made it over a row of houses by about ten feet, went into a stall, out of control, missed the runway, hit on left wing and gear, bounced up, came down on right side, slid quite a ways on the grass. This was a new plane, but it was completely demolished. All ten of us scrambled out and ran, sure it would explode, but it didn't. They later investigated the plane and found it was completely empty of fuel. Spaven did one fine job of bringing it in. None of us even got a bump or scratch.

• • •

DID YOU KNOW THAT...

Of the approximate 95,000 Americans taken prisoner in Europe, about 1 percent died in captivity; of the approximate 25,000 taken in the Pacific, 35 percent died. 2

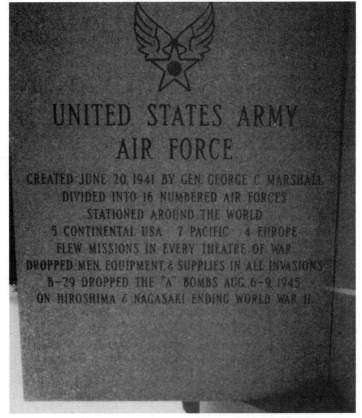

UNITED STATES ARMY
AIR FORCE

CREATED JUNE 20, 1941 BY GEN. GEORGE C. MARSHALL
DIVIDED INTO 16 NUMBERED AIR FORCES
STATIONED AROUND THE WORLD
5 CONTINENTAL USA 7 PACIFIC 4 EUROPE
FLEW MISSIONS IN EVERY THEATRE OF WAR
DROPPED MEN, EQUIPMENT, & SUPPLIES IN ALL INVASIONS
B-29 DROPPED THE "A" BOMBS AUG. 6-9, 1945
ON HIROSHIMA & NAGASAKI ENDING WORLD WAR II.

One of ten panels on monument, Chicopee, MA.
Courtesy Delfo Barabani

DONALD J. CADWALLADER

PAYNE, OHIO

Air Corps, Pilot, 1st Lt., 1942-45,
Basic Training: North Carolina and Nashville, Tennessee
Duty in Europe

I began flying in open cockpit PT-17 aircraft — loved it!
Halfway through flight training my instructor said I needed
more confidence in my safety belt. He had me tighten my belt
and put my hands over my head and lock them together; told
me we were going to roll over. He said that if I took my hands
down, he would wash me out as a pilot. Well, it was what I
needed, and I relaxed and waved my hands freely. It was a thrill
and I passed with flying colors.

Then came Montgomery Field and flying a BT-13 with an
enclosed cockpit and lots of torque. Then Dorr Field, Illinois, to
train in a twin engine AT-10, built mostly of treated wood material. I was pilot on a night trip to Cincinnati, Ohio, and back, not
landing but checking in on the radio. Shortly after leaving
Cincinnati, we lost one engine to failure. I should have returned
to Cincinnati Airport, but the aircraft was stable and flyable,
and I made the decision to return to Dorr Field. We made it fine,
but I was reprimanded for not landing in Cincinnati for the
emergency.

With advance training I was qualified to fly multi-engine aircraft. I asked for, and was qualified to fly, an A-26 low-level
bomber, a new type of aircraft. But co-pilots were needed on B-
17s. At Sioux City, Iowa, after several weeks of training with a
crew of ten, we were to take a night practice bombing run.
Sometimes not all ten crewmen were on these trips, such as
gunners. On this night we had a crew of seven. Everything
seemed normal on checking the aircraft, and we took off when
cleared by the tower. We only cleared to about 800 ft. and lost
one engine. As the co-pilot, I called the tower for emergency
landing and as we came back around, we lost another engine
on the same side and were losing altitude. The last thing I
remember as we cleared a fence was the pilot saying to cut
the master switch. When I came to my senses I seemed to be
okay and the engineer was standing beside me. I couldn't see

the pilot, but there was a large hole on his side of the aircraft and some fire. As I raised up, after unhooking my seat belt, my head hit a tree limb and the aircraft exploded. The only escape was through the pilot's side; we had to go through the flames. The engineer stopped as we were leaving; I pushed him out through the flames and I ran after him with my hands over my head and face. I saw the engineer on fire, stopped him and put out the flames. I tried to return to help the others, but could not reach them for the heat. I received only one burn over my left eye and a cut on my head from the tree limb and a few bruises. The engineer was burned around the face and both arms badly. Two others survived only until that night. The Lord was looking after me somehow.

Donald J. Cadwallader

At the hospital they wouldn't allow me to call my wife, but while the nurse was out, I called. The chaplain and priest were notifying relatives of the crash. When they told my wife I had been killed, she told them she had just talked to me and I was okay. They felt bad about the situation and had to return to base to get the story straight. I was told much later that sand in the crankcase (sabotage) caused the accident.

After a rest period at home, they had me fly the next night in the co-pilot seat with another crew and an observer behind me to make sure I was okay and responsible again. I was then told I could select from a few crews which I would like to join. I picked a New Jersey potato farmer, since I was also raised on a farm; it turned out to be a great crew.

We picked up a new B-17 and flew it, with bad weather and icing conditions, across the Atlantic by way of Bangor, Maine, and Goosebay, Canada, to Iceland.

From Iceland we went to Ireland and left the aircraft there to set up for combat conditions; took train to our base in England. We all were together as a crew most of our stay.

We saw plenty of action on about every mission to Hamburg, Munich, Berlin, Wiesbaden, Cologne, Saurbrucken, etc. At the time of D-Day we flew seven days straight, dropping anti-personnel bombs and blowing bridges and other targets. With all the ships in the English Channel for D-Day, it looked like you could walk across.

Our crew was one of the most fortunate as we had no injuries to warrant a Purple Heart, only scratches and plenty of excitement. There were many holes in the plane from anti-aircraft fire. Some engines were put out of business. Once we had our oxygen destroyed at high altitude and had to leave formation to go down to a lower level quickly to save the crew from passing out. This is when you like to see U.S. fighter escort. We got down to around 10,000 ft., checked everything out, and decided with all four engines running we would be safer on the deck under the cloud layer. Our navigator kept us clear of cities and we returned to England safely.

At one time the Germans were getting desperate and would make a group attack with possibly fifty or more aircraft fighters. On one mission we counted seventeen B-17s falling or leaving formation ahead of ours, and they never touched our group. This was a miracle! Each group started out with 54 aircraft on a mission, almost all wing-tip to wing-tip. It was really hard to see your buddies shot down.

Before our tour finished I took over our crew as 1st pilot and was promoted to 1st Lt. We finished with 22 missions to our credit. Each aircraft had a name and markings on the side for bomb runs and fighter kills, and our last plane was called the Damn Yankee.

And, yes, I am a true American. This is the best country in the world, even if we don't agree on all things.

• • •

ALFRED L. CORMIER
BANGOR, MAINE

Army Air Corps, 1st Lieutenant, 1942-45
Basic Training: Atlantic City
Duty in Kunming, China

If a dog is man's best friend, the same could be said about a pilot's parachute. I got mine shortly after getting my wings. A telegram from my C.O., halfway through my ten-day leave, advised me of my overseas assignment. Back at the base, one of the first things issued was my parachute; not an unfamiliar item but this one would belong to me for the duration.

It took a month of ships and planes to get me to my destination, Kunming, China: to Africa, the Mediterranean Sea, the Suez Canal, the Red Sea, Arabian Sea, Bombay, India, and then Kunming.

There I was assigned to the 322nd Troop Carrier Squadron, flying C-47s. I'd never flown anything bigger than an AT-10, but since the pilots we were replacing couldn't head stateside until we were checked out, it was a quick orientation.

General Chennault was the Air Force commander and his long time friend, Colonel Luke Williamson, commanded our squadron. Our mission was to supply the advanced bases, some of them eight hundred miles away, with supplies and ammunition. This included gasoline in 55 gallon drums, which no one liked for a load. On our return trips we carried ingots of tin, antimony and tungsten to be sent back to the states for the war effort.

Alfred L. Cormier

On our routes we usually crossed over enemy territory several times. Most of the time we were hidden by weather, but on occasion we were given a fighter escort to reach our destination. The Japanese occasionally bombed our bases, and one night my plane got a direct hit on the nose and it burned back to the wing. I lost my camera and field glasses in that incident, but my promotion to Ist Lieutenant eased the pain.

In January, 1945, with the Japanese threatening our advanced bases, I flew a mission to evacuate Suichuan, some 800 miles to the east. It was approaching dusk when we took off from Suichuan with a crew of four and twenty men from a communications squadron that had been stationed there. We were the last plane to leave, the runways had already been mined, and the demolition crew had started to raze the base. Our takeoff brought us over the approaching enemy and we could see the twinkle of gunfire directed at us. Our destination was Chikiang, about 400 miles west, and we were dependent on our radio compass to locate it.

As the hours went by our radio man worked on the long-range transmitter to try to make a contact. We, up front, took turns tuning the radio compass for signs that we were nearing a friendly base; nothing but static emerged from the earphones. This went on for eight hours. We surmised that we had missed Chikiang, so we were trying for Kunming.

As the hours passed, I kept increasing our altitude, knowing that the farther west we flew, the higher the ground rose to meet us. After eight hours and no encouraging sounds from our radios, and the gas gauges approaching empty, I turned east and told the crew chief to prepare the passengers for bailout.

When all had donned their chutes, I gave the order to leave, and they were gone. While I set the auto pilot, my buddy got his chute on, after which I reached for mine; but it wasn't there! Someone had taken my personal chute, the one that had been so painstakingly fitted to me, and my constant companion! It was gone! All that was left was a chute that had been sized for a midget. With help and a lot of struggle, I managed to get it on. All this time we had been putting miles between us and the rest of the crew.

I followed my buddy out the door—that was one long step—and pulled the rip cord. Boy, when that chute fetched up, I thought I'd lost my "cojons." It seemed like hours that I swung through the dark night, seeing nothing until, with a bone-jarring crunch, I hit the earth. The pain finally subsided and I determined that I was still in one piece. Not knowing the lay of the ground, I wrapped myself in the chute and packed it in until dawn.

The next morning I found myself on a cliff ledge about thirty feet from the ground overlooking a river. Before I could orient myself, I saw a commotion on the other side of the river; several black-clothed men were putting out in a boat and heading downstream. Not knowing if they were friendlies, I kept hidden until they had left, and then climbed down to solid ground.

After making my way to a nearby village, I managed to get help for the long walk home. A couple of weeks later I was back and learned that we had been bucking 100-mile-an-hour-winds; that seven planes had gone down that night and that one of our passengers had been killed when his chute failed to open. Mine?

I still have the rip cord to the chute I used and a certificate from the Caterpillar Club. The chute itself was left behind and probably became a wedding dress for a village maid.

After our return to the States, my buddy and I were assigned to Boling Field in Washington, D.C., flying VIPs around the country. Our most notable passenger was General Groves, head of the Manhattan Project, and his entourage, who we flew to Albuquerque, New Mexico, where the first Atom Bomb was tested, although we did not know this at that time.

. . .

DID YOU KNOW THAT...

The "Flying Tigers" were given that name by the Chinese. It was a high honor for the tiger had been an important symbol of their country for many years.

Claire Chennault, formerly of the U.S. Air Force, became a consultant to China and received the rank of colonel in the Chinese Air Force.

The U.S. furnished 100 P-40s in April, 1941, and allowed pilots to take a leave from active duty in the U.S. Air Force to participate in the AVG (American Volunteer Group). Their chore was to protect the 900-mile Burma Road, from Rangoon to Kunming. With all other ports being closed by the Japanese, it was crucial for China's survival that this road be kept open.

Eighteen days after Pearl Harbor the legend of the Flying Tigers was born. Chinese spirit was renewed. Success of the AVG was so great that they became heroes; Japanese pilots didn't want to tangle with them.

When the group's planes were becoming old and unfit, and there were no new ones forthcoming, the Flying Tigers were forced to disband. They were given the option of joining the Army Air Corps, under General Stilwell, but only five pilots out of 250 and 22 ground crewmen accepted.4

EARL G. EDINGER

STEELVILLE, MISSOURI

Army Air Corps, Sgt., Personnel Hqs. & Orderly Room, 1942-45
Basic Training: Ft. Warren, Wyoming
Duty in Pacific

Letter written December, 1943, by Captain to friends back on Oahu:

"...[This is] how you will live the first week in an island base—just in case you ever get in on one of these deals.

"First—how to eat a 'C' ration. One meal of 'C' ration consists of two tin cans, one of which has a key to open it. You sit on the edge of your foxhole and put one can on one knee and one on the other. Open the can with the key. Inside, you will find three lumps of sugar, a small can of soluble coffee, a piece of chocolate, and four biscuits. (These biscuits differ from dog biscuits in that they are round, while dog biscuits are bone shaped.) Dump all this in one hand to get to the bottom of the can in order to get the key with which to open the other can. By the time you get all the stuff back in the first can, you discover you have dropped the key in the mud and lost it. So you decide to use the key which you used to open the first can. Before you can do this, however, you have to first remove the strip of tin which is neatly wrapped about the key. To accomplish this, you grasp the end of the strip of tin between the forefinger and thumb on your left hand, hold the key in your right hand, and pull. After you have gotten your left fore-finger and thumb bandaged at the Aid Station, you proceed to open the second can. This can contains meat and vegetable stew. Since the can is being opened about one half inch from the top, the juice from the stew runs down the side on to your trousers leg. But you have to get up anyway to go get some utensil with which to eat the stuff. You remember that you put your mess kit in either your hand luggage, musette bag, bed roll or foot locker, so you spend 15 minutes fussing and fuming thru these. You finally find it in your gas mask carrier, and take therefrom 1 ea. fork or spoon (depending upon which you like to eat your stew with.) You go back to your seat and eat the stew and biscuits and piece of chocolate. Now you have left the little can of coffee and 3 lumps of sugar. This is where the fun comes in, first dig a little hole in the ground and build a fire in same. Then you fill your meat can 2/3 full of water from your canteen and heat it over the fire. To open the little can of soluble coffee, you first have to remove a little strip of adhesive tape which is wrapped around it. Do not throw this away. It saves you another trip to the Aid Station, because you can use it to wrap up the place where your fingernail was before you tore it off opening the little can. Now put the contents into the hot water. It takes exactly 1 hour and 53 minutes for it to dissolve. Add the three lumps of sugar, stir well and drink. This leaves only your meat can and fork (or spoon) to wash—which you then do. In fact, you finish just in time to draw your 'C' ration for the next meal. QUESTION: When in hell do combat soldiers find time to fight the Japs?

"Next we will take up bathing. All you need is a helmet, soap, towel, and a rope. You tie the rope around the helmet and lower same into a well, filling it with water (the first time Nelson did it, the strap broke and his helmet went to the bottom of the well and he had to get a big fish hook and fish it out). You lather yourself well and pour the water from the helmet over you. Here's an interesting sidelight while on the subject. There I was, standing beside my helmet without a stitch on, when several native women passed. You'll never believe this in a million years, but (before I could grab a towel) when they went by, they casually looked me over from head to toe and what do you think—they never batted an eye. Showed not the slightest expression of surprise, amazement, or any other emotion. My pride has been sorely wounded....

"Now, the next is a rather delicate subject—'How to relieve yourself in the Pacific Ocean.' Of course, there are places to go out over the water, but they are not always handy, so you go down to the water's edge and stand there a few minutes noting exactly how far the water washes up on shore. When you have it gauged exactly (you think) you proceed to do your business. What happens? You guessed it! WHAM! A big wave slips in and slaps you smack-dab on the fanny, immediately stopping any action that might be taking place and filling your shoes and everything full of cold salt water.

"But things are getting shaped up now and we are going to have a nice place here. The morale is extremely high and everybody is ptiching in and working hard and long hours with never a complaint. Why don't those Japs give up? They have as much chance of winning this war as a one-legged man in a butt-kicking contest."

. . .

DID YOU KNOW THAT...

During the war the West Coast was considered a war zone. There were 24-hour Navy and Coast Guard lookouts and patrols. Civilian volunteers also helped with the patrolling, being called the "Hooligan Navy."

Japanese submarines appeared along the Coast frequently in December, 1941, and attacked several ships. During 1942 they appeared less frequently, and then mostly disappeared.

Mines were laid at the mouth of the Columbia River and supposedly it was also protected by the guns and 2500 men at Fort Stevens. However, on June 21, 1942, a Japanese submarine, I-25, came through a group of fishing boats, fired seventeen shots on Fort Stevens, and then left through the same group of boats, undetected. Not a shot was fired.

This same submarine, on September 9, 1942, launched a seaplane near Oregon. The plane dropped two 170-pound bombs in a densely forested area, hoping to start a forest fire. With the forest being wet at the time, this did not happen. But on September 29, the plane tried again, dropping two more bombs. A fire was avoided again for the same reason.

The interior of this giant size I-class submarine included an aircraft hangar capable of holding four small planes.[5]

CLEO HOLLAWAY

ZIONSVILLE, PENNSYLVANIA

Army Air Force, Sgt., Cook, 1946-47
Basic Training: Shepherds Field, Texas
Duty in Philippines

Because he had a job with Western Cartridge Co. washing ammunition shell casings, Cleo was deferred from the Armed Forces three times (and also because he was to be a new father). Two years after the baby was born, however, he was called. He then enlisted because he was told that he would be able to get home sooner if he did.

After Basic Training, Cleo expected to go for training as a paratrooper or in artillery, but was told that the Air Force needed cooks. He, along with about 200 others, was sent to Santa Ana, California, for hands-on training as a cook. They had to prepare for and serve returning troops as they docked in Santa Ana. There were three mess halls with each feeding about 4,400 men. Cooking began at 6:00 and the mess was opened at 6:30. When the doors were opened one had to get out of the way! Pots would hold 20 gallons, large enough for 40 chickens!

The returning troops, 1700 per ship, were sent to a shed after debarking, where they shed their clothes which were to be burned; then they showered and were issued new clothes. Their families were there to welcome them. The cooks had gone all out and prepared turkey and steaks for all, and they could eat their fill. After dinner there were wagon loads of gifts for the returning soldiers, things such as: watches and razors, and perfume to give to wives or girlfriends as gifts. The troops were then housed in barracks for several days while being kept under observation for diseases and parasites.

Cleo was shipped to the Philippines with an advance group of eight cooks. He cooked on board ship for the 2200 troops. The trip took 20 days and he slept down on the third floor where he could hear the water on the bow of the ship. The troops went through the chow lines and stood up to eat. The officers ate the same food as the troops but were served at tables. Those men on KP duty raised the tables to the ceiling on ropes after meals and scrubbed the floor until it shined.

Cleo Hollaway

In the Philippines it rained for four months, which was good for growing rice. Carabao were used to prepare the soil, for hauling, and for milk. "Carabao milk is like cottage cheese. We had a Filipino 'barracks boy' who swept the floor, made the beds, and tidied up. He often brought craft items to sell. I said, 'Hey, Joe.' Everybody was Joe. 'Have you more of those little shoes? I want a pair to send home to my little girl. I'll pay you for them.'" He went running home and soon returned with the shoes.

Troops were warned to watch for booby traps when they went off base. The Japanese and rogue Filipinos had booby trapped everything, even corpses. Cleo and some buddies went off base one afternoon and saw the body of an American on the side of the road. They knew not to turn him over to see who it was, and Cleo warned them to stay clear, but one soldier foolishly tried to take off the wristwatch. It blew up and the fellow lost his hand.

On Sundays soldiers in Cleo's unit sometimes would hire a taxi (jeeps, which everybody in town had), and go up into the mountains to a beautiful pool. It was deep and cold, a welcome relief from the heat and dust, but they had to be on the lookout for snipers. The Japanese held the mountains surrounding Manila. They were holed up in caves. To roust them out, the Americans would rig up a rope and, like Tarzan, swing past the cave or into the entrance and lob in grenades. Then the foot soldiers would enter the cave.

One had to be wary of the Filipinos as well; not all were friendly nor to be trusted. "When they came into camp to get something to eat, we'd have to run them out because they stole everything."

"Others, like the barracks boy and the laundry woman, were very kind to us. The laundry woman did not wish to be paid; we only had to give her soap powder. She brought the clean clothes to us neatly folded and placed on our beds."

All food was shipped in from the United States. One week it would be meat, the next turkey, and then chicken. "The crews liked it when we had steaks. A Filipino man would haul off the guts from the butchers and take them home. Kids at the end of the mess hall would fight over the garbage; the kids were starving." Even so, Cleo said that the Filipinos would not eat our smooth grain rice, even if it were given to them, free.

The base had its own bakery although they sometimes used local white bread. Cleo would often be called on to make up "flight lunches" for the crews leaving on bombing runs to Tokyo. While Cleo was anxious to get home, he wasn't like the homesick fellow who shot off one of his toes so that he would be shipped home. That fellow was put in the base hospital until the toe healed and then sent back to active duty. When Cleo did get to go home, he was given $200 mustering out pay.

Written by John M. Ramsay with permission of Cleo Hollaway.

• • •

DID YOU KNOW THAT...

In 1944 Japan started sending up bomb-carrying balloons. Although most of the balloons were found on the West Coast, some were in North Carolina. Unfortunately, the government had kept these secret so the public would not be alarmed. After finding the one that killed five children and a woman in Oregon, however, government policy was changed. The public was warned not to touch them if found, and to notify authorities immediately. The balloons continued to be found, but there were no more deaths. 6

RONALD J. MIKSCH (Jim)
BELLEFONTAINE, OHIO

Air Corps, 29th Bomb Group, 314th Wing, 20th Air Force
S/Sgt., Gunner, 1943-45
Basic Training: Ft. Lewis, Washington
Duty in Pacific

DONALD EUGENE MIKSCH (Gene)
BELLEFONTAINE, OHIO (DECEASED)

Being twins, we wanted to enlist in the Air Corps together; we had planned that when in high school. Gene was working at Tangers and got a 6-month deferment. In the meantime, I was drafted, Infantry. When they asked that anyone interested in getting into the Air Corps for flight training take a test, I took it, qualified, and was sent to Amarillo, Texas. Because the College Training Detachment, part of the flight training, was full, I was sent to airplane mechanical school; then to Gunnery School at Las Vegas.

Gene, in the meantime, had come in, taken his Basic Training, and was at Ft. Myers. When I asked the colonel at Amarillo how my twin brother and I could get put together, he said to ask the War Department, which we did. They sent a telegram out to Las Vegas to process me immediately and to hold up on Gene's training. We took all our training then together.

At Sacramento we picked up a new plane and headed to Hawaii, to Kwajalein, and on to Guam. The B-29s flew out of the Marianas, which is Guam, Tinian, and Saipan. Our new plane that we got in Sacramento was taken out on a bombing mission by another crew whose plane was out of commission. It got shot up so badly that they junked it. There was another crew that had a lot of injuries, so they sent the crew back to the States for rehab, and we got their plane.

We flew in a 12-plane formation, daylight missions; we were the deputy lead. We lost the lead crew and so were moved up to lead; they gave us a new plane, which we used to fly the rest of our 28 missions.

Gene (left, deceased) and Jim Miksch (twin brother).

In daylight missions we flew up individually and made contact with the coast of Japan. Then we'd circle and get in formation to go in and bomb them. That put us in the air about an hour and twenty minutes.

Gas mileage was a problem. Iwo Jima was a safety stop for us, a place to get gas or maintenance. The P-51 fighters that escorted us were also stationed on Iwo. They were good fighters, but were strictly for daylight missions. If there was a wounded B-29 that had to drop out of formation, the P-51s would stay right with it. But they had no navigation equipment, so we had to navigate them; they couldn't navigate from Iwo to Japan. At that time the B-29 was the Cadillac of the Air Corps, flew about 200 miles an hour. The P-51 was fast and could hardly stay in the air at 200 miles an hour; that was just too slow. The engine would carbon up and they'd start missing, etc. That was no problem if it was clear so they could break loose and do some fast flying to burn the carbon off the engine. But if it was soupy or we were flying in clouds, they didn't dare lose sight of us cause they would get lost. The P-51 didn't have the navigational equipment we had, so they needed to keep visual contact with us at all times, unless they would come to a break in the clouds and pick up another B-29. So they kept wanting us to fly faster; we didn't want to fly faster and use up all our gas in case Iwo was fogged in and we couldn't get any more gas there. Our missions were usually 15-16 hours long.

We had all the fire power we needed, the latest remote control, central fire control system, which was new. We could switch turrets. Very accurate. The front turret had four 50 caliber; lower front, two; upper and lower aft, two; tail gunners had two 50s and one 20 mm; and, if we could keep in tight formation, we could shut the Jap fighters down.

We had good backup; besides the fighters, there were submarines that we could ditch by and they would pick us up.

In back of the pilot is the navigator and radio operator. There is a double bomb bay. There's a tube that runs from the front to the back of the plane and it is pressurized, didn't have to wear oxygen masks. Gene and I were gunners in the two bubbles on the sides. Behind gunnery compartment was the radar navigator. That section was also pressurized. The CFC (Central Fire Control) gunner in the top switched the turrets to whoever needed them. When a Jap fighter came in at 1:00, the CFC gunner would switch the fire power to that direction.

If we had to bail out, Gene and I would have gone out through the round hole in the bomb bay area. We would jettison the bombs and parachute out. The manual jettison for the bombs was under my seat.

There was an unpressurized area in back with the tail gunners. We were trained to never land on the tail. The back door that we could come in was opposite a window, which was a weak spot in the plane. If we'd crash land, it would break off there, and the tail would roll off to the side.

We by-passed a little Japanese-held island, Rota, between Guam and Tinian. There was a little airstrip and we bombed it just to keep the Japanese scared. Don't think there were a hundred on the island. One time we were supposed to drop a 6000-lb. bomb from low altitude to see what damage it would do. We weren't too happy about doing that! We put flak suits underneath our seats, wanted to protect ourselves. But the bomb didn't go off! After that, whenever we were up that way on practice missions, we'd try to drop a bomb from a higher altitude to set that 6000-lb. bomb off. We never did set it off!

Demolition bombs, 500 lbs., were for railroad yards, industrial type. We carried a few up to 2000 lbs. for certain heavy installations, but mostly 500 lbs.

Nagoya was one of the toughest missions, heavily defended. We were scheduled twice for it but never made it.

One time we blew a tire and went off the runway. Another time we had a mechanical problem.

Some of the earlier missions over Japan had trouble because of high winds, up to 200 miles an hour. Sometimes gas consumption, when fighting these high winds, left planes in short supply on their return trip. General LeMay decided we would go in at low altitudes, bomb from 5-6,000 ft. at night. Daytime bombing was usually 10-12,000 ft. We went in individually at low altitude, usually with 100 lbs. of incendiary bombs, with two or three cities being burned at night. The B-29s were designed as a high-altitude bomber, which in those years was 25,000 ft. The atomic bomb was bad, but what we were doing wasn't too good!

B-29, 20th Air Force, 314th Bomb Wing, 29th Bomb Group.
Courtesy USAF.

We probably lost as many planes due to thermo as anything, from the heat rising from these bombed cities in the night raids. The bombed cities were an inferno. Right after we dropped the bomb, we'd go into a column of smoke. Sometimes we flew up several thousand feet. When we went out the other side, with the air rushing down, it was just like the bottom dropped out. One night I looked back in the radar room and the operator was up to the ceiling and still had his seat on! He came down pretty hard! This up-and-down-draft put a great deal of stress on the wings.

We nearly got shot down on one return mission from Japan. With a little flak hole in the fuselage we could maintain pressure; if it was a big hole, we'd lose pressure. We had to go on oxygen then or drop down below 10,000 ft. Once we got to Iwo we felt like we were home safe. But this time the Navy opened up on us. Our pilot took off to the right and evaded them. When we got home we found out our IFF, which identifies the friendly planes for the ships and submarines, was shot out over Japan and wasn't working. So we couldn't blame the Navy for opening up on us.

One time we had to land at Iwo because of engine problems. While waiting for the new engine, there was still some sniping going on, nothing that really bothered us. But a Japanese sniper sometimes would shoot at the men that were manning the airstrip tower. The tower operators would come down out of the tower and run like scared rabbits!

Our next to the last mission I dropped supplies to the POWs. Our very last mission was a show of strength, flying over the battleship Missouri when the peace signing was going on.

· · ·

DID YOU KNOW THAT....

A Japanese soldier, after 30 years, was persuaded to come out of the Philippine jungle, still not fully convinced the war was over. In April, 1946, there were still four Japanese soldiers (who thought they were still on duty) in Lubang of the Philippines. They were determined to secure the island and be ready to guide Japanese troops, who they always felt sure would be landing soon, on the safest routes through the mountains.

Moving from place to place every three to five days, so as not to be discovered, they ate fish, wild buffalo, wild boar, wild chickens, iguana, bananas, islanders' cows, and rice. Knowing how to build fires without much smoke helped to keep their secrecy.

At various times they heard messages over loud speakers, found notes, leaflets, even photos and letters from their families, all saying the war was over, but there was always something suspicious which made them think they were all fake. Onoda felt that if Japan had really lost the war, not a single Japanese person would be left alive because they had all (women and children, too) taken a vow to resist until death.

Finally, after his last companion was shot in 1972, Onoda relented and talked with Norio Suzuki, one of the persistent visitors to the island, saying he could only leave if he had official orders from the Commander releasing him from his duties. Suzuki returned with a Major and orders for Onoda to leave. Onoda returned, after thirty years, to Japan as a celebrity.[7]

JAMES F. SCHRUBB

PIQUA, OHIO

Army Air Corps, Sgt., Photographer and Darkroom Tech, 1942-45
Basic Training: Patterson Field, Ohio
Duty in Europe

I enlisted in the Army Air Corps a week before my 21st birthday; it wasn't long until they dropped the age to 18. There were a few days when I wondered why I had done this as it was the first time that I had been away from home by myself.

I thought that I would be flying in a plane, but, because of wearing glasses, I had to stay on the ground. Pay had just increased from $21 to $50, which was a nice surprise.

I decided to stay in photography since this is what I had been doing at home.

After going to army photo school I was classified as a photographer and darkroom technician. We took pictures of wrecks, fires, dances, and entertainment, and did all the darkroom work.

One year after enlisting (on my birthday!) we shipped out for England on the Aquitania. It was a World War I vintage luxury liner converted to a troopship. They really knew how to stack us in! If I had known at the time that Germany was running subs up and down our coast, I probably would have been a little more uneasy.

We had the duty of showing movies in the evening on the base. On June 5, 1944, the day before D-Day, I had shown the movie and when I came out of the theater, there was a lot of hustle and bustle. Paratroopers, with faces blackened, were getting ready to board planes. They were to go to France that night to guide other paratroopers and glider planes in by radio for the invasion the next morning; we knew that a lot of those boys were not coming back.

As written in the 50th Reunion Newsletter of the 33rd Air Depot Group, there were "...many interesting and challenging tasks; one was to uncrate and assemble gliders, and another, just prior to D-Day, was converting a P-61 Black Widow night fighter aircraft for, on-the-spot-air observation of the progress of the invasion. This was a highly classified project. Maintenance personnel stripped the aircraft of all guns and radar and installed a plexiglass nose, with special radios and seats, front and back. During the first few days of the invasion, an admiral and an army general occupied these seats and relayed the action on the beaches to General Eisenhower's command post in England.

James F. Schrubb

"After the invasion, the Group had an assignment to recover as many gliders as possible, scattered throughout Normandy. They were to patch them up for one time flights, and their pilots would snatch them off the ground and tow them back to England for further use. They were later used in Holland and the assault to cross the Rhine River."

While in England we were fortunate in seeing Bob Hope, Glen Miller, and James Cagney.

After the war in Europe ended we were going to be sent to Japan; however, the dropping of the atomic bomb meant that we would be coming home.

I was never sorry about enlisting and would do it again if I were younger and if it were necessary.

. . .

DID YOU KNOW THAT...

The V-1 rockets, or buzz bombs, used extensively against England and Belgium, originally had a steel wing span of 17 ft. 8.1 inches and was 29 ft. 1.3 inches long. The steel warhead was replaced by a wooden one and the steel wings were replaced with steel-tipped ones in order to reduce the weight and extend the range to 230 miles.

The one thousand-pound warhead flew so low that radar did not always detect it.

Antwerp, Belgium, was a primary target of the V-1s because it had "...30 miles of wharves, 632 hoists, 186 acres of warehouses, 100 million gallons of oil storage tanks, and 250,000 people in it."

In Liege, Belgium, V-1s were coming in every 15 to 20 minutes at peak hours. Railroad tunnels 25 ft. below the steel mill were being used as shelter for people whose homes had been bombed out.

Around Antwerp deaths by V-1s numbered 4,483; injuries, 7,266. The Germans built 34,800 V-1s during the War.[8]

Buzz bomb over Belgium

Damage from buzz bomb in Liege, Belgium, November 1945,
courtesy Sherl Hasler

WILLIAM ZORN

SIDNEY, OHIO

Air Corps, Airplane Mechanic, Sgt., 1942-45
Basic Training: St. Petersburg, Florida
Duty in Africa

The draft notice said: "Men reporting to the Local Board for Induction: The selectee should bring hand baggage only. Trunks and boxes are not to be taken on bus or train. The following articles are suggested: a pair of strong comfortable shoes; an extra suit of underclothing; 3 extra pairs of socks; 2 face and 2 bath towels; a comb, a toothbrush, soap, toothpaste, razor, and shaving soap."

After taking a battery of tests, I got mechanic school, at Biloxi, with Pug Cromes, Sidney, as one of the instructors. Trained on engines 16 weeks; one week on body of plane; one week on hydraulics; then to propeller and engine—electrical, fuel system.

From there we went overseas and took over a French flying school in Marrakech. Got it cleaned up and ready for big planes to come in. Sixteen hundred ninety-nine planes went through that airfield: C-46, C-47, B-17, B-24, P-47. I went to B-24 school but never worked on one.

William Zorn

We didn't have to worry about where the runway went, just sand, anyway. The runway wasn't gravelled; sand was packed, but lots of it still blew off. All planes had to wait for dust to settle after each one took off.

The hangar was bombed before I arrived at Marrakech. German paratroops were landing near the field. A lot of French equipment was hit but didn't hit any of ours.

Temperatures there ran 140 degrees during the day and 80 by 4:00 A.M. We didn't touch much metal during the heat of the day. Didn't have gloves, either. Tried frying an egg on the wing, but it didn't work.

This was transient headquarters, part of the Ferry Command; women flew planes in the U.S. from manufacturer to overseas embarkation point but were not allowed to fly overseas.

Marrakech was a small base, 300 at the most, out from town five or six miles. An old bus, that was a real joke, ran into town, but usally we could get a ride in a jeep.

We had apartments, two to a room. Got meat, bacon, sometimes. Had fresh eggs. Native woman washed our clothes on rocks. Clothes didn't last long that way, though.

Bob Hope came in at the airfield, but since we didn't send a car to bring him in, about four city blocks, he wouldn't come. We had a small PX.

First B-29s came through; we weren't allowed to go out near them, but the French ran around all over. The Air Transport Command was taking the B-29s to Japan via Karachi, India, on what was called the Rocket Run, the supply route.

Saw four or five men from Sidney coming through our base: Bill Deam, Fred Barker, Merlin Campbell, Dick Davis, and a few others. The artist, who painted a lot of the pictures on the nose of bombers, was at our base.

Some planes, crippled or low on fuel, came in here on way back from bombing Ploesti. On bomb runs Allied planes would drop leaflets having pictures of destruction and said (in German): "Hamburg, August 1943. What does this picture prove? That the German air force cannot even protect the cities that can be attacked from England. Just as soon as the Allied bombers begin to operate out of South Italy, the German Air Force must begin to stretch out of South Germany, Austria and the Balkans. And then the German Air Force is supposed to protect East Germany from the ever approaching Soviet air power. And that means: Less protection for all of you."

William Zorn

I got transferred, as a mechanic, to Cairo, a large base about 30 miles out from town. We caught a little train into town. Had a couple of weeks' schooling for C-46, which had 2800 Pratt Whitney engine; the C-47 had a smaller engine. It was the workhorse, would practically fly itself. One engine could be out and it would still come through. Was used for paratroops and pulling gliders.

About the C-46 (Curtis) we said, "A tisket, a tasket, 2-engine flying casket." It had to have two engines to fly. The C-47 would fly on one engine and you could nurse it back, but not the C-46.

There was a machine shop and I met Schemmel from McCartyville, who was working on a Monarch lathe there.

President Roosevelt came over while I was in Cairo. Three routes had been picked and prepared. No one knew which he would take, but he went through the southern part of Africa on a 3-tail, 4-engine Constellation. The crew I was on was chosen to service it.

We were responsible for our work; had to sign forms listing what we had done. Someone had to go on test hop with the pilot. You never knew when you were going to get picked, so you did a good job.

There were engine inspections after 25, 50, and 100 hours. Engines were changed, but that job went to the hangar. All types of planes beyond repair were put in the salvage yard. If we needed a part, we got it there.

We, six on a crew, would start the engines up after working on them and taxi the plane around the field. There were few tire problems. One was making noise and a Coke bottle was found inside.

In Cairo we had lots of USO shows; National and American League baseball players came; and had a nice PX, as well.

I was pretty disturbed by the Red Cross. In the middle of the night guys would come in to get coffee and donuts and the Red Cross charged for them; also for cigarettes, four in a package, which on the back said, "Donated by——."

Supply parts came on planes; large engines went by ship. Gasoline came by boat and was trucked to bases. Troops went over by boat, very few on planes.

After V-E Day, most of the bombers and large pursuit planes were brought home, and then sent to the Pacific. Small planes were left. One B-17 they brought back for war bond sale had 500 holes in it. The sheet metal men were trying to get them all covered up.

Courtesy William Zorn

DID YOU KNOW THAT...

A Florida woman, living in Paris with her French husband, saved the lives of many American airmen who had been shot down on bombing runs. Being part of the French and Belgian Resistance, she cooperated with those who rescued these airmen and sent them from contact to contact on their way to Nazi-held Paris.

On June 7, 1944, one day after the Normandy invasion, while she and one airman acted as scouts ahead of a group of ten, they were confronted by police and arrested. She was told she would be shot the next day. Fortunately, this did not occur, but she was sent to a work camp north of Berlin. Shivering in the cold, having very little food, being forced to do heavy labor (building roads, loading farm wagons with manure), her weight went down to 80 pounds. They had shaved her head, she was infested with lice and racked with dysentery. In February 1945, with the war winding down, she was given clean clothes and sent to a camp on the Swiss border where French troops reached her. In May she was driven to her husband in Paris where, with his love, she recovered her health. Besides receiving France's Legion of Honor and many other awards, she treasures the cards, letters, and gifts she still receives from the men she helped. 9

French recognition of American soldiers' sacrifice — Normandy, 1944
Courtesy WAC Museum, Fort McClellan, AL

70

EFFECTS OF THE ATOMIC BOMB NAGASAKI, JAPAN

As told 50 years later to Wanda Briggs and John Stang
Tri-City Herald — Tri-Cities, WA

'A blinding flash of light filled the sky'

The little home is tucked away in an alley, so narrow neighbors wait politely for each other to walk past.

Along the flagstone path and stairs leading to Akiko Sakita's home, cats cluster and flowers flourish.

Sakita's father inherited the tiny plot of land and built a home on it that later would be destroyed by atomic fire.

Today, Sakita's eldest son has been given that same piece of ground, on which he has built a home now shared by three generations.

In 1945, from this small corner...Akiko watched the atomic destruction of the city of his birth. And at that location, he rebuilt his home and his life....

...Sakita told his story:

By the summer of 1945, "Japan had already lost the war," he said.

But the war waged on as Japan's military leaders vowed to fight to the death of the last man, woman and child.

...his parents rented a small piece of land outside the city....They were there Aug. 9, 1945, building what they hoped would be a safer shelter.

Back in the city, 16-year-old Sakita finished the graveyard shift at the Mitsubishi arms factory and returned home. At that same factory four years earlier, torpedoes were made to bomb Pearl Harbor in the sneak attack that pushed the United States into the war.

Sakita recalled, "It was so hot, so humid when I got home that morning, I couldn't sleep. I took off my shirt and went out into the backyard to do wash and cool myself."

Through the open back door, he heard the clock chime 11A.M.

"Almost at that moment, I heard the faint drone of airplane engines in the sky...behind my house.

"Oh no, not another air raid," I thought....

"Suddenly, a loud full boom like the burst of an anti-aircraft shell sounded in the direction in which the airplane would have passed, and just as I looked up to see if it had been the enemy, a blinding flash of light filled the sky and my body was showered in a wave of intense heat."

He felt a searing pain on his face and threw himself onto the ground with his eyes shut. Sakita was about a mile south of the center of the blast.

The upper half of his body was badly burned. The family's home was pushed over like a "flimsy matchstick toy" and Sakita was trapped by debris.

He managed to squeeze free. The long row of houses along his street was broken wood and rubble. Nearby factories were enveloped in flames, and thick smoke churned into the darkening sky.

Directly north, Sakita could see hundreds of people stumbling through the smoke toward the nearby mountains.

"I suddenly realized I, too, should flee for my life."

Barefoot and shirtless, skin peeling from the left side of his face, he turned and ran toward a cave dug into the steep hillside behind his home.

That shelter was crammed with people hiding for their lives. Sakita could not get inside.

He clawed his way up the burning hill behind the cave and came to a road halfway up....

"The ground was strewn with countless numbers of corpses. I could no longer bear to walk among them. I jumped into a sweet potato patch, tripping over the vines as I ran."

After two days of wandering, he made his way to a makeshift hospital. "Two or three nurses were desperately trying to care for the injured, but they were hopelessly outnumbered. It became obvious that however long I waited, my turn was not going to come.

A nurse threw a small tin of petroleum jelly to him. "It was pointless to wait for more. I left, and started home."

The road home was barred by civilian guards. He tried to get through. "My parents and sister may be there. Please let me go look for them," he pleaded.

Guards turned him away, and Sakita wept. "I lamented over the fact that I might never see my parents again and wondered how on Earth I would be able to go on living alone. I did not know what to do."

He roamed aimlessly, looking for friends among the dead. He spent two days and nights in the middle of a pine grove, hungry, bleeding, in pain and in shock.

On the third day, he made his way to a relative's home and collapsed into a coma.

Those relatives carried Sakita on a pull cart...to another temporary hospital....

With no doctors, nurses treated his wounds with mercurochrome and zinc ointment. He regained consciousness at the end of August, his sores covered but festering.

He learned later his parents were walking home...when the bomb exploded. They were carried to a makeshift hospital...where they spent a month recovering from their injuries. They died several years later from what Sakita said were radiation-related illnesses.

In the next four decades, Sakita, now 66, was hospitalized 14 times—the longest period for 30 months—and underwent 10 operations. "Sometimes I feel a great weariness."

...."There must never be another Nagasaki. Your family and mine must all be able to live in peace, without fear."

Reprinted with permission from the *Tri-City Herald*, Tri-Cities, WA, Wanda Briggs, and John Stang. 10

President Harry Truman's decision to drop an atomic bomb on this city freed Chonu Su from a life of slavery.

"America was right to drop the plutonium bomb and end the war Japan started," Su said.

His view is not popular in this industrialized city of nearly half-million.

But neither is Su. He's a reminder of a time many here would like to forget.

During the war, Japan replaced its dwindling labor force by enslaving thousands of Koreans. Su was captured when he was 14 and dragooned to Nagasaki in 1943.

He remembers vividly the spring day he was torn from his homeland. He was weeding a cucumber patch outside the tiny hut he shared with his grandparents when five armed soldiers came for him.

"The men said I must go to Japan and work. But I said, 'I could not, that I needed to stay to grow vegetables and care for my grandparents.'

"The men said, 'You will come.'" Su turned and ran, but was caught and beaten.

In April 1943, he arrived in Japan via ship. That year, about 12,000 Koreans arrived in Nagasaki. Most, like Su, were captives. Some were willing immigrants.

Su survived beatings, torture, near starvation and the atomic bomb.

"I will never forgive the Japanese government for what it did to me. They took my life and made it theirs."

...Su was given a Japanese name he never felt was his.

His first job was at a coal mine. For five months, 12 and 14 hours every day, Su mined coal. Black dust filled his eyes and lungs.

The scrawny Su grew weak on the daily diet of soybeans and fish scraps. When he no longer had the strength to work, he was beaten again.

When he recovered, he was assigned to the Mitsubushi shipyards, where he was taught how to melt metal. He was working there two years later when a bomb with the force of 2,314 tons of TNT exploded a mile away.

"There was a huge noise, a boom, and 80 percent of the ship I was working on was destroyed. All around me, people were dead."

Su was caught under a mound of metal that tore through his skin and sliced open his kneecap. He struggled free and stumbled to the Mitsubushi dormitory where he lived, but his dormitory, near the center of the bomb blast, was ashes.

He limped to yet another dormitory and found it filled with "frightened people, groaning with pain. Around me it was like a red ocean, so many houses were on fire."

Su stayed hidden for two days. On the third day, civil guards found him. They marched him to the...district of Nagasaki that took the bomb's heaviest toll.

Bodies were layered. The stench fouled the air. "Clean them up," Su was told.

For the next several days, he pushed a garbage cart filled with charred corpses to an open field. "It was so bad, I can't tell you how awful. Bodies were black, they fell apart and I swallowed toxic gas."

Mass cremations followed in that open field.

Each night, the exhausted Su returned to the dormitory to yet more death. "My Korean friends died right there in front of my eyes."

Soon, Su's hair fell out. His lungs were infected. His gums bled. And he was hungry.

"I was only a 16-year-old boy and I was Korean, so I was not lucky. There was no help for the likes of me."

...It wasn't easy. In post-war Nagasaki, nobody would hire the youth with the hacking cough who had retaken his Korean surname the same day Japan surrendered. He survived on the black market....

Su had no home, no mat to sleep on, no coat to keep him dry. He ate bits of rice and raided garbages to fill his belly.

Five years after the atomic bomb, his lingering lung ailment was diagnosed as tuberculosis.

"...I still feel fierce anger toward Japan. I was compelled to come here, and have known only a life-time of discrimination.

A slave for always, that's what they made me."

His rancor extends to his country. The Japanese government paid 3 billion yen to compensate Korea for loss of life and property during the war years. None of that money came to Su, now 66.

If he could, he would visit the United States. "I so respect America. It is a country of gentlemen who set me free when they dropped that bomb."

Reprinted with permission from the *Tri-City Herald*, Tri-Cities, WA, Wanda Briggs, and John Stang. 11

POW Says Nagasaki Bomb Saved His Life
'I would not have survived'

Elias Veerman believes the atomic bomb saved his life. On the day the bomb was dropped on Nagasaki, the now retired Oregon shoe store owner was a prisoner of war working at a coal mine just outside the city.

He was a Dutch sailor who spent about three years as a prisoner, forced to work in a shipyard on a Nagasaki harbor island. He was transferred to a mining camp outside the city in February 1945.

The prisoners heard stories they would be herded into trenches and buried if the Allies invaded Japan.

And during air raids, the prisoners were herded into a cave.

Finally, it dawned on Veerman the cave would have been blown up with the men inside if an invasion occurred.

"This [atomic] bomb saved a lot of lives. It saved my life. I would not have survived an invasion. They would have just wiped us out," said Veerman, 71....

Veerman, who was an 18-year-old living in Dutch Indonesia when war broke out in 1941, spent almost the entire war as a prisoner.

Drafted into the Dutch navy, he had little time to train before Japan forced the Allies to abandon the island of Java.

Veerman was on a transport ship evacuating people to Australia when it was captured by a Japanese battleship.

He was held several months at a camp in Java, where he was beaten and saw other men tortured.

And he was forced to watch two prisoners, recaptured after escaping, dig their graves before being beheaded.

"I didn't see the execution. I closed my eyes. Some of my friends still have nightmares. They were so cruel. They broke the rules of decency."

In October 1942, Veerman and other Dutch, British and U.S. prisoners were shipped to Fukuoka Camp No. 2 in Nagasaki harbor, where there was no escape.

They worked in a shipyard, where Veerman, armed with a broom, swept ships....

Prisoners were beaten often. Forgetting to bow to a guard brought blows.

Veerman was hit once on the rear with a baseball bat for losing his cap. And a Japanese marine hit him on the face, cracking his jaw, for warming his hands over a riveter's fire.

"I don't understand how these people loved to do these things."

Veerman endured other beatings. He also had to have foot surgery and a broken molar removed, both times by a prison doctor without anesthesia.

Finally, the prison camp got a new commander, and the beatings stopped.

One day, a never-smiling Japanese shipyard worker sent Veerman and another prisoner on an errand to his home in Nagasaki.

The worker's wife greeted them, and fed them rice, fish, soybeans and seaweed soup. The two discovered the errand was a ruse by the unsmiling man to get them a good meal.

By mid-1944...Red Cross parcels began to show up at the camp.

In February, 1945, Veerman and other prisoners were sent to a coal mine camp at Itah, on the other side of a mountain next to Nagasaki....

Then came that August morning. Veerman was walking across the camp compound when, "the daylight was drowned out by a white light. Then came a boom. There was a light that shivered. It shivered for a few minutes. Then the white clouds came over.

"I saw the flash. But I did not know what it was."

No one at the camp told him what had happened.

The last atrocity took place Aug. 13, when the camp commander spotted an American who ate his lunch too early and kicked the man to death.

The next day, a U.S. plane dropped pamphlets nearby. One side of the pamphlets showed a clock reading 11:55. The other side showed a clock pointing at noon with a city of flames.

The guards became more friendly.

On Aug. 15, another plane dropped pamphlets. They read: "You are free. Japan has surrendered unconditionally."

Veerman and the other prisoners stayed at Itah for a few weeks. Red Cross workers told them about the atomic bomb....

Eventually, they were taken to Nagasaki by train. "The only thing there was the train station."

But what a scene it was. A U.S. Army band played "When the Saints Go Marching In" as the train arrived, and nurses danced with the prisoners. For the first time in his life, Veerman had a Coca Cola and a doughnut....

In 1957, he moved to the United States....His attitudes toward the Japanese today appear split, sometimes focusing on the savagery he witnessed and sometimes recalling acts of kindness.

"I don't hold a grudge today."

Reprinted with permission from the *Tri-City Herald*, Tri-Cities, WA, Wanda Briggs, and John Stang. 12

Destroyed City Rises from Ashes

....."No trees or other plants will grow there for 70 years. It is recommended all residents find a suitable place to live elsewhere," the government message read.

Dr. Takashi Nagai refused to go. The physician and radiology professor had lost his wife and his home a few hundred feet from Ground Zero, and he wanted to stand his ground.

Lacking radiation-measuring instruments, he watched the ground.

"After three weeks, we found a swarm of ants, and they were vigorous and strong," Nagai wrote in 1946.

"After a month, we found worms in large numbers. Then we found rats running around. And I began to think that if small animals could survive, human life was also possible."

So Nagai built a hut on the rubble of his old home, where he lived until 1951 when the 43-year-old physician died of leukemia, a disease he had prior to the bombing....

Indeed, Nagai's courageous stand was correct. Within a few days of the bombing, radiation had decayed to safe levels. And long-term environmental contamination never appeared to be a problem, according to Yutaka Hasegawa, director of the Nagasaki branch of the Radiation Effects Research Foundation, which has studied atomic bomb survivors for 48 years.

Following Nagai's lead, others began to leave the huddled groups of survivors who were living in primitive dugouts elsewhere in the city and built huts in the destroyed area. Gradually, the huts were rebuilt into houses.

Wheat and green vegetables were planted in the bombed area, but the first crops of corn and sweet potatoes were disasters....

By nature, Japanese don't like to discuss humiliating experiences," Aguilar said, adding, "The bomb could be considered the ultimate humiliation of all."

For decades, many survivors would talk only with close friends about their experiences. Even 50 years later, some survivors won't talk to their grandchildren about the bombing.

But within a year of the bombing, Nagai wrote a book, *The Bells of Nagasaki*. "He was the first in Japan to write about the bomb," Aguilar said. "No one would open up his life or write about the bomb. He wrote about the war, but had no bitterness about the bomb."

....U.S. occupation forces banned the book in 1946, but the Americans finally allowed publication in 1949 when an appendix describing Japanese atrocities in the Philippines was added. That appendix was dropped when the U.S. occupation forces left.

Nagai's writings helped mold Nagasaki's response to the bomb, said the Rev. Diego Yuuki, a Jesuit museum director...."In Hiroshima, they became angry. In Nagasaki, they prayed," Yuuki said.

And after the prayer, Nagasaki set about quickly to rebuild itself.

It was a monumental task: approximately 30,000 homes were destroyed or damaged. Along with the homes, two arms factories, a steel works, an iron foundry, two hospitals, a medical school and part of a shipyard were destroyed.

The blast was contained between two mountain ranges on the east and west, funneling the damage about 2½ miles north and south of Ground Zero. Nearly everything within three-quarters of a mile from the blast's center was destroyed.

But the main Mitsubishi shipyard, the primary military target in the city, escaped major damage. And that proved to be a key in Nagasaki's recovery....

Today, shipbuilding is the biggest industry in the city of 450,000, employing about 11,000 of Nagasaki's work force of 180,000. Shipyard customers come from all over the world, including the United States....

Reprinted with permission from the *Tri-City Herald*, Tri-Cities, WA, Wanda Briggs, and John Stang.13

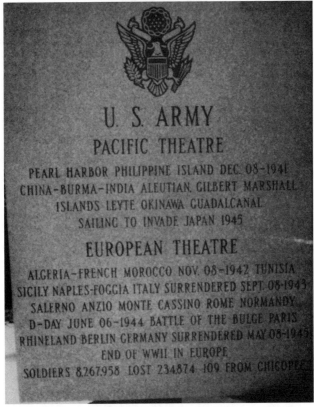

U. S. ARMY
PACIFIC THEATRE
PEARL HARBOR PHILIPPINE ISLAND DEC. 08-1941
CHINA-BURMA-INDIA ALEUTIAN, GILBERT MARSHALL
ISLANDS LEYTE OKINAWA GUADALCANAL
SAILING TO INVADE JAPAN 1945

EUROPEAN THEATRE
ALGERIA-FRENCH MOROCCO NOV. 08-1942 TUNISIA
SICILY NAPLES-FOGGIA ITALY SURRENDERED SEPT. 08-1943
SALERNO ANZIO MONTE CASSINO ROME NORMANDY
D-DAY JUNE 06-1944 BATTLE OF THE BULGE PARIS
RHINELAND BERLIN GERMANY SURRENDERED MAY 08-1945
END OF WWII IN EUROPE
SOLDIERS 8,267,958 LOST 234,874 109 FROM CHICOPEE

One of ten panels on monument, Chicopee, MA.
Courtesy Delfo Barabani

DON J. BIGGS
TOLEDO, OHIO

862nd Engineer Aviation Battalion, Cpl, 1943-45
Basic Training: Jefferson Barracks, Missouri
Duty in Europe

Lived in quonset huts in England; tents, otherwise. Had permanent KPs, 25 in a squad. One guy stayed up and kept fire going in pot-belly stove. Had coal pile and had to guard it from civilians.

Being in service was lonesome, but I enjoyed it. Spent almost 15 months at Raydon Airfield between Colchester and Ipswich, England. The Germans used to fly right over it going to London, called it The Great White Way. The British would turn the search lights on and light up the whole airdrome, all concrete. Some of us thought the reason the Germans didn't bomb it was so that when they invaded England, they'd have a nice airport to use.

After infantry went through a place, then we came in. Had inspection every morning, even in fighting areas. When on the move, we had to take down tents and take them with us. We carried guns but couldn't shoot them. When our guys took over an airdrome, our job was to get it ready for our own planes to come in. We unloaded 28 boxcars of cement one day, all in burlap bags, from those 40 x 8s.

We came to Cherbourg along Omaha Beach and started up through France. Our unit could only go so far and then we'd have to send trucks back to get more gasoline. We carried a water tank behind the truck, which would carry maybe 250 gallons.

At St. Lo we relieved the 833rd. They had made all the runways; we made the aprons. We were told that most of the 833rd were killed on that airbase. They were fighting on one end and trying to get the bulldozer on the other. Sometimes one side of the airfield was secure and the other wasn't.

At Liege we had seven or eight B-17s coming in. The drome wasn't ready. Had a road through the middle of it, but there was a big dip in the center. These big planes could make it in, but a P-38 tried it. We kept shooting red flares to warn them off, but they came in, anyway, put brakes on and went over just like at slow motion. Didn't get hurt but messed up plane.

I was on a 30 mm machine gun, digging in. "Don't fire! The enemy will know where we are!" I said, "Why not? They know where we are." Our company had to be blessed. We were right along the river in an old glass factory. We got chased off the airdrome; they bombed the hangar and the next day we moved out. One guy fell off the hangar there and lived. They were throwing 88s—those are big shells!—at us. A lot of them were duds. I was on a machine gun one night and a buzz bomb was coming right down at that factory, but it turned and went into Liege. You could hear them for miles. We were close to where the Battle of the Bulge was. They were going to leave our company to blow up the airdrome in case the Germans didn't, cause we were right there on that main highway at Liege; could see down in the river where they were fighting and could see tracer bullets.

In Germany had a big hangar on an airdrome that we had just gotten into. Free French sneaked up on us. "Understand a group of German soldiers are around here." They went through the hangar; found the Germans in a basement we didn't know about. We had been there for three or four days; the Germans could have come out and killed us all.

POWs had barb wire about 10 feet high. If they were bad they had to stand all the time. Only had 25-30 guys. They were eating venison; we were eating K-rations. In Germany had POWs cooking for us.

We had fighters, P-47s, taking off. A fellow from Indiana ran out there. Bombs on plane killed him when the plane didn't make it.

A B-17, on Thanksgiving Day, came straight down and crashed. We found pieces of that aircraft all over.

German civilians were practically starving. One man with a family to feed brought his wife and wanted her to have sex with anybody, just to get money. Captain took him out. Really a sad case! Wonder how anybody survived!

It took us four weeks to come home on a Liberty ship. The ocean was so rough, and we never knew which way that ship was going to go, sideways, or what. When they started those engines in Marseilles, France, everything vibrated.

DID YOU KNOW THAT...

The supply of guns was so critical that the roofs of buildings around the White House had wooden dummies rather than the real things. Some of the ammunition for the real guns was the wrong calibre.14

• • •

RALPH BOERGER
NEW BREMEN, OHIO

Army, Staff Sgt., Medic, 1942-45
Basic Training: Camp Grant, Illinois
Duty in Europe

Had eight weeks of medical training. Went overseas in June, 1943, arriving in Oran, North Africa, just after the African Campaign ended. After some training, the division boarded ships for the first beachhead battle of Palermo, Sicily. From then it was fighting every day. On to Salerno, Naples, Anzio, Rome. The division encountered more heavy fighting in Munich, Germany. On April 29, 1945, we liberated the Dachau Concentration Camp.

I never missed a day of combat, first being an aid man, then litter bearer, then jeep driver. And then I was put in charge of 36 men in the aid station.

The citation accompanying my Silver Star said in part: "A heavy concentration of enemy rocket and mortar fire landed near the battalion aid station and set fire to adjacent buildings and the ammunition pile of a nearby mortar platoon.

"While others sought cover, Technician Boerger, on his own initiative, left his position to remove a trailer laden with gasoline, parked next to the aid station. The enemy shelling continued and the ammunition began to explode, showering fragments through the area and igniting the tarpaulin on the gasoline trailer, but Technician Boerger ran to a truck, maneuvered it into position, coupled it to the trailer and pulled the gasoline a safe distance away.

"His quick thinking and courage undoubtedly saved the men sheltered in the aid station from serious injury and reflects credit upon himself and his organization."

Ralph Boerger

• • •

DID YOU KNOW THAT...

As American MPs marched prisoners through a town in Italy, one woman in the crowds yelled, "You're all right now; you're all right now!"15

BUD A. CLEMENT
PIQUA, OHIO

Army, Pfc, 10th Mountain Infantry Div., 87th Reg., Co. L, 1943-46
Basic Training: Camp Hood, Texas
Duty in Italy

After Basic our new orders said we were now in the 10th M.T. Division. Seeing the period by the M and the T, we all agreed that we were getting a good deal, out of the infantry and into the motorized transportation division. Big mistake! We had been put from the infantry into the 10th Mountain Infantry with all the mules and snow skiers and rock climbers! Back to Camp Swift, Texas, we went.

The rest of the Division had trained in Colorado, learning to ski and do rock climbing. By getting in later and going right to Texas, we missed that part.

As soon as the 10th Mountain Division was at full strength we headed for Italy on the USS West Point. At first my pay was $50 a month. On going overseas everyone was made a private first class and received $4.80 more pay. When arriving overseas, another $10 was added. In combat with small arms fire overhead, I got the Combat Infantry Badge with another $10 increase. From then on I received $74.80, and all the snow I could eat, a foxhole, and ski clothes. Because the Mountain Division was classified as a special force, we were to get $10 extra per month; however, we never saw that $10. In 1949 I received a letter stating that we were still going to get it; after that, I never heard another word about it.

The 10th Mountain Division had the best equipment, mules and skiis and weasels (on tracks). The mules had been adapted to battle areas, having had surgery so they couldn't bray nor hear. It was the only full mountain division in the world. I don't believe that any of the group ever used their skiis, but we did rock climbing on the mountains, using a rope.

The Germans and Japanese had mountain troops but not as many as ours in the States. We were called "Roosevelt's Glamour Boys."

Senator Bob Dole was in the 10th Mountain Division, 85th Regiment. He was hurt on Reviva Ridge before we got to Mt.

Belvedere. We lost a lot of good men in these battles in the northern Apennines. We went on through the Poo Valley to the Alps and were at Lake Gard when the war ended.

One of our officers came and told us not to fire our weapons any more, that the war was over. The German officers told their soldiers the same thing. They didn't tell the Germans who won the war for a few weeks. We were rushed up into Austria to keep the Germans from going through the Brenner Pass back to their home. Then we went to Yugoslavia where Tito wanted to take Trieste, the seaport, from the Italians. Everyone was guarding everyone else and only we knew why—a real hot spot to be in! We stayed there until the Germans were entered in a POW camp.

According to an article in "The Piqua Call" October 10, 1996, special bread had to be baked with a heavy crust for the 10th Mountain Division so that it would keep in the mountains. A man in the Piqua area, Richard Ayers, said he prepared 49 million pounds of bread while stationed in Italy.

• • •

DID YOU KNOW THAT...

Being easy to ship and assemble, 32,000 quonset huts were made during the war, the first ones being shipped overseas in June, 1941. In post-war days, some provided shelter for those who had lost their homes in the war.16

RICHARD W. DAVIS

FT. WAYNE, INDIANA

Army, Pfc., 76th Infantry Div., 2d Squad, 2nd Platoon, I Co.,
3rd Battalion, 417th Regimental Combat Team, 1943-46
Basic Training: Jefferson Barracks, Missouri
Duty in Europe

I was working with the 3rd Army under General George Patton.

Following the relief of troops by numerous divisions, we pursued the remnants of Hitler's attack force across northern France, Belgium, and Luxembourg, halting at the Sauer River near Echternack, Luxembourg. For about ten days we held the OPLR (Outpost Line of Resistance) along the western shore of the Sauer and overlooking Germany. On two occasions I was on a four-man reconnaissance patrol across the frozen river. Fortunately, we were not discovered by the Germans but did find many trip wires to set off explosive charges or alarms.

Richard W. Davis

On February 6, 1945, we attacked Germany across the Sauer at night at Echternach. We did not succeed in reaching the German side that night due to German artillery fire (88mm) and their knocking out the Army Engineers' pontoon bridge which was destroyed time and again on February 7 and 8. The river had risen to a rushing flood stage due to thawing ice.

On the night of February 8, 1945, we succeeded in crossing the Sauer in assault boats through rushing water. On the German side we encountered barbed wire and mortar fire which wounded several men.

A small group attempted to flank the Germans' positions on the heights above the Sauer. Within 200 yards we encountered a mine field which wounded two and mortally wounded another one. Sgt. Kittleson and I were knocked down by concussion but were not wounded. Pfc Katz came forward immediately, but just as he reached the wounded men, he stepped on another mine and was killed instantly. I was knocked down by concussion and thought I was blind, but found that my poncho had blown up over my face.

We moved into an abandoned small house right in the mine field and were fortunate that it was not booby trapped. A German patrol came near but didn't try to attack or enter the house since the mine field was around it.

Later we probed our way out of the mines and rejoined the company in front of the Siegfried Line fortifications. We attacked those individual fortifications with everything we had: rifles, machine guns, grenades, satchel charges, a flame thrower and a bazooka. By Friday, February 16, (my 21st birthday) our section of the Line was clear and we were relieved and sent back to a rest camp in Luxembourg for four days.

Fifteen of our men were killed and 20-30 wounded in this battle.

Trier, on the Mosel River, fell without much resistance, but on the other side (Eastern side) we encountered a line of German infantry and tanks. I was wounded in the left arm and another fellow was killed by a machine gun. Fortunately, I was in a position to attack the two machine gunners with a hand grenade and succeeded in taking out the position. The Army saw fit to award me the Silver Star and Purple Heart. However, it was no act of bravery; it was an act of desperation to save myself.

After three weeks in a hospital in Metz, France, I rejoined my company, and we moved rapidly across the Central German plain, sometimes riding on tanks.

Just outside of Weimar, where Hitler's 3rd Reich had been born, was the concentration camp, Buchenwald. The sight of people suffering and murder there were indescribable and sickening.

While returning to Germany on a C-47 after a 10-day furlough to Nice, France, I heard the news that the European War had ended with Germany's unconditional surrender.

All in all it was a great experience which I will never forget, and I will always remember the many good friends who died in Europe. They were not as fortunate as I to return to this great country.

. . .

DID YOU KNOW THAT...

One African-American who is still living, and the survivors of six other African-Americans, received the Medal of Honor from President Bill Clinton on January 13, 1997.

These men were members of a crack tank battalion that Gen. George S. Patton had personally solicited to help the 3rd Army drive the Nazis out of France in 1944.

The white officer in charge of this group said that POWs were treated better than his men. At that time African-Americans were used for menial tasks only.

After great heroism, the captain recommended Ruben Rivers for the Medal of Honor, saying: "I've never met a man like Rivers in all my life. He and the other men were treated like hell, but proudly waded into battle like the patriots they were."

Senior officers thought it was a good joke. Not until May, 1993, in a study of the awards process of WW II, was it admitted that there might have been racism in the decorations process.

The time to issue medals had expired, so it took an act of Congress to award these long-overdue honors.17

WILTON E. DICKE

NEW BREMEN, OHIO

Army, Tech. Corporal, Jeep Driver for Battalion Commander, 1942-45, WW II
Basic Training: Jefferson Barracks, Missouri
Duty in Europe

The 411 AAA Gun Battalion left New York in January, 1944, aboard the Queen Elizabeth. Most of the fellows had a small job to do, as guard duty or KP. Two days out we hit a big storm with waves 15 to 20 feet high. Most of the fellows got seasick. I stayed in my bunk most of the day and ate nothing. We landed at Glasgow, Scotland and then on to England for more basic training, practicing what we were taught in the States. On June 9, 1944, we landed in France. While unloading the jeeps into the water to get to the beach, the one driver refused to drive because the water was about three feet deep. I was asked to take his place. That's how I became a jeep driver for our Battalion Commander. He did not say much to me as everything was kept secret, only told me when and where to drive.

One day I drove my Commander, a Major, and a Lieutenant to Paris for a meeting. That's how I had my picture taken at the Arc de Triomphe De L'etoile.

Wilton E. Dicke

Our unit was composed of Hdq., A, B, C, D Batteries. We were separated once in a while because fighting was severe. One night I drove six hours straight in the dark to a new location to find places to set up guns. I had a Commander, a Major, and a Sergeant with me and the Major had to get out several times at a crossroad to read the signs, making sure we were going the right way. I did a lot of driving because the Commander always had to check on other line batteries. Quite an experience one day: A Captain, Colonel, and a Major were with me in the jeep when one of our army tanks lost its steering while making a turn and ran up the side of our jeep. Luckily, only the Captain got a slight injury. But I soon had another jeep to drive. The Commander called back to where our Battalion Hdq. was stationed and they brought another jeep.

Wilton E. Dicke

At the Battle of the Bulge, we were strafed by German planes as we were driving. I jumped into a foxhole with the Commander. This happened about three miles from the front-line. Another night a German bomber came over and dropped several bombs and one landed about 500 feet from where we were camped. It made a lot of noise. That plane was shot down by our guns. The next morning we saw the big hole the bomb made.

After the war ended in May, 1945, we were stationed out-side of Munich, Germany. Driving through Munich, I saw most of the buildings damaged and some completely destroyed. From here I had a chance to go sightseeing with my Commander. We went to Dachau Concentration Camp. Prisoners were all gone, camp was cleaned up, but the gas chambers and fur-naces were still there. The odor was still very strong.

Since my Commander was interested in architecture, we saw some churches and cathedrals. Both had received dam-age, some more than others. Some stained glass windows were all right, but most of the paintings were gone. Also saw the the-ater at Oberammergau, where the Passion Play is performed every ten years. I was able to go back in 1980 and see the live performance.

· · ·

DID YOU KNOW THAT...

The A. J. Miller Company, pre-war manufacturer of funeral cars and ambulances in Bellefontaine, Ohio, converted in 1941 to war-time work, increasing workers from 150 to 500. Major pro-duction was of the nose section for the C-46 cargo plane. They also manufactured "...gas tanks, floors for fighter planes, air duct systems, wing panels, exhaust stacks, fuselage and engine slings, airplane tow-bars, cowlings, cockpit enclosures, and many other small assemblies." [18]

WAYNE E. FOGT

SIDNEY, OHIO

Army, T/Sgt., Ordnance Supplies, 1942-45
Basic Training: Camp Barkley
Duty in Pacific

Boarded an old Norwegian freighter, called the Roosevelt, headed for Australia. It took 25 days, zigzagging en route. In Brisbane the temperature changed about 50 degrees every day. After four weeks we headed for Milne Bay, New Guinea. There we slept in tents until the natives built barracks for us up off the ground.

I was assigned to the tool and equipment warehouse. It was like a hardware store except that we did not collect any money when filling a requisition. After the sergeant was transferred, I was put in charge. We had lots of Hobart welders for other companies to requisition.

Wayne E. Fogt

During the 18 months at Milne Bay we sent supplies for each invasion up the coast of New Guinea.

In a field ordnance depot at Lingayen Gulf I sorted ordnance supplies that were unloaded on the beach. Later our company moved to a small town called Lubau; set up our warehouse in the building where the Japanese kept the prisoners on the Subic Bay Death March. It was here that Bob Reineke from Port Jefferson came in. My brother-in-law also flew in to see me.

My buddy and I were looking for someone to do our laundry. The first person we saw said that she would do it. She also invited us into her family's home and introduced us to her parents and brothers and sisters. The father was principal of the Lubau School; the oldest two daughters were teachers. We played cards and listened to Rose play the piano. When they had dances at the school or at the neighbors' tennis court, my buddy and I went with the four girls: ages 23, 22, 20, 16. Clark Field was not too far from Lubau, and when they would send trucks to the small villages to take townspeople to dances, the girls' father would not allow them to go unless John and I went along.

Our tents were set up in the church yard. Many times we were going to or from the shower, with only our towels wrapped around us, when the Filipinos were going to or from church.

I had many people staring at me because they had not seen red hair.

A Filipino said he'd seen a Japanese soldier fishing on a nearby pond. Seven or eight of our company got their rifles and surrounded him. When the Japanese saw them, he stood up and killed one of our soldiers before he was killed himself.

Made a move to Manila, which is 100 miles south of Lubau, and set up our ordnance depot in an old shoe factory, which had been bombed and burned. Tarps made our roof; our sleeping area was on second floor. The engineering company poured a cement floor, which was used as a dayroom and dance floor; even had a jukebox. At times they invited civilians and neighbors to come to dances.

I took over the small arms parts with the tool and equipment supplies. Sometimes boxes would arrive with the small arms parts torn open so the springs, clips, etc. had to be identified by looking at books and break-downs of different guns.

Later we loaded up all our supplies and headed for Nagoya, Japan. Spent four weeks on a ship waiting for Nagoya Bay to be mine-swept. When we unloaded, our vans were parked inside an airplane factory that had been bombed. Some planes were still setting on assembly lines; we'd throw a rope around them and pull them outside.

John and I never smoked, so one day we were selling our cigarettes to the Japanese; John was on one side of the street and I was on the other. An MP came up to John and asked if he knew where Leavenworth, Kansas, was. We got out of the cigarette business pretty quickly!

Our motto while overseas was: Home Alive in '45! I just made it in time for Christmas.

Fifty-one years after leaving Lubau I received a phone call from one of the sons of that family who had befriended us. He had been living in California for 25 years. Now I am communicating with the whole family. The story of their life in the Philippines during the Japanese occupation, as written later by one of the girls, is quoted below:

The Japanese Occupation by Benita Saplala Yap

December 8, 1941. Daddy and Inang told us not to go to school although we were dressed for the celebration of the feast day of Our Lady of the Immaculate Concepcion. I was a Senior leader and potential valedictorian for the fourth straight year. So I pleaded to go to school. But to no avail. Daddy was adamant. (After liberation, all seniors at the outbreak of the Pacific war were declared graduates). Our parents summoned their tenants to prepare garetas for transporting things to the barrio where our rice lands were located. We prepared for evacuation. Everyone in town had the same idea. Animals that could be bought were killed and prepared for future consumption. Excess things were given away. The carabao-driven carts had to come again and again to bring livingroom and diningroom sets, beds, aparadors, piano, clothes, food, silverware, kitchen utensils, chinaware, glassware, and live animals including the feathered variety.

Rumors were rife. The air was electric with news of the Japanese creating havoc from town to town. News of comfort women, raping and killing persisted. But no one thought the war could last for years. Daddy and Inang tried to make us understand the difficult times ahead of us, and how we were to conduct ourselves and preserve our virtue at all costs.

At first it seemed that life was just a round of activities for us, a prolonged vacation from school. There was a lot of going from one relative to another, attending this or that party for whatever occasion. Everyone had enough to eat and clothes to wear. War seemed far away. There seemed to be no difficulties on the horizon. The days swiftly turned into weeks and into months. Then slowly the months dragged by as people now started economizing in earnest for commodities became leaner and leaner. Lack of vital necessities followed, unemployment was ever present and hunger was at the door. Strangers started drifting into the barrios asking for work, for food, for clothing. Medicines were becoming difficult to procure. The "herbolario" was finding his place under the sun. Daddy's knowledge of herbs was coming into play very often. The Death March brought relatives with malaria, dehydration, fever, shock. They were treated as best as could be and were fortunate if there was a doctor nearby. Plants with known or even of doubtful medicinal qualities were searched for and used. Some got well; others died. Still the war went on. The Japanese now had their garrison in town, in the public schools.

To keep body and soul together, some individuals were ready to do anything. Unlikely couples allied which could not have happened prior to the war. Tenants with land left by their masters had more than enough food. Many came to ask them for help or to beg for food. War became a great social leveler.

Daddy and Inang decided to turn to business. A sari sari store was tended by us elder girls. On market day, Ating Miniang sold clothing materials. Barter was the chief medium of exchange. When there were few customers in our store, Ating Rose would play the piano placed at the rear of the tindaan. That could be one reason why we never lacked buyers to our modest store. The foresight of my parents in acquiring some rice land was heaven sent for we were able to barter palay with whatever we needed. Titong usually went with male relatives to town, to gather fruits in empty yards, or to catch fish, shellfish or get vegetables at our place. In our relatives' gardens, they usually found fruits and more vegetables. Our brother matured greatly.

Where before we used to go to social gatherings and party with Titong, now we joined groups for communal work like gathering camotes, cleaning palay, harvesting fruits. We received our due share as workers. These increased the home larder.

As time went on, the Japanese soldiers started to forage into the barrios for food. Whenever Japanese sightings occurred, Inang would tell us to dress the native way, baro at saya with shawls to cover our heads. Everyone had a clothes bag containing clothes, money, jewelry and some food in case we got separated. We used to hide in sugar cane fields all day, sitting still for long periods, slacking hunger with the sugar cane stalks and waiting for the all-clear signal. Relatives and friends devised a system of communication, using the tree branches along the way. The one farthest from the group would move a certain branch when Japanese patrols or trucks were coming. The next lookout did the same and so on down the line. We were very fortunate no one in our group was molested. Sometimes we were alerted at midnight. We stayed near rivers or canals, getting water to drink by scooping out nearby sand to form holes filled with water. When the sand settled down and the water cleared, we drank it. We also hid in bamboo clumps or other trees covered head-high with overgrown weeds. We were getting scared every day. Sometimes we heard of people we knew who were tortured or died. We also hid underneath rice hay stalks where rooms were built. Bamboo tubes supplied air inadequately. Bedpans took care of toilet needs. It was very stifling and claustrophobic. Yet we managed to stay many times in such shelters till the Japanese wisened up to the trick. We ate at unholy hours and bathed when we could. Such activities caused many sicknesses and some heart attacks.

When the Japanese stayed in the town, they soon received instruction from their higher-ups to open the public schools. So a portion was used as a Japanese garrison and the rest as school. Daddy was called and he had no option but to obey the ruling from the Education Department. We returned to our house in town with him and found it looted, partially destroyed, and ill used. Some Japanese soldiers stayed there. Mosquito coil burns were all over the place; part of the kitchen walls were used as firewood and our oven range was thrown out of the window into the yard. We had to clean the house to make it livable again. We patched the walls as best we could and returned most of our furniture and things into the house.

An order soon came for school officials and teachers to study the Japanese language. Daddy decided to make me his proxy, contending he was too old to learn a new language. I was the only teenager studying Nippongo, learning to write Katakana. We used Hanasi Kotoba. We learned to write slowly in Hiragana. Conversational Japanese was stressed; songs were learned, especially their national anthem. I learned to count and write simple messages. An old Japanese cook came to our house one day upon hearing the piano played. He taught us simple songs and danced to them, usually with closed eyes. He talked often about his children. He helped me in my Japanese studies, stressing the different forms of address. He brought vegetables in exchange, he said, for allowing him to listen to music. Daddy stressed politeness and civility since he had seen too many instances of Filipinos being struck for impoliteness to the conquerors. Soon I graduated with a certification written in Kanzi. Now I was a Japanese sensei or teacher like Sensei Shimizu. I was sent to Sexmoan (Sasmuan now) to teach Japanese in the public school for a while. I was also able to make use of what I learned when I acted as interpreter among my neighbors. A doctor used to ask me for help whenever he needed to bring a patient to the hospital. Using the honorific form of address, I invariably got a special pass for doctor and patient.

Once I went to the barrio with Inang during the rice harvest. We saw Japanese soldiers getting our palay and those of our neighbors. They were loading them into trucks. Inang asked me to help as everyone was bemoaning Japanese cruelty, leaving each family without rice for many months. When I spoke in Japanese, the soldiers were pleasantly surprised. Pleading with them to give each family some sacks of palay, they laughingly complied. When I said "Arigato de gozaimashita" instead of just "arigato," they looked more surprised and even gave extra sacks of palay to Inang....

Life in the town somehow normalized, when there were no more threats of killing in the area where we lived, which was in the town proper. The threat of being pointed at as anti-Japanese by pro-Japanese sympathizers or as Japanese collaborators by the guerillas kept many people afraid since some believed that among those killed were innocent people.

The young people in town formed informal groups. One such large group was our M club....Afternoons saw us socializing and eating. Old snapshots were brought out again and again....We learned to make shoes out of bakya by putting cloth tops with embroidery or recycled ribbons or lace and tying them at the back and front. Thread meant unraveling old clothes, especially khaki pants which gave tough wear. We fashioned new clothes out of old curtains or tablecloths....There was a lot of borrowing books, telling stories and quoting or making up poetry.

....As the year limped one into the other, we learned via the grapevine that the Japanese were now retreating. Again we went to the barrio and again we took cover whenever the soldiers passed by for they were desperate. We knew those who were killed or raped and it made for more anxiety and fear. Everyone was panicky. Mental cases were on the rise. Our relatives did not want us to expose ourselves in the open, such as bathing near the open wells....More news came. This time it was of Americans liberating the Filipinos. There was fear and wariness especially among the older ones that those coming might also commit injustices to the suffering victims of the war.

Liberation

When news filtered into our barrio that the Americans were spreading goodwill and meant no harm, everyone was filled with hope that the end of the war meant the end of despair and suffering. The Americans came into town and stayed in front of the church square. People assumed to be Japanese collaborators were taken away. The expression "peparimla de sacung," cooling of feet, meant permanent oblivion for the accused. Some were not really collaborators but it was difficult to talk for fear of being mistaken as pro-Japanese.

It was only years later that I learned even Daddy was accused of being pro-Japanese by the guerillas simply because he allowed the public schools to open. He maintained that he had received orders from his superior to do so and it was his duty to obey. It was also his livelihood. He had to be civil to the Japanese who came to the house seeking respite from their work by listening to music and teaching us to speak Japanese. In return, they sent food as tokens of appreciation. He was believed for they sent him home relatively unharmed.

I also learned about Inang's ordeal at the hands of the Japanese. It seemed that when Inang was asked by her relatives to help identify a body found floating on the river if it was really their second cousin, the Japanese learned of it. So all who were by the river side were rounded up. For three days there were endless interrogations, accusing them of being guerillas. Inang maintained her innocence, stating that all she did was to view the cadaver with her relations, for there was difficulty in recognizing a bloated body with cuts and wounds. Daddy succeeded in having her released to his custody.

The Americans offered to help repair the schools and even the destroyed houses of the populace. Roads and bridges in town were fixed. Daddy entertained them in our house as he was also entertained in the army headquarters. These Americans who came to our house brought dried eggs, flour, candies, newspapers. Some like Wayne (his story above) brought hometown magazines.... Medicines were given and even clothes exchanged hands. A camp cook taught me how to bake bread on improvised utensils. He brought ingredients when he learned we had not tasted bread all these years. When I learned the knack of simple baking on claypots, I was asked to demonstrate how it was done in some houses. I am sure part of the success lay in the eating of pan Americano. For my efforts, I was usually given some native delicacy for our family.

Then Americans left the town. The euphoria generated by the liberating army stayed. Now everyone was enthusiastic and wanted to do something.

Benita Saplala Yap, Philippines

Benita, the writer, became a teacher and has given permission to quote from her book, *Our Lives.*19

WHAYLAND H. GREENE

BELCHER, LOUISIANA

Army, S/Sgt., Rifleman, Platoon Runner, Squad Leader; 1943-46
Basic Training: Camp Fannin, Texas
Duty in Pacific

One of the best things I can remember about WW II is the real close friends I made. The men I fought with became like brothers.

One of the worst things I can remember is that some of these same men that saved some of our lives, or helped save some of our lives, were killed or wounded badly as we looked on. In some cases they died quietly and peacefully, while others were begging for mercy and wanted to be killed quickly to get away from the pain. After fifty years it still hurts to think back about some of them.

In Leyte, Philippines, all hell broke loose for us. They loaded us into trucks. When an infantry soldier is put into a truck he knows he is not going to mail call or the chow line or anything like that because we walked everywhere we went except crossing the water. We knew someone needed us quickly or we would have been walking.

In a distance we could hear artillery, machine guns and rifle fire. As we passed a large army cemetery with all those rows of neat graves and white crosses, (and some of those graves didn't look too old), and also looked at those rows of new graves already dug, it made me think—and those guns kept sounding closer and closer. Most of us probably realized that some of us weren't coming back alive, but we always thought it would be the other man.

We unloaded from those trucks before we got too close. They didn't want the trucks to get damaged because it would take too long to replace them. If we got killed, all they had to do was call up the draft board and they could call up a few more thousand eighteen-year-old kids.

On Leyte we were wet day and night for almost the 47-day battle. Can you picture sleeping in a hole with water three or four inches deep, and sometimes more, for 47 days and night? Keep in mind that the holes we slept in were different holes almost every night. We would make a push and when we went as far as we could, we would dig a new hole. A hole was the best protection available to us other than the Good Lord. Picture being cut off from your ration supply line and doing without food five days; sleeping only one or two hours at a time; waking up to eat a can of cold meat and spaghetti and halfway enjoying it because you were so hungry. Imagine not having even one warm meal for 47 days. When you opened a can of C-rations you would have to fight flies off continually that were moving from dead Jap bodies to your can of C-rations. I never go to sleep now without giving thanks for food, water, and shelter.

Whayland H. Greene

There were always dead Jap bodies lying around the battle area. The Japs were not able to recover their dead as often as we were, because they were usually being pushed back pretty fast. We had to be careful when we stopped to search the bodies because sometimes they would booby trap their dead.

Can you picture burying one of your close friends who was killed near you and wrapped in a poncho; and going back days after the battle was over, digging him up and putting him on a litter and carrying him for miles on a narrow jungle trail? The odor was almost unbearable.

The fighting lasted a lot longer on Luzon, but we were not in the mud and water all the time, never out of food more than one day at a time. We were real short on water part of the time; this had to be brought up in five-gallon cans on Filipinos' backs.

We were still fighting the same Jap soldier that was familiar with the terrain, well trained, well disciplined, and unmerciful. There are pictures of places they took over where they tied live civilians to trees and posts and used them for bayonet practice.

As a patrol would return, we would meet them and ask, "Did anyone get hurt?" The next question would be, "How many Japs did you get?" American lives were real important to us, but Jap lives meant nothing. I am sure their feeling toward us was the same. As we got older and the war long behind us, every life seems important and I think that is the way it should be. I know now they were doing what they were told to do by a group of misguided leaders. They were very conscientious and determined soldiers and loyal to those misguided leaders. When the war was over and they were told to quit fighting, they were very humble to the point that you could not believe the way they were just a few days before.

Lt. Kedrick was our platoon leader toward the end of the war, and I do mean leader, not driver. He was outstanding! He was always out in front of us. He slept in the same hole with us, ate out of the same can of C-rations with us, and did without food when we did. He could be as mean as any Jap at times and as gentle as a Sunday School teacher in the nursery department when he wanted to. As an example, after the war was over and the Japs came in and surrendered, we were leaving the area where we were fighting, climbing a tall mountain, with the Japs mixed in with us. A Jap soldier was carrying a sick or wounded Jap on his back. He carried him until he himself fell to the ground. Lt. Kedrick put the sick or wounded Jap on his back and carried him. The other Japs could not believe their eyes—you could see the surprise on their faces.

When you see all the white crosses in a military cemetery (or a picture of one), stop and thank God for those who gave so much. Each was doing what he or she was told to do and sometimes even more. A lot of the fighting was done by 18 and 19-year-old kids right out of high school, kids who had to become men almost overnight. They were gathered from all over the United States and given a gigantic job to do. With lots of love for their country and fellowman, lots of determination, lots of sweat, blood, and tears; with excellent leadership, and last but not least, a tremendous amount of help from God, they were able to get the job done.

May God continue to Bless this Great Country and the People who live in it and may we who live in it be a little more deserving of that blessing.

To You Beautiful WW II Nurses

Even if you are seventy to eighty years old now, in the eyes of every WW II veteran you will always be beautiful.

There is no way we can say "thank you" in the way we would like to. I am going to attempt to say it for the thousands that did not get home, the thousands that have died since WW II, and the thousands that are still alive. The best way I know to do this is to use some of my own experiences, then you can multiply them by thousands, and maybe you can understand what I am trying to say.

My first twenty-six days in real combat was a frightening experience. I was on Leyte Island, had thirty-one inches of rain in thirty days, and we were out in all of it. We got cut off by the Japs and had to do without food five days. We had some of our close friends killed, others wounded. Some of us had killed our first Japs. Some of us were nineteen years old, scared to death. We had been sleeping in wet holes twenty-six nights. We were just about as miserable as we could possibly be, and on top of that, real homesick.

I got a bad case of jungle rot on my feet and was sent to a hospital that consisted of a long tent with canvas cots. They took care of my feet almost immediately. Then they were busy with seriously wounded soldiers, so I didn't receive much attention for a few days.

Portable hospital

After about the third day, a beautiful young nurse, probably about twenty-one years old, came to my cot. She said, "You haven't been receiving very much attention; we have been real busy with the wounded. How would you like to have your back rubbed down?" I could not believe she could spend that much time with me. She asked how old I was and when I answered "nineteen," she said, "You look about sixteen." When she said that, I knew she had at least looked at me. She then asked where I was from and I said "Louisiana."

You can't imagine what that four or five minutes meant to me. I am sure that each of us fell in love with her as thousands of others fell in love with the nurses that spent a few minutes with them. So after fifty years, we all would like to tell each of you "Beautiful WW II Nurses" that we are still in love with you.

Reprinted from *Grateful Soldiers... Not Great Soldiers* with permission of Whayland H. Greene, author.[20]

• • •

DID YOU KNOW THAT...

In 1862 President Lincoln established the first National Cemetery "for the soldiers who shall die in the service of their country."

"Now 2,406,170 veterans or family members are buried in 130 national cemeteries in 39 states, the District of Columbia and Puerto Rico." [21]

Sitka National Cemetery, AK

DWIGHT L. HALEY

CHATTANOOGA, TENNESSEE

Army, Staff Sgt., Topographical Section, Surveys for Artillery, 1942-45
Basic Training: Ft. Sill, Oklahoma
Duty in Europe

I was the son of a circuit riding Methodist preacher in Waynesboro, Tennessee. When my military career began, I had been working at the Redstone Arsenal in Huntsville, Alabama. After our physicals and I.Q. tests at Ft. McClellan, Alabama, my group was celebrating our good physical and mental condition when a huge sergeant told us were were going to be punished for our noise. He had us fall out—that's army for "Come with me." We marched to Battery Street and policed the area— that's army for "Pick up everything that's not growing, and if it's too large to remove, paint it."

Dwight L. Haley

When we went to pick up our army clothes, the only thing that fit me was my necktie. When the command "Left Face" was given, I had to reach down and turn my shoes with my hands.

Next came our assignment to training camps. I saw I was in trouble when the man in front of me was asked what he did in civilian life; he worked for Dr. Pepper. The sergeant said, "Put him in the Medics." I was lucky—went on a troop train to Ft. Sill, Oklahoma—two large barracks bags and a duffel bag to carry. I didn't get seated 'til the train pulled out, and I just left my bags in the aisle; the officer in charge came along and stumbled over them. After a few choice words he said, "Private, get rid of those bags!" Trying to carry out orders, I raised the window and threw them out. That was a mistake! As I got off the train the supply sergeant was standing there with a statement of charges to sign—that's army for "You only get one third of your pay 'til those clothes are paid for."

After training as a gunner on the 105 Howitzer, I learned that I was to attend Officer Candidate School and become a "90-day wonder." Anyone whose I.Q. was 110 or over had to attend. I quickly told them I didn't want to be an officer and a gentleman—that's army for 2nd Lieutenant. I had already heard they were expendable, and even our own troops didn't have much use for them. I flunked the entrance exam and was held at Sill as cadre at the training center.

My first group could not carry arms—they had brooms, shovels, etc. After one training session of this, I asked to be transferred to a line outfit. After another session of training political appointees, ranked from lieutenants to colonels, they decided to get even with me. I was sent to Madison Barracks, New York, located on the Canadian Border near Watertown. To add insult to injury, this outfit was made up of Yankees. I found out soon that this was an Observation Battalion and would be my permanent unit. To acclimate the Yankees to warmer climate, we were sent to A.P. Hill, Virginia, for further training. Then on to Tennessee for maneuvers. I really hated this; we were bivouaced 22 miles from my home.

After about a month of this we went to New Jersey and hitched a ride overseas on a converted luxury liner; landed in Oran, Africa. After selling mattress covers, cigarettes, and chocolate bars, we got enough gas money and drove to Bizerte, Africa. Were disappointed that we didn't get to see Dirty Gertie from Bizerte.

Italy surrendered and we loaded on boats and landed in Naples. This started the long march. Got as far north as Monte Cassino and bogged down for quite a spell. Got impatient and loaded on more boats—landed at Anzio and Nettuno and established our outfit. This was where Nero fiddled while Rome burned. We fiddled while waiting for the rest of the army to catch up to us. They finally arrived and we kept going until we reached the Brenner Pass (Italy and German Border).

Now, what did I do? Briefly, I earned four battle stars and the good conduct medal, one beachhead landing. Oh! I captured forty German soldiers. We were cleaning up pockets of Germans near the end of the war. An Italian came up to me and said, "Sergeant, there are several German soldiers in my barn loft and they want to surrender." I jumped in my jeep and went to get them. As I arrived, it dawned on me I didn't have my side arms on; I nearly panicked. Then I thought about Alvin C. York who gobbled like a turkey and came up with a lot of captured soldiers. I got a large rock in each hand and brought the prisoners in.

When leaving for the U.S., I received a letter from Lt. Col. Nichols, which included the following: "...Your courage and endless humor was an inspiration to the men and a large factor in maintaining the high morale...."

• • •

DID YOU KNOW THAT...

The Tuskegee, Alabama, airmen became famous in WW II, not only for their accomplishments in the air but because of winning the battle of racial segregation in the military. Even though they had been accepted in a special Civilian Pilot Training Program at Tuskegee, completed ground school and flight instruction with scores equal to white candidates, they were given only menial jobs and refused enlistment.

Finally, after much controversy in the military, as well as among civilians, the War Department approved plans for an Army Air Corps all-black Pursuit Squadron, the 99th.

After being taken into the Air Force in July, 1941, there was quite a delay in sending them into active service, into battle. With interception of Eleanor Roosevelt, the 99th Fighter Squadron eventually received word it was going overseas in April, 1943.

Arriving in Africa, they received twenty-seven P-40 Warhawks and advice from experienced combat veterans. At Tunisia they received congratulations from both Major Jimmy

Doolittle and Gen. Dwight D. Eisenhower. Later becoming part of the 332nd Fighter Group and a component of the 306th Fighter Wing, in their role of providing bomber escort and ground support, missions included Ploesti and Berlin as well as Sicily, Anzio, the Monte Cassino Abbey.... They had flown, besides their original P-40s, P-39s and P-47s in combat, and in mid 1944 received P-51 Mustangs. Because of the all-red tails on their P-51s, the 332nd became known as "The Red Tails."

Because it was difficult to get replacements for these black pilots, many of the 332nd flew up to 125 missions, while 50 was the normal cutoff point for white pilots.

Gen. Arnold said that the eyes of Negro America were upon the 99th Fighter Squadron. "...the experiences and accomplishments of the Tuskegee Airmen served as a focus of pride and encouragement in the decades to come and ensured that, eventually, in war or in peace, there would be no more segregated skies." [22]

"...the 99th's precision flying remained unmatched until the advent of demonstration flight teams after the war. Ground crews excelled as well, performing engine changes in one-third the time usually required." [23]

SHERL HASLER
BLOOMFIELD, INDIANA

Army Engineer Aviation Battalion, T/5 Sgt., 1942-45
Basic Training: Richmond, Virginia
Duty in Europe

On my first day in the army we stood in line for shots; then it was on to the clothes-issue line. My feet were measured for shoes by standing in a sand pile, holding two buckets of sand. Then my track was measured. On down the line, I was handed a pair of size 12 shoes. I told the Supply Sergeant that they were too big, that I only wore size 7. He said, "They'll fit!"

Sherl Hasler

Moving down the line, the shirt I was handed looked like it would go around the neck of an elephant. When I told the PFC that the shirt was too big, he replied, "It's your size, soldier, move on." By then I decided to keep quiet about the pants.

When I dressed in my uniform, the knot in my necktie hung down on my chest about where the top of my shirt pocket should be, and my pants wrapped around me like an Indian blanket. I have always thought that Bill Mauldin was in that line and got his ideas for his famous cartoon, Sad Sack, from me.

Mariposa

In May, 1943, 15,000 of us loaded on to an ex-luxury liner, The Mariposa. We did not go in a convoy as the ship had too much speed. We were escorted by planes out as far as their fuel would permit, and then picked up by planes from England when they could reach us.

The trip was uneventful except for one round with a submarine. On reaching Liverpool we were unable to disembark as the harbor was being bombed. By train the next day we went to Raydon Wood, England. At the time we disembarked and marched toward the airfield, an air raid occurred. The train was strafed and bombed and all the train crew members were killed.

Raydon Air Base was about half completed when we, the 862nd, took over from the 833rd Engineer Aviation Battalion which had started the Base one year before. P-47s, P-38s, and P-51s were flying from Raydon and soon there were B-17s.

Raydon Air Base, England

Heavy equipment, 862nd

Apparently our group crossed the channel at different times. I was on a ship in the channel when the invasion started, but some went 8 or 10 days afterwards; some as much as a month later. The ones I was with went on Utah Beach just beyond Point D Hoc. We could not move inland for several days because of being hemmed in by hedge-rows. A sergeant came up with some kind of apparatus to put on tanks and bull-dozers and that opened things up. After the break through at St. Lo, it was a foot race until we got into Belgium. Winter had hit hard, the worst in history.

We had worked on several airfields on the way up. We now had 36 hours to lay down an airstrip, made from pierce steel plank, on a sea of freezing mud, snow, and ice. When the last plank was put down, three hundred C-47 cargo planes with supplies were circling for landing. When unloaded they reloaded with wounded and frostbite cases. I saw people loaded on those planes with no meat on their toes, just bone. I, too, had frostbitten feet but not to that extent. I always tried to get my shoes off at least once in a 24-hour period and massage my feet to get the circulation back.

Steel-pierced plank runway constructed by 862nd, Belgium

We worked on an airfield a short distance from Bastogne. Soon after the battle started and the fog lifted so the planes could fly, we watched the air drop of supplies at Bastogne. The German army got to the Meuse River but never made it across. We knew then it was all over if we could withstand the cold weather.

• • •

Sherl Hasler in gas mask

German prisoner quarters, Furstenfeldbruck, Germany

German prisoner stockade, Furstenfeldbruck, Germany

B-17 after direct hit

Bridge 862nd crossed over Rhine River

GEORGE HUCKLE

BOYNTON BEACH, FLORIDA

Army, Sgt., 1942-46
Basic Training: Camp Roberts, California
Duty in Europe

When we were on the train after Basic, all pre-med students, we thought they would take us as Medics. When we passed up Ft. Leonard Wood, St. Louis, Missouri, where the Medics were trained, we thought, "Well, we must be going into the Air Corps."

No, kept going. Ended up at Camp Roberts, California, in the infantry.

Infantry training; job assignment, company clerk, which was great. Months went by, though, and I was getting a little bored. They were looking for volunteers for the 10th Light Mountain Division, which would start training at Camp Carson, Colorado. That appealed to me cause I used to ski a lot in high school. I had to be certified or recommended by some mountain climbing club or a certified ski club. It so happens that outside Cadillac, Michigan, there was a ski club and my best friend's older brother was president of it. I wasn't that great a skier, but I wrote to him and by return mail I received a letter telling about what an accomplished skier I was, etc. Sent in the application and about ten days later I got a letter back. Everything was in order, contingent on my passing the physical examination. When I went to the base hospital to get this physical examination there were about twenty other young fellows getting exams. I thought it was rather strange because the examination was a little more than the usual one. Since I wore glasses they had three ophthalmologists test my visual acuity. After all this, they passed me, but it took the greater part of a day. They called us all in another room, asked us to sign the papers. We were all supposed to raise our hand and take another oath that we were willingly volunteering for the paratroops. The truck was waiting outside the door to take us to the training center. Wait a minute! I had no interest in jumping out of airplanes! Well, I got out of that, fortunately!

A year or so later I was transferred overseas as an infantry replacement, just a few weeks after D-Day. Two days after we got to England I was the only one in the unit that wasn't shipped out. I sat in England maybe a month doing nothing. My time came up, got orders, went on troop ship, which was really an old British Channel steamer. On board was a Special Service unit with Mickey Rooney, Terry Bartholomew, Jackie Coogan—we all played poker while crossing the Channel.

Got to Le Havre, living on C-Rations, in tents, in the rain and cold. Packed us on troop train. I can remember in my home town they used to have a 40 & 8—that's what we were in—forty men and women packed in those little boxcars. It was a miserable train ride; took two days and two nights through the outskirts of Paris. We were sitting in some marshaling yards outside Paris, and off in the distance we could just barely see the top of the Eiffel Tower, so we knew we were in Paris. I thought that the greatest thing that could happen to me would be to get a three-day pass in Paris.

The next day they called most of the guys I was with, and then it was my turn. When he said we were headed for Paris, I didn't believe him. Then he said, "The truck leaves in ten minutes. Load your gear." It turned rather warm and the sun came out that October day. As we drove into Paris, I was all eyes and they took us through the center of the city right to the Hotel Majestic. At that time it was the headquarters of the U.S. Forces in Europe. They took three of us in. Remember the old cartoon of Willie and Joe? That's what we looked like. We were in the infantry—had full field packs, steel helmets, leggin's. Hadn't had a bath or shower for several days, dirty, grubby. They took us in that hotel and up to Gen. C. H. Lee. Gen. Eisenhower was Commanding General of U.S. Forces and Expeditionary Forces in Europe, but Lee was actually the technical Commanding General of U.S. Forces in Europe. They ran all the nuts and bolts, the communications by and large, the Red Ball Express. Communications is what I ended up being in. Lee was a very spit-and-polish general and here comes the Ernie Pyle rejects! The secretary was a WAC major and he said to her, "Take these men. I believe they are to be assigned to Col. —, but be sure he has them billeted, shaved and showered before they return."

The Majestic Hotel has now been taken over; the French Government donated it to the U.N. and it is now the U.N. Conference Center. It was used by the Germans as their headquarters before we got there.

I worked there as a clerk—me and my Remington Automatic. Had learned to type in high school. When I went into service they put us through the usual stuff and asked if anyone could type. I was put in a room with about ten other guys and we were given some stuff to type for five minutes. So, anyway, they found it in my file. I guess I was just at the right place at the right time. At least it was better than the paratroops!

By the time I got to Paris it had been liberated for six or eight weeks. Things were still in turmoil. Still a little shooting around with the Free French, the collaborators, and the German deserters who were still in the city at that time.

I worked in the message center; everything funneled through us. We were concerned about identifying 5th column infiltrators; some were dropped in Paris—paratroops. So the city was really buttoned up. Everyone had to be off the street at dark. MPs and even French police had to be off. Had to carry our ID, our Paris assignment card, our unit where we worked. Each day we had to have a special pass, dated, for 24 hours only. All leaves to city were cancelled. The word was out—shoot on sight! Very suspicious! We worked around the clock, and when we had the swing shift, 4:00 to midnight, we had to walk home 1½ miles, past the curfew hour. Eeriest sight standing under Arc de Triomphe with not one person, nor one light, nor car, nor dog. As the three of us were walking down the street, a jeep with four MPs came up, two guys had Thompson submachine guns; the third guy had his .45; the driver sat with his hand on a carbine. Even though we had a legitimate reason to be out, we had to do some fast talking!

The closest I ever came to combat was the one and only air raid my second night there. A half dozen German bombers got through somehow and dropped some bombs on the city. They dropped one only about three blocks away from us.

The greatest thing after being overseas and eating C-Rations, was that the government had taken over a lot of facilities, including a restaurant in which the only thing GI was the mess sergeant whose job was to punch our meal ticket.

That winter of 1944-45 was pretty bad for civilians. Transportation had been all bombed out, communications were down, no heat except in public buildings at certain hours. The military had some. There was no food available for them; ours was all shipped in. But what those cooks would do with those powdered eggs and powdered milk, all the fruits and vegetables in the can! They had the wheat and they would make delicious fresh rolls and omelets that melted in your mouth. What meat we had was Spam. They took it and, if I didn't tell you what it was, you wouldn't know it was Spam. I never ate so well. Only missed ice cream and a glass of milk.

The British had taken over entertaining the troops. So Lawrence Olivier and all these great British actors were there in the plays. And we could get tickets for the opera.

Around the end of 1945 headquarters were moved to Frankfort for the occupation.

A couple of months before V-E Day, early spring, after the Battle of the Bulge, up to about the time they crossed the Rhine, there had been a big attrition in infantry, and particularly in platoon leaders. They were having problems getting replacements from the States. So in March they did two things: They started putting out directives for all the rear echelon officers to free up about 10 percent of enlisted personnel for reassignment to infantry, regardless of rank and length of service. Some of these guys they called up were master sergeants and had never fired a gun. Supposedly they would be given a little training. They were issued an M-1 rifle and one clip of ammunition; the next day they put them on a truck and sent them up to General Bradley.

They were also running out of platoon officers, so they started an OCS (Officer Candidate School) deal. I knew Germany wasn't going to last much longer and I figured this training would last ten or twelve weeks. By the time I got through this, the war should be over, hopefully in Japan, too.

I was there a few days before Roosevelt died. They closed it down about a month after V-E Day. I was there on V-J Day, too. No place to celebrate and nothing much to do. V-E Day meant much more to the people in Paris.

• • •

DID YOU KNOW THAT...

The WW II destroyer escort USS Mason, commissioned in Boston on March 20, 1944, was the first warship in U.S. Navy history with an all-black crew. For the crew's action in escorting six convoys across the Atlantic and for guiding twenty ships to safety during a fierce storm, each man received a letter of recommendation in his file, albeit they were not received until 1996. 24

• • •

NEIL H. JOHNSON
GLENMORA, LOUISIANA

Infantry, Captain, Company Clerk, Duty Liaison Officer, 1940-45
Basic Training: Camp Blanding, Florida
Duty in Europe

At the end of the war in Europe, we assumed occupation duties in the area. I was assigned to temporary duty with the Allied Military Government. My primary task was to assist in returning people, displaced by the war, to their countries of origin.

Innsbruck was a "choke point" because German and Italian railroads were of different gauges. We had to provide food and shelter while awaiting trains from Italy.

In one camp we had some 2500 Russians and some 1000 persons of other nationalities from central Europe. We also had a number of people who were classed as displaced persons. No country would claim them. The Russians were unique because they didn't want to return to Russia. They claimed they would all be killed. We put them on the train at gunpoint.

One such person was Hulda from Kiev. Her story: Mother was German; father a Russian professor. When the Germans attacked Russia, the Russian police arrested her father and he never returned. When the Germans overran Kiev, Hulda's mother claimed her German citizenship and obtained employment with the German army. When the Germans recaptured Kiev, Hulda went west and stayed near the Germans. When the war ended, Hulda was in a camp in Austria. She was fluent in English, Russian, French, German, and conversant with most of the languages of eastern Europe. She was very useful as an interpreter. Hulda really had no home and her desire was to marry a GI and come to the States.

We freed a group of some 250 Russian girls who had been taken prisoner soon after the Germans attacked Russia on June 22, 1941. They worked in a factory building Hainkel planes. They said that early in their captivity the guards tried to molest them. They invited one in and sent him back over the fence, one piece at a time. No more attempts by the Germans. They also complained that Hainkel treated them better than we did. He gave each of them a pint of milk for breakfast every day.

I also met Mike, an Italian, in a camp in Austria. He stood behind the gate cursing Mussolini, Hitler, Stalin, and anyone else he could think of, all in perfect Chicago English. When he was small, Mike's parents had come to Chicago and become citizens. In 1939 Mike returned to Italy to visit his grandparents and was taken in the Italian army.

When Italy got out of the war, Mike was taken by the Germans to work in a munitions plant. They were making artillery shells and Mike said that the workers sabotaged as many shells as they could get away with. Mike really felt he should be rewarded with a trip home, along with our troops. We put him on a train to Bolzano, Italy, and told him to see Mussolini for passage to the States.

I met a group of about twenty men who were claiming "stateless person" status. I never really knew where they were from or where they wished to go. They had an intense dislike for Italians; they were armed with nightsticks and used for police in the camp.

Because of the difference in rail gauge between German and Italian equipment, the home-bound Italians had to change trains in Innsbruck. We took them off the train and pro- vided food and shelter for them until the train came from Italy. We also deloused them with D.D.T. Our twenty stateless men thoroughly enjoyed spraying the travelers with D.D.T.

We picked up a trainload of Italians going home, about 500 people, including fifteen full colonels, all of whom claimed the same date of rank; all wanted to be in charge. That problem was solved by appointing the one that spoke some English to the rank of Brigadier General. His first question was "Who pays me?" Answer: "See Mussolini."

The 442nd Regimental Combat Team, the well-known and respected Nisei or Japanese-American citizens, were on our right flank when we relieved the Third Division for our first combat. I visited the 442nd and was told we should not run patrols that night. They would patrol our front as well as their own. I was to tell our front line troops to wear helmets at all times. The 442nd patrols carried only knives, and they liked to slip up to a foxhole and check the helmet shape. Wrong shape and the head was lost!

I do not wish to repeat my experience in the war, but the memory is priceless.

• • •

DID YOU KNOW THAT...

The Japanese-American unit, the 442nd Combat Team, earned 18,143 medals during five campaigns in Italy and more decorations for battlefield bravery than any other unit of comparable size. While all Japanese-Americans had been placed in internment camps, these Nisei pleaded with the War Department to be allowed to fight for their country. In January, 1943, the President authorized them to serve in a separate unit, with mostly Caucasian officers, primarily because the Army was desperate for men. The 442nd became known for its aggressiveness and spirit in engaging and destroying the enemy. 25

FRED J. KELLERMAN

CINCINNATI, OHIO

Army, PFC, 131st AAA Gun Battalion, 1943-46
Basic Training: Ft. Bliss, Texas
Duty in Europe

The Battalion's principal weapons were sixteen 90 mm high velocity guns which were later supplemented by 16 quadruple-mounted 50 caliber machine guns.

When moved to Camp Livingston near Alexander, Louisiana, a battalion dance band was started. Its initial function was to complement a burlesque-type stage show that was produced by various members of the 131st and presented for the battalion's entertainment. My dad sent my saxophone and clarinet. Afterwards the instruments were boxed and went with us.

Boarding the Mauretania in New York, we crossed the Atlantic Ocean, without escort, arriving at Liverpool, England. From there we were transported by train to Staffordshire, Camp Blackshaw Moor near Leak, where the battalion received its guns and vehicles. By motor convoy we went to the marshalling area at Dorchester and then to Port of Weymouth and boarded LSTs. A heavy storm forced the ships back to Southhampton Harbor. Two days later we left again and landed on Utah Beach in Normandy, France.

After moving from place to place, we set up a gun defense at Dinant, Belgium. During the first week at Dinant three German soldiers were killed and six were captured as they were trying to reach their own lines by filtering through territory held by the Americans. Later the gun batteries were heavily engaged with enemy aircraft.

We moved to Luxembourg, the scene of a High Command Conference being held by General Eisenhower and attended by Generals Bradley, Simpson, Hodges, Patton, and others.

At Maastricht we met continual heavy enemy fire. The battalion underwent 177 raids and engaged 192 enemy aircraft. The battalion submitted claims on 15 Cat Is and 10 Cat IIs.

Here, too, the buzz bombs came roaring in; 742 were over the battalion area. There were no injuries but some close calls.

While at Maastricht the dance band was reactivated and played for dances in the evenings for the battalion and other troops nearby. Maastricht girls were brought and returned to their homes by truck before our men were returned to their batteries. One dance in Holland held a special significance for one corporal—he met an 18-year-old Dutch girl and they were later married.

When the German Army launched its major offensive in the Battle of the Bulge, we were not run over but they were very close. With the air strikes complementing the offensive, a low-flying German plane dropped a large bomb which narrowly missed our battalion command post and hit a row of houses across the street, killing 21 civilians and injuring many others.

On March 24, 1945, a massive artillery barrage initiated an attack across the Rhine River. A vast air armada—889 escorting fighters, 1696 transport planes, 1348 gliders—brought 21,680 paratroopers and glidermen to the attack. It was a spectacular sight; the whole sky was filled with aircraft.

A number of transports and bombers were hit by enemy gunfire. A B-24 bomber that crashed into an ammo dump nearby caught fire. Our colonel and two others pulled the crew safely from the plane. The fire spread to the ammo dump, which exploded with a massive roar and fireball. Regrettably, three men from the 131st were at the ammo dump and lost their lives.

When moving to Rheinberg, a number of our group were assigned to guarding prisoners of war en route to collective centers. The prisoner totals grew by many thousands each day.

After V-E Day and moves here and there, we were assigned to Berchtesgaden, the mountain resort of Hitler and all of his top staff and generals. With Germany's surrender, it was turned into a rest area for GIs.

Having a talented dance band available for special dignitary functions was a major consideration in getting the 131st assigned as the Occupation Force for the Berchtesgaden area. It was the primary attraction for all military and political officials; therefore, the band was again reactivated and played many engagements. On a few occasions we had Dave Brubeck sit in with us. After the war Dave achieved international fame as a jazz musician. The band also went to Paris on a three-day pass and sat in with a French band playing at the Eiffel Tower.

Before leaving Europe, some of us were assigned to Augsburg and filled in with a band there.

. . .

DID YOU KNOW THAT...

On September 16, 1942, the first of thousands of gliders, made by Ford Motor Company and WACO for the Air Corps, successfully completed its 45-minute demonstration.

The cargo glider was originally designed by WACO Aircraft Company of Troy, Ohio. Carrying thirteen men, a jeep, or one of the largest guns, the CG-4A was towed by a C-46 or C-47.

By holding costs down to $15,400 rather than the $25,000 of the other sixteen companies manufacturing gliders, Ford became the dominant supplier.

Gliders, being built mostly of wood, were difficult for early radar to detect and could land silently on almost any open field or stretch of road. 26

WACO glider, WACO Museum, Troy, OH

ROBERT LANGHORST

CINCINNATI, OHIO (DECEASED)

Army, Staff Sgt., 1941-45
Basic Training: Ft. Thomas, Kentucky
Duty in Europe

At Camp Barkley passes were handed out on Friday at retreat by First Sergeant, a married man. One Friday he announced, as usual, "Of course the married men go first." Cancienne, a cajun from New Orleans, who loved to go into town and get with the women, blew up. He shouted, "Married men first, that's all I hear, married men first. When we get overseas and get down in the trenches, and they say, 'Over the top, boys,' by God, married men first!"

When going overseas, we landed at Oran, Algeria, and then were on our way to Sicily. Soon we were dropped off 100 yards from shore, in water well over our heads. I had a full field pack, two medical kits, and a litter.

We formed up a few hundred yards from shore and set up an aid station. Captain Baker and I were taking care of the wounded. There was small arms fire in the trees above us, and everyone else was under a truck or behind a tree. One fellow came rushing up crying, wanting to go back to the ship he came from. Captain Baker decided we should move back about 150 yards behind a small building.

Robert Langhorst

That night Germans came over and bombed the supply ships off shore. Tracers filled the sky. Then suddenly the air was filled with parachutes. A perfect move by the Germans; they would wipe us out! One of the paratroopers huddled over his tommy gun—I was in my foxhole with only the knife my brother had sent me. The trooper came up a small draw—if he came on this side of the building, I was finished—he went on the other side. A plane burning furiously came down and slid to a halt, across the road. The trooper stopped at a small tree and yelled, "Hey, Joe!" At that time everyone shouted, "American paratroopers!"

It seems that after the Germans had bombed the ships in the harbor, they left. Soon the American paratroopers from Africa came over. I believe that 28 planes were shot down and many casualties occurred from their shooting us and our shooting them—mistaken identity! We picked up eight dead in our immediate area. The plane across the road was filled with skeletons of paratroopers.

Our Regimental Headquarters was informed an hour later that we would have paratroopers coming over. Thus it went, the first day of combat.

At Anzio there were many incidents: A litter squad leader, while holding the Geneva Cross overhead, being shot through the wrist. Being rattled around in a foxhole when a nearby truckload of ammo was hit. A terrific explosion, mortar fire raining down while we were in a culvert and a wounded G.I. nearby on a litter. But what saddened me most was having my buddy, Lou Simon, killed. I still think about him. I wrote to his mother. She wrote back, wanting to know how he was killed. I couldn't tell her he was blown to pieces with a German shell.

Our grumpy major told me the Germans had shelled that night and put one right through his tent (the only person on Anzio sleeping in a tent). The shell nudged a rubber basin, splashing water in his face, waking him. Needless to say, it was a dud. He rolled over and went back to sleep. Within a week he had gone home.

One of our guys, Jack Jobe, was scheduled to go home. They kept him in the rear so he wouldn't be hurt. When he pushed off from Anzio, he got a ride to Rome—he had to see Rome! He was killed by a sniper.

Our last invasion, No. 4, was coming up. Unlike the first, Sicily, we were well informed, well trained, and we carried medical kits and just two chocolate bars. As we were going in, a destroyer put down a barrage and it seemed as though the whole beach erupted in a terrible explosion. We had casualties, but it was a relatively easy landing. We pushed inland and set up an aid station. After a regiment has been together through a lot of combat, one unit depends on and helps the others, a sort of dependency takes place. So it was with our kitchen. We had pancakes for breakfast!

We were moving up one day when the Germans shelled us. An ammunition truck was hit up ahead. When we arrived, there was only debris and some guy's intestines were in the trees overhead. The sights of war—unbelievable!

A tanker came by our roadside aid station, looking for graves registration. He had a "10 in one" ration box with him. He said, "My buddy is in the box. I want to see that he has a proper burial."

John, a good friend of mine, was with his unit in a small town when a German plane dove down and dropped a bomb. A little girl was blown and shattered against a wall. John became an exhaustion case. He insisted on staying around the aid station, saying he would eventually be all right. But his crying went on and on, so the captain sent him to the rear, to a hospital unit. Another good soldier was a casualty; not an obvious one, but nevertheless, a casualty.

We were still in a leapfrog position and one day we pulled onto the lawn of a huge chateau. We set up our tent, and shortly the kids started coming around. I gave a couple of them cigarettes and chocolate bars. Then a very pretty girl on a bicycle came by and said in broken English that her brother had fallen and hurt his leg. Would we take care of it? About that time a brand new lieutenant came rushing over and said, "I'll take care of this." The girl had caught his eye. Some time later a woman came by and said, "You have been so kind to my children. We would like for you to eat with us." A buddy and I went; not much to eat, but the pretty girl was there. We traded addresses and pictures. Thereafter when the lieutenant was nearby, we would whip out the picture and tell a few lies.

We didn't see many Germans in our aid station. One day we did. He was SS and had just a flesh wound in the upper arm.

The major, being Jewish, took a look at the SS on the collar and refused to treat him—he knew about the concentration camps. I do think he was relieved, though, when I bandaged the guy up.

Spending Christmas in the basement of a house, we had a scrubby tree with some radar tinsel on it. When we retreated, the engineers came in and booby trapped the toilet.

When we crossed the Rhine River, it was like another amphibious landing. We had 105s (artillery) dug in, shooting point blank at the Germans on the other side. While waiting to get into our duck (amphibious vehicle), a G.I. came around the corner of the building with a German in tow. The G.I. had a 45 and was screaming at the cowering German, threatening to kill him. This went on for several minutes, disturbing everyone, 'til someone said, "Take him behind the building and shoot him or shut up!" The G.I. immediately quieted down. He really couldn't shoot anyone in cold blood.

Our last battle was at Dachau. One of our other regiments took the concentration camp, but we were there shortly after. When I saw all those naked bodies piled up in the corner of that large room, ready to be put in the furnaces, I knew what I had been fighting for!

We were escorted through the compound by an English soldier who said he was an inmate. We saw this huge room with sprinkler-like attachments in the ceiling, that the gas came through. After the people were gassed, they would clear the room, then drag the bodies into the furnace room, where I had seen them piled up. Then into the furnaces (eight, I think). We saw dead guards in the moat that surrounded the place, machine gun emplacements, some mean-looking large dogs.

The division brought in a hospital unit to care for the survivors. They still died by the hundreds every day; they were too far gone.

We were stationed in the town of Dachau after the war for six weeks before I was flown home. That time in Dachau was the most pleasant of my 25 months overseas. We were not supposed to fraternize with the Germans, but I figured that did not include the kids that came around the aid station. My favorite was a 9- or 10-year-old girl named Frieda. She was one of those intended for the "Master Race." She knew her mother, but had no idea who her father was; she was being raised by an elderly couple. In a letter after the war she said that they didn't have enough to eat. My mom and I sent a huge package, which she acknowledged in minute detail.

Some of what I have written seems a bit facetious. I didn't at all want to minimize the horrors of war, but, waking up each day, wondering if you'll be alive tomorrow, you have to keep your sense of humor; without it you'd go crazy. With 511 days of combat, 4 amphibious landings, 4 months of being shelled and bombed on Anzio, I do feel as though God was looking over my shoulder.

• • •

DID YOU KNOW THAT...

England had bomb shelters, with different levels, in their subways. Each person was permanently assigned a numbered bunk. There were lavatories with running water and also a food canteen. A separate level was for sick or infectious patients, another for those needing treatment and consultation. [27]

LOUIS BOSYK

COLUMBUS, OHIO

American Child Caught in Throes of War

I was born in America, as were both by parents. My father's people were Russian; mother's, Austrian. All came to U.S. around 1900.

When my mother's father came to the U.S., his name was Elkus. Immigration didn't understand him so they asked what his trade was. He was a schneider, a tailor, so they said that was his name.

My father's father was brought here by a cousin whose last name was Feinstein. The cousin said, "You'll have to change your name; it's too foreign sounding, too Russian." So he changed it to Feinstein.

Bosyk is my mother's mother's maiden name. My mother's grandfather was a very wealthy man, lived in a 150-room house in Vienna, Austria, that was over 300 years old, full of magnificent things. He was a politically important person, had a title; read, wrote, and spoke 16 languages. The family had been importing and exporting for hundreds of years, so was known all over the world. Cousins, aunts and uncles were all involved in the business and lived in the big house with my great grandparents.

The family came to Austria in 729. I have the document, in Latin, in a bank in Switzerland, giving us permission to settle in the area that is now Vienna. In Europe, even at the turn of the century, especially if you were a Jew, you needed a paper to allow you to travel. You couldn't go from town to town. In Russia, Jews weren't allowed in what was called Russia proper. This was in the Czarist time. They were in the Ukraine, Poland, Estonia, Latvia, the Crimea, what they called Holy Russia, Mother Russia.

Jewish parents, in Czarist times when a child was born, gave it a different last name so that it would be registered as an only child and it wouldn't have to go into the service. If he was not an only son, at 10 years of age he would be taken into service for 15 years.

Louis Bosyk

I had a cousin born in Poland, which at that time was Russian Poland, and in order to go to school he had to pass a test and get the highest mark. His father had to pay for four gentile children to go to school in order to get his Jewish child into the public elementary school.

We had another house in Vienna on the Ringstrasse. When the emperor, in the 1860s, decided to tear down the fortification wall (all cities were ringed with walls), noblemen and wealthy families built the Ringstrasse. We built a house there that was much smaller than the other one we had, 40 rooms. Part of the family used it, and we had offices there where the family worked.

When the crash came in America, my mother, along with my father, brother, and I, went to visit her grandparents in Vienna. My great grandfather said, "Why worry about the situation over there? Just stay here."

We did stay but then in November, 1937, my mother, father, and brother went home to the U.S. because her youngest brother was getting married. They didn't take me because I was small, only 4½ years old. In those days you didn't fly; you had to take a boat, going either to Germany or France to get it. They left me with my great grandmother, intending to come back at the end of April or May.

I had a good life with my great grandparents up until the Germans came. My great grandfather was a good, kind man, and I was very close to him. Even though they were in their 80s, they were very outgoing people and the house was always full.

We had gardeners and stables, carriages and sleighs. It snows a lot in Vienna.

For my 4th birthday we had a party that I will never forget! We had a big formal dinner, a ball, and three hours of fireworks. The diningroom and ballroom were beautiful and everyone was dressed in their finery. I had never stayed up so late before. The fireworks didn't start 'til midnight; they were in the conservatory, room made out of glass with palm trees in it. They had the Old Imperial Eagle (the coat of arms of Austria), the Kaiser (next to last emperor of Austria), Franz Josef, Austrian flag, my picture, and many decorative fireworks. And, oh, the reflections on the snow! And they played music when they did the fireworks. I had a magnificent birthday! I was little but still remember it.

My 5th birthday wasn't too great. Grandfather was dead and it wasn't lavish. After that I was in Paris, and there was nothing for birthdays. I never had a birthday card. Birthdays, I think, are very important. Every other holiday is everyone's day, but your birthday is your day.

In the meantime the threat of war came. There were loud speakers in the street and the Chancelor spoke, March, 1938. He told us that Hitler said there wouldn't be any onslaughts because we were German people, part of Germany, and no reason to annex us. There would be peace. That was the 11th and on the 13th German soldiers crossed the frontier; by the 18th Hitler was in Vienna. The Jews in Germany saw it coming on. Most of the German Jews did get out.

After Hitler came to Austria, you had to fly a Swastika from your house. My great grandmother wouldn't do it. The Gestapo came and asked why we were not flying it. She said, "Because we are Austrian, not German." There was a to-do and then they shot her right there at the house. She was 99. If it hadn't been for a servant who grabbed me and hid me in the basement, I probably would have been next. Late that night he took me to a cousin in Vienna on the Prada. I stayed with her from March until I got a permit to leave in November. By that time it was very bad in Austria for the Jews.

Because I was an American and we could pay some money, I was given a permit to leave Austria. The first eleven days the Austrian Gestapo took over. After that Himmler said the Germans should take over; the Austrians were too brutal.

At the end of November I got the permit, left by train, going to Zurich first, to a cousin's; was almost six at that time and traveled by myself, had a private compartment. Just like a stewardess does on a plane, they take care of kids. Everything, ticket and meals, had been paid for; my passport was validated.

I spent a week with a cousin in Zurich before they shipped me to another cousin in Paris. I stayed in Paris from December, 1938, and then they started trying to get papers for me to go to the U.S. I led a normal life but didn't go to school because I couldn't speak French. It started getting bad and there was a threat of an invasion. Cousins continued going to the American embassy and asking about the papers, writing my parents.

When things started getting shaky, my cousin went to the head of the Russian church in Paris. My father's father, a Russian, was an artist who studied in Paris and did fresco ceilings, gold leaf, marble, interior of palaces. He worked for the Czar, Alexander the 3rd and Nicholas the 2nd. This head of the Russian church in Paris had been the private priest of the Czar prior to the revolution and knew my grandfather. So my cousin went to him and said, "We're waiting for papers, but if things get bad and we have to flee, can you take him?" I was almost seven. He said, "Yes, if it gets bad, bring him here and we'll take him in." And that's what happened. When the Germans came, first the French Gestapo took over. They were very bad. For every Jew they turned in, they got 350 francs.

We were going to leave at midnight and head for the South because the Germans hadn't occupied all of France. After starting, Joseph said to his wife, Regina, "I left the cat locked up in the store. The cat will die." The wife said, "Joseph, don't go back. It's too dangerous."

"How could I leave an animal to die?" Unfortunately, he got caught. The neighbor came and said Joseph was taken by the French Gestapo.

Then we had to flee. Regina's son was about 1½ years old; I was seven; Regina had a bad heart. We took to the streets and headed south. Outside of Paris we met a Christian woman, about 40, who had a farm. She took us in and kept us for quite a while, and when we were ready to leave, she said, "You know, Regina, it would be very difficult for you with a 1½ year-old child to make any time. Leave him here. I will take care of him 'til you get back." She kept him all through the war.

Traveling at night, too dangerous in daytime, we went as far as Marseilles. Regina stayed there and I went on to Nice where there was a Russian Orthodox Church. After about six months there was a threat that the Germans were going to occupy Nice, so the Metropolitan (church official) sent me east.

I walked through Italy and Greece, into Turkey. The gypsies were very good to us and helped a lot. They are a people with their own language and their own culture. The Germans did not like them because they were always moving around, and they weren't pure, and all that nonsense. They fed and took care of me and took me from place to place. There were a lot of people running in those days, not just Jews but people who were being harassed politically and religiously. It either brought the best out in people or the worst.

I got to Russia at the end of 1940 or beginning of 1941, and the Germans didn't come 'til the spring of '41. At first I was in the North, but when the Germans came, I was shipped down to Moscow where I spent most of the war.

I went from one Russian church to another. The letter I carried from the Metropolitan in Paris instructed the Russian priests to take me in and hide me, which they did. The priests arranged with gypsies and partisans to get me farther on. I couldn't have done it on my own.

I spent five years in the Russian Orthodox, learned Russian eventually, church Russian, the catechism, the service; was an altar boy, and went through the whole thing.

Close to the end of the war my great aunt in Moscow, who I saw once or twice a week, said to me, "As soon as the war ends, you must leave or you will be stuck here the rest of your life. You have no papers. We don't know where your parents are. Just get out of Russia. You'll have to fend for yourself. If you stay here, it's no good."

So the day the war ended, that's what I did. I took what she gave me and started walking west. I was 12 then. She said, "Go while there are a lot of celebrations and confusion. As soon as everyone settles down, you won't be able to get out. Now I don't want to get rid of you, but it's not that great here."

I followed, asked people which way was west. People were

so displaced. There were concentration camps in Poland, Italy, Romania, Hungary, Czechoslovakia. People were out and going back home. Roads were packed. Soldiers were coming back. Refugees, people looking for families, looking to see if they had anything to come back to.

After the war was worse than during the war. During the war you only saw what was happening where you were. There were no newspapers; no one had a radio. You only knew what was happening around you. You didn't know what was happening five blocks away. After the war when you started to walk, you saw all the destruction and the people coming out of the camps. Your mind can't envision a human being looking like this! You can't envision four buildings standing where a whole city once stood, where thousands and millions of people lived! The destruction! They bombarded Moscow something like 21 days straight and Leningrad like two years; there was hardly anything left! This is mind boggling! Everything was desolate, absolute confusion!

I first went to Vienna, walking, riding, on trains. I was a kid, so I got picked up quicker. You ate whatever you could. If you were hungry, you filled your stomach up with leaves. Plenty of people would rob something just to go to jail, because there they fed you. In Russia there was very little to eat, but at least we had potato soup, bread, tea.

When I got back to Paris, we had a little store. The first time I saw oranges and bananas, I didn't remember what they were. It had been five or six years since I had seen them.

When Stalin's daughter came to the U.S. a few years ago, she wrote in her book that her grandmother was very upset during the war because she couldn't get sour cream. We were very incensed over that because we were starving in Russia. Stalin was one of the worst individuals you could ever come across! He killed millions and millions of his own people, just to kill them! In Russia you didn't dare disagree with him. Americans can't understand that because they are always taught to think and to express opinions.

We have many Russian Jews in the U.S. These people never had to think for almost 80 years. They were told to do every-thing. They didn't make decisions. They were told where to work, whether to work or not, whether they were a doctor or a street cleaner they got the same money. So the mentality is different.

When they come here, they can't cope with making their own decisions.

It was the same in Europe when the wall came down. Two generations were brought up under Communism and were taught to do as they were told. They didn't think. They were punished if they thought. One girl said, "Now that I have freedom, what do I do with it?" Americans take for granted, since they've always had freedom, that people know what to do with it. But these people don't.

Americans are very politically naive. Most of them don't care who is in the White House if they can pay their bills. In France when there is an election, every person, from the smallest child, knows about every single candidate, and they know that man getting in or out will affect them in every single way. And the election is on Sunday so you can't say you don't have time to vote.

And here in the U.S. so many people don't care about the vote! It bothers me because I've seen the other side of the coin. I saw the devastation. America has been very fortunate. There has been no war on this continent since the Civil War.

Most European countries after the war paid people to have children. You received x amount of dollars or pounds or francs for every child you had. In less than 40 years they had two great wars that ruined the economy and killed off their male population. In England I once heard a GI say there were a lot of spinsters. Then a woman said, "Yes, all our men were killed off in the two wars." Americans don't realize that and what it does to a country.

You say to a young person: "Did you vote?"

"I don't bother with that nonsense."

"What do you mean? That's your right! You don't know how lucky you are to have the right to vote!"

And people make light of it! This is your life! This country is in trouble and no one is doing anything about it!

Continuing with Vienna: That was the first place I went back to when the war ended, but I really didn't know it. I was a child; it was bad times. I didn't know the streets or the neighborhood. I remembered where my cousin lived and went there. In the movie, "The Third Man's Theme," they showed a big ferris wheel in an amusement park. My cousin didn't live far from there. I went there and found no one; stayed about three weeks; it was very bad. People were walking around with pictures asking if you'd seen this one. They had divided Vienna up like Berlin, four zones: Russian, British, French, and American. Completely encircling Vienna was the Russian zone, so no matter what zone you came from, you needed a gray card to get through the Russians into Vienna. Even in the 50s when my parents came to visit me, they couldn't get a card to go through the Russian zone. This lasted until around 1955.

Our house on the Ringstrasse is still standing but not in great condition. Across the street there was a sub station of the Gestapo, and when they were pulling out at the end of the war, they didn't have time to take all the records; they demolished the building and the blast damaged the front and side of our house. The German government paid to repair that part. The servant who saved my life, and his wife, were living there as caretakers until about 15 years ago when he died.

I decided my best bet was Paris and started west. After about 2½ months I arrived in Paris, not being able to speak the language; spoke Russian, little bit of German, most of the Slavic languages, Ukrainian, Polish, but not French. In the neighborhood where my cousin had lived, I couldn't find her or anyone I knew. The little store was boarded up. Maybe three or four months later I saw Regina near the store. After listening to my story, she said she wasn't very well, had no place to live, no money to pay rent. I told her to go back to her apartment.

The Paris government had been Vichy and the French Underground took over. All you had to do was point to someone and say he or she collaborated, and they took him out and shot him. DeGaulle was in England and was not recognized as the government. The Allies arrested all of the Vichy government because they had collaborated.

We only had electricity three hours a day because they didn't have coal to run the generators, so we used to go in the Metro (underground train) to stay warm. They had to heat that. They had to generate electricity to keep the trains running. The Metro stayed open until 1:00 and then we had to come out. We had no gas; anything that was wood was broken up and burned.

Money was worth nothing. Every day there was a surcharge. If you bought something and paid 200 francs, the next day that same item was 600 francs; the next day, 900 francs. The money was useless, just like tissue paper.

Going back to Regina. She didn't know what to do. On the way back, she picked up Simon, her son, from the woman that kept him all during the war. He wasn't very well. They couldn't get much to eat. The soldiers were very good to us, gave us food.

She didn't get the old apartment back, but near the store was an old house, about 400 years old. She got one room with an alcove and a carpenter in the neighborhood made a floor and walls for us and a partition out of wood and glass so she could have a bedroom. We got two leatherette chairs that opened up into a bed; Simon slept in one and I in the other. The carpenter was French, not Jewish, so had been there through the war; he didn't have to flee. Thank God for him; we had a place to live.

Our only water was in the hallway. There was a cabinette (toilet). It was like a hole in the floor with two footprints, no toilet bowl or seat; you squatted. That hole was the toilet, with a pull chain. You had to go in with a candle. It was like the black hole of Calcutta! And you couldn't turn around; it was narrow! The stairs wound around, and back in the corner of the hall was a little 12-watt lightbulb. In apartments there the lights aren't left burning like in the U.S. You press a button and have x amount of time to get upstairs. On each floor there's a button in case the lights go out.

Philip, a friend of my cousin Joseph, showed up after three or four months. They were in Palestine together before the war and were in concentration camps together. My cousin didn't survive, died in the camp. Before the war Philip was a big husky fellow; when he returned he was like my finger, so thin—but he survived!

Philip opened a little store. With three customers inside, it was full. If it weren't for him, we wouldn't be alive. Somehow or other he got a pushcart with two big wheels. It tilted; you had to hold it up. We didn't live too far from the old market, about a 15-minute walk. That man would get up at 4:00 in the morning, push this cart to the market, pack up all the produce, bring it all back, set up the store, and sell. He opened at 6:00A.M., closed in the afternoon for a couple of hours. He had to stay open during the lunch hour because people would buy food for lunch; things close down there for two hours. Then he'd go back in the afternoon and stay until 8:30.

Finally, Regina paid someone to bring water into the house. She had a three-burner gas hotplate that she put on a table, no stove. Eventually we got a gas heater. She had a little cabinet to put the groceries in, a table, and a little wardrobe to put our few clothes in. That was all the furniture.

Immediately after the war people were very anti-Semitic. They wrote "Jew" on our window and broke our windows. People got right back to hating one another. The only ones that were a little sympathetic were the ones that really got hurt by the Germans. A Protestant woman whose son had been taken out and shot had empathy toward us because she understood that the Germans killed for no reason; the average Frenchman didn't care.

My grandmother's cousin, Anna, went to the U.S. in 1933 from her part of Austria, which after the first World War became Romania. She saw what was going on when Hitler took over and told all of her family to get out, even giving them the money for escape and to start a new business. Unfortunately, they didn't listen. Before long the war came and they were all in concentration camp, and the only one to survive was the mother and the youngest sister with her husband. Anna's oldest brother, his wife, his children, and all the other brothers and sisters perished.

After WW II that part of Romania became Russia. When Anna's mother came back from the camps, she was about 79 years old. My cousin went to the Russian consulate in New York and said, "You know, my mother is elderly. She really can't do anything for you. If anything, she is a hindrance. You will have to support her cause she's in her late 70s. I'll give you any amount of money if you will let her leave the country." She was too old to make it all the way to America, but there was still Palestine. They wouldn't do it.

Finally in 1950 they allowed Jews to leave Romania, only the old, though, in the beginning. I think it cost $175 a person. They could go to Israel. Anna supplied the money, so they all left, but somehow, her mother wasn't getting anything. They found her in a tent with mud floors in winter; she had double pneumonia. There were no direct telephone lines to Israel at that time. It took us 2½ weeks to arrange a phone call, $75 a minute. So then they got a letter to a cousin who got her out, found her an apartment, and saw that she was taken care of.

I went back to Vienna for the reopening of the opera house in 1955, and I didn't need a card to get through the Russian sector. At the end of the war, the last day, an American bomber thought the opera house and cathedral were a railroad station; direct hit on them. Demolished the opera house. They weren't supposed to bomb it because Vienna was an open city like Rome and Paris.

In 1955 they rededicated the opera house. My great grandfather had played an important part in the establishment of that opera house, so when I wrote and said I would like to come for the opening, I was sent tickets and went. There was a party and Jack Kennedy was there.

Our family was connected with the opera house going back to Mozart's time. My great uncle was the musical director of the Imperial Opera House in Berlin under Kaiser Wilhelm. My uncle said that when he got invited to the palace he always ate dinner before he went because he never had time to eat there. Wilhelm ate so quickly, and there was always a long reception afterwards. The Kaiser would eat maybe two bites of soup and they'd take the plates away. He had a shriveled left arm and didn't like people looking at it, so he would eat very quickly. Court procedure was that when the emperor finished eating, everyone was finished.

During the three years I stayed in Paris after the war, my cousin went to a meeting of a Jewish organization. Whenever people went to the U.S. from Europe, they established societies in the U.S. to help others who wanted to come over from the same European towns. Regina went to one of these affairs in 1948 and met a man from New York. While talking, Regina said her husband had family in New York, but she didn't know where. "What's the name?"

"Same as mine, Bosyk." That's the name I went by in Europe because I didn't know a family name. I had lost contact; I didn't know my parents at all. The last time I saw my father and mother and brother I was 4½ years old. The next time I saw them I was 15 or so. My relatives over there didn't know my mother's married name; she and my father grew up in America.

"But where do they come from?"

"It is now Russia, but it was Poland and then it was Austria."

When she gave the name, the man said he was born in that town. "You know there's a society from there." After getting all the information from Regina, he went back to New York. When he went to the society, my grandfather's cousin was there. "Why are you asking about Bosyk?"

"I was just in Paris and met Regina Bosyk." He told about the family, and the man replied, "Well, my cousin is married to a Bosyk." He went up to my grandparents, told them the story, gave them Regina's address, and that's how we got in touch. I came over in May, 1948, just got here when Israel became a state.

The relationship with my parents wasn't very good. I had grown up and was 15 and used to doing as I was told. When living in a monastery you do as you are told, and it was an era when you had to do as you were told; it was a matter of my safety. I didn't ever ask why. The parents weren't used to my being there. Maybe they had guilt. I don't know. I wanted a close relationship; I hadn't had a mother or father. I had a brother that was five years older than I, and he wasn't very friendly. I lived with my parents from 1948 to 1952 when I went to service. Then I came back in 1956 and stayed for a few years. I left then and went back to Europe.

My grandparents were very good to me. He was head Jewish leader in Tammany Hall (Democratic Party). President Wilson sent them as a special commission in 1919 to Geneva to try to get Palestine for a Jewish state; and he was at the Peace Conference with President Wilson. I have the pen that was used in the Peace Conference by President Wilson after the first World War.

When I went back to Vienna, they were having an organ concert in the restored cathedral. I sat there in the Catholic Church and saw all these old people praying. I said to myself, How did all this happen? Look at all these people. They're praying; they believe in God. How did it happen? Later I went to an elderly couple and expressed these feelings. She said, "My dear boy, 30 years ago they were not old. They were the ones who were wanting to kill us." Then I saw the picture. I didn't look at these old people and think that 30 years ago they were my age or maybe a little older. I can understand how younger people who have never experienced this can say, "Oh, this never happened," because I went through it! It really plays tricks on your mind. Even though I lived through it, I still had this reaction. And, of course, in the serenity of the church, with beautiful music and an elegant cathedral, it puts you in a different frame of mind.

When I went home in 1965, there was a Jewish student who was clubbed to death at the high school outside of Vienna. There was a big resurgence of anti-semitism. The Danube runs into a canal at a certain point, where you get to the old Jewish quarters, and on the wall of the canal, "Nazis kill again." There were only two small synagogues open.

One last thought: You have to realize that Judaism is a religion, not a nationality. Jews come from all over the world. People fear what they don't know.

. . .

WILLIAM E. LEIGHTY

SIDNEY, OHIO

Army, S/Sgt., Criminal Investigation Det., 1944-46
Basic Training: Ft. McClellan, Alabama
Duty in Pacific

I remember being packed and prepared for the invasion of Japan when we received word that "The Bomb" had been dropped and the end was very near. Our departure was put on hold for a few days and then cancelled. Such a happy time!

Being a life-long Republican, I still give thanks to President Truman for his decision to drop The Bomb. A Democrat saved a lot of lives, possibly mine, and I give him a lot of credit for having the intestinal fortitude to follow his convictions.

• • •

DID YOU KNOW THAT...

With men going off to war and the increased production demands for defense, Monarch Machine Tool Co., Sidney, Ohio, hired and trained 500 women in all facets of factory work.

Patriotism and the desire of each one to do his/her part resulted in workers only getting one day off every three weeks and in taking no vacations. This dedication was nationally recognized in October, 1941, by Monarch's receiving the coveted Army-Navy E Award for outstanding contributions to the defense effort. "By the end of the war, its pennant contained five stars, a record unmatched by any other Ohio machine tool company." (A star was awarded for each 6-month period thereafter for which you met the requirements.)

Monarch employees worked on many critical projects: "The 40 millimeter Bofors anti-aircraft gun, which helped turn the tide against the dive-bombing Japanese Zeros in the Pacific, contained Monarch parts." Monarch "manufactured the power takeoff units for the aircraft engine used in the British Lancaster and Halifax bombers." Lathes, which they shipped to a mysterious address, were later found to be used in the "Manhattan project, which resulted in the production of our first atomic bomb." 28

A W A R D

OF THE

U. S. NAVY BUREAU
OF ORDNANCE FLAG

AND THE

NAVY "E" PENNANT

BYRD LEROY LEWIS
ARTESIA, NEW MEXICO

Army, T/5 Corporal, Radio Operator, 1942-45
Basic Training: Camp Maxey, Texas
Duty in Europe

Sailing from England, we crossed the English Channel and landed on Utah Beach, probably about three weeks after D-Day. We fired our first shots of the war as we approached St. Lo, France.

We crossed most of France in Patton's 3rd Army, but later were transferred to the 7th Army. We spent 297 days in combat without relief!

After the St. Lo breakthrough, our forward observation group was supporting a tank division. We were on a hill overlooking a tank battle taking place just below us. We were directing artillery fire on German tanks, supply trucks, infantry, or anything German that we could see. Just behind our hill was a small French town with probably 3,000 population; the main street ran straight down the middle of it. Our artillery battalion was about two miles behind us receiving our firing directions. About sundown we got a call telling us to return to our firing battery because we were being transferred to another tank division. We loaded up the jeep, made our way down the back side of the hill, and drove down the main street of the small town. The streets were full of jeeps, supplies, and American soldiers. There were some medic, supply, and infantry units ready to move up the next day. We left the town on a paved road that ran about one-third of a mile, then made a sharp right, went down behind a steep embankment, and then made a sharp left to a straight road leading back to our battery.

It was dark when we got back to B Battery to eat our supper. We mainly had C-Rations three meals a day, which meant one can of something–a choice of stew, hash, or beans. After our meal, we pitched our pup tents and went to bed.

About five o'clock the next morning the captain woke us up and said that the transfer was off and that we were to return to the same tank unit that we had been supporting the day before. We should go by the tank division headquarters, which was on this side of the small town, for further orders. The four of us each ate a can of C-Rations, loaded the jeep, and started down the road. By this time it was daylight.

Byrd Leroy Lewis

Thinking that it was unnecessary to go by the tank division headquarters, since we were certain they would send us to the same location as yesterday, we headed straight for the little town. Suddenly a German artillery shell screamed in and hit about fifty yards to our right. Shrapnel was flying all around us. Willie, our driver, said, "Where did that come from?" and slowed down. We knew that the Germans couldn't see us from the other side of the hill beyond the town. I said, "Aw, go on. It's just a stray shell." Captain Lewis immediately said, "Don't stop here, Willie! If they can see us and we are stopped here, the next shell will be right on top of us!" So Willie picked up a little speed and kept going toward town.

I noticed some dead GIs on the right side of the road and said, "I don't remember any dead GIs here when we drove through last night." No one else could remember them, either. On the left side of the road there were some dead Germans, and we couldn't remember seeing them. Looking straight ahead down main street, there was not a person nor a vehicle of any kind in sight. Just before dark the night before it had been full of GIs and army vehicles. This was very strange. By the time we were approaching the first building of the town, Captain Lewis told Willie to pull over behind a building so we could talk. Maybe we should go back and check with the tank unit headquarters for orders after all!

Willie wheeled the jeep around and headed back down the road. Bullets started flying behind us by the thousands, at least it seemed like thousands! There were German machine gun tracers all around us. We knew that between the tracers that glowed there were four bullets that did not glow and could not be seen. Also, there were rifle bullets zipping by, and immediately the German artillery shells were falling close enough that we knew they were trying to zero in on us. Willie shifted gears and picked up speed. He had the jeep going as fast as he dared and was zigzagging to dodge the bullets. I wondered how he was going to make the sharp turn to the right when we got to it, if we got to it! Somehow, Willie slid around the turn to the right, and we went down behind the embankment where we were safe from the machine gun and rifle fire. Thankfully, the German artillery stopped, too.

We were still not home free; there was more trouble ahead. When we made the sharp turn to the left and headed down the straight road leading back toward our battalion, there was a column of American tanks about 200 yards away, coming toward us. When the men in the front tank saw us, they stopped the tank and turned the 75 mm gun barrel down toward us. They naturally thought we were Germans. Willie slid the jeep to a halt. We jerked our helmets off and started waving them in the air so that they could see that we were Americans, standard procedure for identification. The tank commander in the front tank raised the hatch, stuck his head out, and motioned for us to drive on up. We pulled up beside the tank and he yelled, "What in the hell are you guys doing up here?" Captain Lewis explained that we were trying to get up on the hill where we were yesterday to direct artillery fire, but that we had run into trouble. The tank commander asked, "Didn't you guys know that the Germans counterattacked last night and retook the hill and the town?" No, we didn't know, but we sure found out about it as soon as we got back to town!

Miraculously, none of us were hurt; however, the jeep had some holes in it and one or two of the men had holes in their jackets. We all knew full well that this had been another narrow escape!

In the above incident, when we came to direct artillery fire, there were no French civilians in sight. We hadn't been there very long, however, until they came out of their basements where they had been hiding. There were two or three men, several women and children. We were the first Americans they had seen, and they were overjoyed. We tried to wave them back, afraid they would attract the German artillery observers' attention and give our location away. We couldn't wave them back, so we tried to explain what might happen; that didn't do any good, either. They were so happy; all wanted to hug and kiss us. They brought out cognac, wine, and food and spent the whole day with us. Fortunately, the German forward observers didn't see us. No other forward observer days were that pleasant!

I had noticed some dead German soldiers, barefooted, lying in the ditch. As soon as there was a lull in the fighting, the French civilians came out of their basements and pulled the boots off those dead soldiers, if they could get there before the bodies had stiffened. Shoes were rationed and very difficult to find. Also, the French had been mistreated by the Germans and hated them so much that wearing the dead German's boots was like wearing a badge of honor.

I mentioned that we usually had C-Rations three times a day. Actually, we had a kitchen truck and two cooks that prepared meals whenever they could. Most of the time they prepared a breakfast of powdered eggs or powdered pancakes, bacon, toast with butter and jelly, and coffee. Sometimes they would prepare a simple lunch if the fighting situation permitted. All in all, the cooks did a great job when you consider the adverse conditions they had to work under.

When we were directing artillery fire we usually took K-Rations with us. A K-Ration looked similar to a Crackerjack box. It contained a small can of potted meat, two or three hard crackers, a chocolate bar, a sack of instant coffee and of lemonade, and three cigarettes. Even though we complained about the food, we knew that it was nutritious and gave us the energy we needed.

Courtesy Sherl Hasler

Letter to the Editor: THE HOLOCAUST DID HAPPEN!

After viewing 60 Minutes' presentation about people who said they did not believe that the Holocaust actually happened, I felt compelled to write.

I, along with many other WW II veterans, know that it did happen–we saw the horrifying evidence! I am an Anglo Protestant veteran, and I wish to set the record straight.

I was an American soldier in the 250th Field Artillery Battalion supporting the 45th Division when the concentration camp at Dachau was liberated by units of the 45th Division on April 29, 1945. Dachau was one of the many death camps where the German SS troops killed Jews and political prisoners during WW II.

By the time we had reached Dachau, I had alredy seen so much killing through France and Germany that I thought I had seen the worst, but when we went inside the prison camp, I was over-whelmed! The grotesque bodies, the awful stench, and the skin-and-bone survivors made me sick at my stomach all over again. Those sights will be etched in my memory forever! I saw battle-hardened soldiers crying and others vomiting as they saw the stacks of skeleton-like bodies from the gas chamber. Some rooms were filled with bodies that were stacked like cord-wood, and many other bodies were stacked in huge piles waiting to be burned in the furnaces that were still warm. The gas chamber was still filled with bodies that hadn't been removed. It appeared that the Germans had tried to run as many of the prisoners through the gas chamber as they could as the American soldiers were approaching Dachau. Also, other bodies were lying around or huddled in corners where they had been shot by the SS troops just before the Americans came in.

Setting on a railroad siding at the prison camp were 39 boxcars filled with dead bodies. These prisoners had been crowded into boxcars, shipped by rail to Dachau, and had died enroute. In addition to the 2310 bodies in the 39 boxcars, there were over 9000 other bodies in huge piles stacked here and there around the prison camp. Of the 31,000 survivors that were rescued that day, many are still alive today to tell firsthand what happened in Dachau.

Today we have many veterans still living who liberated the many death camps and saw firsthand the horrible scenes like I saw at Dachau. Because there are fewer of us WW II veterans each year, it is crucial for us who do know that these atrocities did happen to speak up. I suggest that other veterans who participated in the liberation of the death camps write letters to the editors of their newspapers and tell their eye-witness accounts, as I have done.

Sincerely, Byrd Leroy Lewis, Artesia, New Mexico
Reprinted with permission of Byrd Leroy Lewis

JOHN MADER
HOUSTON, OHIO

Army, 150th Ordnance, T/4, 1942-46,
Basic Training: Ft. Warren, Wyoming
Duty in Pacific

In the Orderly Room there was a bulletin requesting four volunteers for the 251st Remount to take horses to India. After I volunteered, the Captain called me in and said, "John, I don't know anything about horses. Would you tell me some of the boys in this company that could handle horses." There were 25 or 30 that wanted to go.

John Mader — living quarters, New Caledonia, 1944

In about ten days they took us to Dumbea Valley in New Caledonia, where they had 2300 head of horses. In the early part of the war the island was guarded by our cavalry. The war progressed north and they had no more use for the cavalry, so the cavalry went into the infantry. The horses went with the remount, which is a quartermaster.

When the ship came in, the SS Virginian, a regular horse boat which I think was used in WW I, had regular stalls in it. We walked 300 head in one day, about six or seven miles from Dumbea to the harbor. These were riding horses, a cross between thoroughbreds and Arabian, all Australian-bred.

On the ship they tied the horses to a pick line, a rope; at night they continued to load horses. There were three hatches with flying stalls, a door on each end. You lead the horse in, close the doors, in front and behind him, and up it goes, over and down the hatch. Only one horse at a time, but it goes really fast. There's men down there putting them in the stalls.

The next day we went back and got 300 more head, loaded our gear, and were on our way. It was such an old ship, went really slow, only about 8 knots. We used a lot of old ships in WW II, but this one had been made strictly for horses, three decks with stalls on each deck. Sixty-eight men took care of the 600 horses. Had to take a lot of feed.

John Mader with cavalry horse, New Caledonia, 1945

A boat escorted us out of the harbor and stayed with us 'til dark. Subs stay around the harbor, about eight miles out.

Went down around Tasmania. On the other side of Australia is Freemantle; stopped there and took on fresh vegetables and milk. After a day and a half we started across the Indian Ocean over to Ceylon, which is now Sri Lanka. On our way we had some losses on the top deck. Horses got dysentery and then they'd bind up. They cut them up in pieces and threw them overboard so the sharks would get them; otherwise, they would float. Didn't want the subs or ships to see them. Just before dark we'd throw the manure over. We had to guard these horses at night, go around and check them. They were in strange stalls, had chains on each side of their heads. Once in awhile one would get his foot in that chain. We each had a flashlight (ship was in complete darkness), so we'd take the foot out. This flashlight was an ordinary GI one, with cardboard around it and a little peep hole. You couldn't light a cigarette, either.

From the time we loaded the horses 'til we unloaded them, it was forty-six days. Fed them bran and oats hay, cut but not threshed. I was an Acting Stable Sergeant and had to see that the 68 in my hatch were fed and watered. The ship made its own water, using sea water. In the morning we had sick call, same as in the Army. The Captain (veterinarian) and his corpsman came along. Sometimes a horse would bump its head or something. The horses got off the ship in good shape; lost only five.

We got to Sri Lanka. Then up the Bay of Bengal to the Ganges River, which is really muddy. On the Ganges River you have to wait until the tide goes in to take the ship up the river. We went about eighty miles, I think, docked at Calcutta. The Chinese met us and took 300 head on a train. Next day we took 300 head to Ramgar on a train, eight horses to a little car. That was the last we saw of the horses.

After a few days we went on a truck convoy back to Calcutta, over dusty roads. It was a dirty place. They cook with dried cow manure; you can imagine how that smells. They butcher right out on the street, no refrigeration.

When the war was over, some of those horses they gave to the Indian government; the rest were shot and put in a deep hole. No feed there. Tigers would kill them.

When we got down to Ceylon, it was nice and we were

sleeping out on the deck. Mosquitoes were pretty bad. About five days out I started getting sick; started to shake. On the fifth day, pulling in to Freemantle, there were five of us sick. They met the ship with the medical truck and took us to Perth, about ten miles. I had malaria and was put in the Army Hospital. The other guys had dengue fever. The ship went back to get a load of mules to take to Burma. I was there thirteen days, lost eighteen pounds; had 106 degree fever. They took good care of me. My doctor was an American Naval Officer, had a big sub base at Freemantle. No American army there. Australians were so friendly. They'd come to see their relatives and come over to see me and thank me for helping to save their country.

From the hospital I went back to that naval base; did a little guard duty. Finally a ship came in and they put five of us on. Proceeded to Melbourne and then Sydney; then on a ship going to New Caledonia and back to my original company.

Motor vehicle assembly line of 150th, New Caledonia, 1943

The 150th was a motor vehicle assembly unit. They couldn't ship trucks down there because they take up too much space. They crate them all. They crated weapons carriers, 6 x 6 trucks, jeeps, trailers–we had an assembly line; assembled 10,000 GMC trucks, 6 x 60s, in New Caledonia. I think maybe the motor was in the chassis. At the end of the line they ran them right into a place where they tuned them up and they were ready to head up north. Everything that went up north was new; some of the stuff that came back from there was used in non-combat places. Eleanor Roosevelt came down our assembly line one day.

No trouble with malaria after I got home. Had several flare-ups, though, in New Caledonia. In Perth, Australia, they give the guys pure quinine, didn't have atabrine. New Caledonia had no malaria. Up north the company clerk in the chow line would take our name, hand us a pill, watch us take it, and check our name off.

GMC truck assembled in New Caledonia, 1945

New Caledonia had 30,000 troops on it; had five general hospitals. Whole convoy of ambulances would meet ships, take the sick ones and get them well. Every day there'd be a plane go to New Zealand and bring milk up to the hospitals. Men who had been agriculture teachers got jobs of farming. They'd take boys out of the company to help on the farms. Those valleys were high productive land, rich, black soil. They put in one crop right after another, using the little John Deere tractors sent from the U.S. They fed 30,000 men on that island and put vegetables on the ships. And the French were starving to death (French island). Java and Tonga people did the work.

Our company was in New Caledonia a little over two years and then went to the Philippines, about 80 miles north of Manila. Again we assembled trucks and jeeps. Were going to go to Japan in the 5th wave, invasion. As luck would have it, the war ended. We had to go up, anyway, but the war was over. Stayed five or six weeks. Did more assembling up there.

When in the Philippines there was an outfit like a tank. One of the guys said, "We could really use that. If we got something stuck, it would pull it right out." Our captain went to bed that night and the crew that was working just slipped that thing on there. When we got to Japan, we had a whole field of them.

In Yokohama we slept in tents and it was cold. Had little stoves. That Japanese coal is so dirty. We had to clean out the stove pipe every day.

General Stilwell was going to get all those horses to use as pack horses in Burma. When I arrived home, I learned that Dr. Bailey, veterinarian in Piqua, had used one of the horses with General Stilwell; also Delvin Miller, who was a trainer and driver of standard bred race horses, from Meadowlands, Pennsylvania, and known all over the world.

• • •

DID YOU KNOW THAT...

Hershey's, at the request of the Army in 1937, developed a four-ounce chocolate bar, high in energy, that would withstand tropical heat. Between Pearl Harbor and 1945, troops consumed 3 billion bars, Field Ration D, each with 600 calories. Wanting the GIs to save it as emergency rations, the Army asked Hershey not to make it taste too good. However, in 1943, a better-tasting Hershey's Tropical Bar was developed.[29]

LEE McCOOL

NORTH OLMSTED, OHIO

Infantry, T/3, Litter-Bearer and Aid-man, 1943-46
Basic Training: Camp Fannin, Texas
Duty in Pacific

As battles go, the fight for Biak Island would not rank along-side of Tarawa, Guadalcanal, or Iwo Jima, but for the men of the 41st Division, Biak was a four-letter word for Hell.

The division had been the first to sail to the southwest Pacific and had participated, along with several other outfits, in the fighting in the Buna-Sanananda-Salamua areas along the southeast coast of New Guinea. This campaign was to prevent an invasion of Port Moresby and Australia.

After more than 76 days in combat, the division had been pulled back to Australia for a rest and to take on replacements. A large number of us were assigned to the 186th Regiment; I soon found that I had become a medic. We spent several weeks before our first landing learning the fine art of litter-bearing and becoming company aid-men.

From April 22, 1944, to the middle of May, we newcomers had our "baptism of fire" during the landings in the Hollandia area of Dutch New Guinea. Being our first taste of combat, we thought it was really bad, but it was merely a warm-up for the Biak landings.

Biak (pronounced Bee-ack) lies off the north coast of New Guinea in Geelvink Bay. The island did not have dense jungles as the division had encountered before; this one was composed of coral, with soil being a very scarce item. The little water to be found was almost undrinkable. We relied mostly on rain water, caught in our ponchos and helmets, to supply our needs.

The island was honey-combed with caves and crevices. Some holes were just large enough to hold a small Japanese, while others were large enough to hold hundreds of troops. These caves had to be systematically cleared, which was to slow our progress.

After the usual naval bombardment, strafing, and bombing runs by the Air Corps, our regiment, plus the 162nd, landed on the south side of the island, about eight miles east of the first of three airstrips. We met only light resistance and, as the 186th held the beachhead, the 162nd swung down the coral road toward the west and the airstrips. Running parallel to the beach were a series of ridges, two- to three-hundred feet in height. In places, the ridges ran a quarter of a mile back from the road and in other areas were right above the road. In these latter spots, the Japs kept the road under mortar and machine gun fire from the caves above. The 162nd took many casualties for five days and were finally forced to retire back along the road until an alternate route could be found to the airstrips. This area boasted the first tank battle in the Pacific between U.S. and Japanese forces. Several of their tanks were destroyed with no losses to our own.

On June 1, the 163rd rejoined the division at the beachhead and took over that area while our regiment scaled the ridges. The object was to proceed westward, come in over the ridges from the north, and take the airstrip.

Getting over the ridges with all the equipment we carried took until mid-afternoon. Reaching the fairly flat ground past the ridges, we were told to set up our perimeter there for the night. To that point, we had run into little opposition.

On the perimeters, we always dug slit trenches for two men so that during the night, one man slept while the other kept guard. In most instances, Gerry Lovett of Providence, Rhode Island, and I shared the same trench.

That night Gerry and I spent several hours hacking away at the coral, trying to get our hole deep enough to give some protection. Our entrenching tools were bent, and we had quite a few blisters on our hands. We even utilized a ball-peen hammer we found in an abandoned Japanese truck.

Just as we finished our hole, the order came down for everyone to move over one hole as two other men had moved into the perimeter somewhere down the line. Because we had spent so much time digging, we were not happy, but complied.

Sometime during the night the Japanese threw five mortar rounds into our immediate area, all landing within thirty feet of our hole. The last shell exploded so close to us that we were showered with coral.

When daylight came, we got out of our trench to stretch our legs and make a quick cup of coffee. We discovered that the two men who had taken our hole had both been killed by that last shell.

Moving from one hole to another had never happened before nor after that. It made me think of that old saying—when your time is up, it's up. Evidently, Gerry's and my time was not up.

For the next five days we worked our way westward and on June 6 we were ready to scale the ridges and move on to the airstrip. No heavy opposition had been met except for occasional sniper fire, one strafing by Jap Zeros, and nightly probing patrols by the enemy.

The next morning we climbed the ridges with no enemy fire in our sector, but as we reached the bottom of the cliffs near the airstrip, we were pinned down for awhile by machine-gun fire. After these pockets were eliminated, we proceeded to the east end of the strip about noon and began to set up defense positions between the strip and the beach; then all hell broke loose.

Artillery shells began falling all over our area, all coming from the ridges we had just come through. The Japanese had let us onto the strip, knowing that we would be surrounded on three sides: from the ridges to the north, the beach roadblock on the east, and Japanese positions on the west end of the strip.

We hurriedly set up an aid station in an abandoned enemy gun emplacement and the next several hours, still under fire, were spent bandaging the many wounded and carrying them back to the emplacement.

We were to find out later that their large guns were mounted on rails. When our tanks returned the fire, they merely rolled them back into a cave and waited out the shelling.

T/3 Carl Berg from Eugene, Oregon, the non-com in charge of the regimental aid-station, had, two days before, been sent back to a hospital on the beach, suffering from malaria and running a high fever. The morning we climbed the ridges to take the strip, he rejoined us. He was still running a high fever but told us that he felt guilty taking a bed in the hospital when so many wounded were coming in. Minutes after we got onto the strip, a shell landed in front of him, killing him instantly. Carl was liked by everyone and was missed by all of us.

The Japanese kept us pinned down on the beach for four days until the line companies broke through to the west and northwest and drove the enemy back into the large caverns, which had become known as the "Sumps." During those four days, supplies were brought in by landing crafts at night and the wounded taken out. Our dead were hastily buried near the beach.

By June 20, the 34th Regiment of the 24th Division had joined the party, concentrating on taking the two remaining airstrips. The 186th set up a roadblock to prevent the Sump occupants from escaping to the north for possible rescue by the Japanese navy. For two nights they tried to get through and lost over 200 men in the process. We lost only one man.

The remainder of the campaign consisted of mopping up small pockets of the enemy. The road along the beach to the east would be under occasional fire until it was finally cleared the latter part of July.

Our patrols were still working inland by October, cleaning out straggling Japanese.

We were to make other landings in the Philippines at Palawan Island and on Mindanao, but none of these had the frustrations of digging out the Japanese, one hole at a time, that was the case on Biak. Few men of the 41st will forget those months spent on "the Rock."

. . .

DID YOU KNOW THAT...

"The first production M4 Sherman tank built in this country was completed at Lima (Ohio) in March 1942 and sent to the Army's Aberdeen, Maryland, Proving Ground for testing." Most of the 1,655 tanks built at Lima were sent to England or Egypt. This was about 3.2 percent of the 49,000 M4s constructed.

Lima's government tank contracts were cancelled on September 30, 1943. But they continued with the M32 tank recovery vehicle, building 46 between June, 1943, and August, 1944. "Snow tractors, M12 tank gunnery trainers, and deep water fording M4s were also built at the plant during the war."[30]

THOMAS McMILLAN
FRITCH, TEXAS

Army, Staff Sgt., Machine Gunner, 32nd Infantry, 1944-46
Basic Training: Camp Wolters, Texas
Duty in Pacific

When we secured Leyte, then we made the big invasion on Lingayen Gulf between Baguio and Manila. On the way over, about 50 Japanese suicide planes bombed us. They always hit at night. The kids flying the planes didn't know how to land those planes; they only knew how to take off and fly into a ship. One kid, 12 or 13, dived into our ship, glazed the bow, and bounced out over the water. The sailors got him; he could speak good English, could talk to us. He had his funeral before he left Japan.

We had orders not to open up machine gun fire at night because the Japanese could see that fire and get us one way or another. They'd jump in the foxhole with us with 25 lbs. of TNT on them, pull a little string, and that would end the firing.

Foxholes had to be close so Japanese couldn't crawl between them. We were standing there talking one morning and I heard sniper bullet fire. That bullet caught my good buddy right in the temple and his hot blood sprayed right across my face.

We'd set one gun on the perimeter; captain's headquarters would be back. Machine guns would be set up so the fire would come from two angles and cross, shooting "graze and fire," which is knee-high fire. Then we'd go back sweeping the ground. We'd set up booby traps all around our perimeter before dark. The Japanese would run cattle in to set them off before they came in. They'd kill their own people, cut their throats if they were wounded.

We started pushing on into the mountains, hand-to-hand combat. We were so close to them, pushing them. They were moving so slow that sometimes we'd fight days and nights before we'd ever get two or three hours' sleep in the afternoon. We'd fight in daytime; Japanese fought at night. They'd always get us about 11:00 at night.

Thomas McMillan

We used Filipino ration trains to bring us food and beer. We'd capture the Japanese and guard them day and night so nobody would hurt them. Then the Filipinos would take them back down and interrogate them. They wouldn't get a mile out of camp and we'd hear gunshots. They weren't going to get any information out of those boys! They'd take the clothes off of them; Filipinos were running out of clothes.

Had orders to take a little village down on the river where there were 29 Japanese intelligence officers. When we got there, there were about 600 of them; naturally, they pushed us back. Then they moved out one night. Seven of us were sent on a patrol around that high hill. The Japs had machine guns firing down on us, right down in our camp. We had to go up there and knock those machine guns out. We went in behind them and set the dead grass on fire. Those guys down there along the river where we had our camp set up said those Japs would run and jump off that cliff. They'd be on fire, and they had TNT strapped to them; would blow up right in mid air.

The 600 or so moved back in and pushed our company back five miles; left us seven up there. They didn't know what was happening to us, whether or not we were alive. We were there five days. We were in enemy territory, no contact with our company. Four of us got back; the other three were killed, either their throats cut or a bayonet through them. We had nothing to eat, ran out of rice, no water, and we were about gone. Rats and snakes and everything else crawling all over us. We could see the Japs crawling around in the weeds. They'd yell, "Hey, Joe, what ya doin?" like they were Americans.

The reconnaissance planes came in and spotted us and they told headquarters there were four GIs coming that way. But those Japanese would kill our people and then dress in GI's clothes, so you couldn't tell whether they were our men or not. The only way we got out was that they came in there and threw a heavy smoke screen.

We went back up the mountain, up to the top. We were so tired and weak that we disarmed our guns and threw them away, along with our helmets; they were so heavy. Those Japs were right on us; we literally outran them. When we got back to our Company, I was so tired and exhausted that they said I laid right down beside a 155 Howitzer that bounced back every time it went off; slept all afternoon.

We got regrouped. When we went up there on the frontline we had full company strength of 206 men. After six months of hand- to-hand combat and they pulled us back to get replacements, we had 29 men. That's when I went from a private to a sergeant cause I was the only one left in the machine gun section.

We got new men and went back up again. That first night I was going around checking my men. Two guys had made a long foxhole, put grass down, laid their blankets out, had their little pillows under their heads, their shoes off. "What's going on here?" "We're getting comfortable." I said, "Get your shoes on! Man, you don't pull your shoes off up here!" "There's no Japs around here." I said, "I'll tell you what. Between 10:30 and 11:00 you'll wish you had your shoes on cause you might be running back down that rocky hill." Those old boys were so scared. And the next morning they said, "Man, as soon as we heard those old Japs chattering out there, we slid in those shoes! We're not pulling them off any more!"

We, the 32nd Red Arrow Division, captured General Yamashita and 45 troops. We just took over Yamashita's little empire. He was a big man, weighed 240-250 lbs. They started tunneling on one side of the mountain and came out the other side. They had room after room inside with beds, cooking facilities, curtains hanging on the door. Had Filipino women there. We got them out of there and marched them down the mountain and to the stockade. There were photographers and news reporters with us up there on the front line, so they got pictures.

I burned a machine gun up firing at the Japanese. They were coming right at me with their bayonets fixed and I just blew them up. The captain got killed, so the lieutenant took over; my assistant was shot, so the lieutenant was feeding bullets into my machine gun. I fired 2500 rounds and the barrel of that gun was red from being so hot. The Lieutenant got the Silver Star.

I was decorated with the Bronze Star for bravery in action. But I wasn't brave; I was just trying to survive.

Then we tried to convince the Japanese that the war was over. They were on one side of the mountain, and we were on the other. Our little reconnaissance plane dropped pamphlets saying that the war was over and they should give up. A PA system was set up, with speakers on the ridge line, and Japanese used it to tell their men that the war was over and to give up. Their soldiers shot those speakers all to pieces and blew them to bits. They weren't going to give up!

I went thirteen days and night with rain, rain, rain during the monsoon season; sat there in mud, day and night, had to sit there on the hill, even to sleep. With the other guy and me it was an hour on guard, an hour off guard, 24 hours a day, 7 days a week. When I pulled my shoes and socks off, blood ran out of my feet, and I still have problems with them.

I had malaria, jungle rot, long hair, lice. They sprayed us with DDT, then cut our hair. I had been on the front line six months. There were only two of us that didn't miss a single day of combat. Some of the guys would go back to the rear echelon, lay on a cot and rest, cause up there you'd just get so weak you couldn't go any longer. Down there they'd get them on their feet again in a few days and send them back up.

Thomas McMillan, Japan

I wouldn't take anything for my paid tour—Australia, New Guinea, Philippines, Japan—but I was scared to death that my boy would have to go through what I did. I was *so* lucky to get out alive!

• • •

DID YOU KNOW THAT...

Over 500 German POW camps, built throughout all the U.S. except in Nevada, Montana, North Dakota, and Vermont, held 119,401 prisoners. According to the Geneva Convention, prisoners could be used for labor if they agreed and if they received compensation. The 95.6 percent who wanted to work were used as "...groundskeepers, clerks, truck drivers, painters, carpenters, plumbers, warehousemen, musicians, cooks, hospital orderlies, draftsmen, highway workers and more."[31]

Most of these camps were similar to our regular military bases. In the canteen coupons could be used which had been received for their labor. Their work coupons could also be deposited in a savings account which could be withdrawn at the end of the war.

Newspapers, magazines, and books were available, many of the books being pro-western, hopefully indoctrinating the prisoners with the principles of democracy. Also, some of the more promising prisoners were chosen for a top-secret army program in Rhode Island. They were to be trained for helping with the occupation government in Germany at the war's end.

In the camp at Galveston, Texas, prisoners were studying English and agronomy. They had indoor and outdoor recreation areas and were allowed to swim in the Gulf; they had an orchestra and a drama group, plus 250 books in the German language. Apparently POWs were so pleased with their treatment that they donated $442 of their coupon money to the YMCA and $353.07 to the International Committee of the Red Cross. There were some violent Nazis, however, who had to be separated from the others.

"Many Americans, just coming out of the depression, looked on these living quarters with envy, called them 'The Fritz Ritz,' criticism that continued throughout the war."[32]

AFANASYEV
PYOTR MIHAILOVICH

UFA, RUSSIA

Army and Civilian Defense Work

Recently I read in a local paper: "The largest cemetery in the world is in Petersburg (former Leningrad), where 500,000 WW II victims are buried." For many people it was just a curious fact, but for me it was a painful flashback of my soul, for I happened to be a witness of those tragic events; day after day our number decreases and soon there will be no live witnesses at all.

Formerly I lived in Leningrad, where in 1939 I finished a technical course at the Leningrad Naval Electronics Trust, and then was directed to work as an electrician to the Naval Factory of Middle Neva. At that time its major products were battleships. The factory was located 15 miles from Leningrad, but our office was downtown on Neva Avenue.

At the beginning of the war I was drafted for the army, but soon I was returned to the factory as a specialist of the defense sector and was freed from further draft. My factory was working on a project of the minesweeper T-27. I was included in the technical crew of the ship for final maneuver tests. At the artillery armory tests I had to work right under gigantic gun-barrels while they were shooting. It seemed the sound of every blast tore your soul inside out and apart. Nothing, even the thickest earplugs, helped. The tests were successfully conducted in the Gulf of Finland. The ship immediately was put in active naval duty, and we returned to the factory.

Every day the front line was coming closer and closer to Leningrad. One after another countless barges full of urgently evacuated children went up the Neva. Tugboats pulling the half-built ships from Leningrad's factories followed them. Gigantic lines formed in front of every grocery store, and in a matter of a few hours everything that could be eaten was gone.

We could see the almost endless hordes of German bombers fly towards Leningrad to bomb the city, but a part of their fatal "cargo" was dropped on our factory. We had to hide in trenches that crossed all the territory of the factory back and forth.

Afanasyev Pyotr Mihailovich

Soon the ring of the blockade locked as the Germans had bombed and burnt all food storages, and the terrible famine started. It got even much worse in winter.

Every month I had to walk to the office downtown to receive our wages, food cards, and the production assignment for the next month.

In October, 1941, I came in a notion store to buy myself a kind of luminous badge that many inhabitants of Leningrad wore at that time in order not to bump into each other in the darkness of lightless porches. A young saleslady quickly wrote something on a sheet of paper, wrapped the badge in it, and, pale and trembling, handed it to me. I unwrapped the paper and read: "Do you have at least some bread crusts? I'm dying." What could I answer? I was in exactly the same situation! But the next day I came to the store and brought the crumbs I could find left from my factory rations. The girl was not there. I asked for her, and the new woman quietly said, "She's dead."

Day after day it was getting worse. The railroad bridges were blasted; dead bodies of the starved lay on both sides of the road; trains froze into the track, deformed by the blasts of bombs. Trucks full of dead bodies went one after another up Neva Avenue. The dead were dressed in the clothes they were in when death came. Near the Moscow railway station two frozen bodies were put on the icy road in order not to let the cars stick.

In the end of November, 1941, my friend Alexander Mihailov and I were given an assignment to fit up the central fire post on a ship guarding the Smolny House (Smolny House for Leningrad was like a White House for Washington). On my way to work I stayed overnight at my friend's apartment on Liteyny Avenue. In the morning I was awakened by a strange rumble, as if somebody were loading big logs on a truck. When I came outside, I saw two men loading the dead frozen human bodies, brought down by the people in this apartment building.

When I came closer to Smolny House I found myself in an unnatural twilight. A huge rope net was stretched over the building and the nearby trees, and all kinds of masking materials (tree branches, straw, grass) covered it, thus hiding the building from the German planes bombing the city. On the Neva bank I didn't see any well-armed, massive-looking ships; there was a regular river tugboat standing at the moorings, frozen in ice, with two anti-aircraft machine guns that the crew used to constantly shoot at the German aircraft "hanging" in the sky. This was the ship I was supposed to work at; we were quartered there together with the crew of sailors. At night we woke up because of a deafening noise and rumble. Our ship first went up, then smoothly down, and started swinging, although last night it was solidly frozen in ice. In the morning we found out that the Germans were to drop a 500 kg (1100 lbs.) air bomb on Smolny, but they missed, and the bomb fell into Neva. We were blasted into the air by the force of the bomb and the Neva was cleared of ice all the way through its opposite side.

In the morning we started installing the new anti-aircraft weapons on board, under the never-stopping fire from the already-installed guns. When the sky turned into a cloud of smoke and fire where a German plane used to be, the shooters cheered and hugged each other, like a soccer team after a scored goal. Although in such terrible noise and mess of fight it was really hard to determine whose missile hit the Nazi plane; (other anti-aircraft batteries continued fire simultaneously) each artilleryman thought that it was his missile.

The Nazis kept flooding the city with millions of leaflets from their planes. In the streets the leaflets weren't that obvious on the masses of bricks from the destroyed buildings, or in the black, sooty (because of bombing) snow. But Neva was literally hidden under layers of paper, which gave instructions how to properly be taken prisoner by the Nazis. The procedure was supposed to be as follows: rifles should have been hung behind the back, barrels to the ground, and we should have been moving towards the German trenches, keeping straight up with our arms up and shouting: "Heil Hitler!" If a person didn't have a rifle or a gun, he or she was supposed to follow the same orders, anyway.

To everyone who allows to be taken prisoner in the described manner, the Nazis promised to give a piece of land for a farm and a cow. We know the real cost of these promises from stories about the concentration camps such as Oswenzim, Maydsnik, and hundreds of others.

The Nazis particularly hated the Jews and members of the communist party. Here is the text of one of the leaflets: "Kill a Jew and a political leader! Brick their mugs!" And on the back was a picture of how to do it practically.

Before the New Year, 1942, the Nazis filled the city with leaflets of the following content: "People of Leningrad, eat up your beans and prepare wood for your New Year's coffins." We couldn't think of beans or even coffins! Everything wooden, including furniture, was burnt to heat the half-destroyed homes.

In January, 1942, we were transferred to the battleship Banga that stood in the ice of Neva, 10 kilometers from Leningrad. The ship was armed with long-range 150 mm guns, which kept firing at the Nazi troops at Pulkovo, Pavlovsk, and Pushkino. There were two more workers from the Leningrad Naval Factory coming with us. One of them died the next day, and the other one, younger, tried to look cheerful, although he was bloated from starvation. I asked him how he was doing, and he said that he lived comparatively well—his neighbor worked at the bakery and her room was often "visited" by rats. So this worker put a mousetrap near the hole that rats came from, and almost every week he added fresh rat meat to his tiny ration. He died on the third day at Banga. Every day it was getting harder and harder to work. Deafened by the constant noise of artillery, weakened by hunger and cold, we kept installing the equipment, raising the effectiveness of fire.

Once, in a hot gunbarrel, an unshot shell exploded. The barrel, torn apart, landed far on the ice of Neva, and we, relieved, were happy to get at least a little rest. But we were wrong; the next day a new gunbarrel was delivered on the sledge made out of logs and pulled by a tractor from the Obuhov factory. We had to work again for 24 hours to replace the blasted barrel, and the gun immediately joined the battle after repairs.

Women and teenage children worked 24 hours a day at the Leningrad defense factories, producing the necessary equipment. All the factories were powered by the only power station miraculously left in the city. It worked on log wood and peat.

Spring of 1942 was an especially hard period for Leningrad's inhabitants. People couldn't wait til the grass showed up in the ground to ease the sufferings of starvation. But for many, the grass meals were fatal. People died after filling themselves with several poisonous kinds of grass.

At that time I looked like a human skeleton from a museum. But, unlike the museum's one, my skeleton was covered with skin in greenish down, and had still some life inside. I had to crawl up from ship to shore because I didn't have enough energy to walk up the slope of the footbridge.

By the May 1 holiday we finished working on the Banga. The next day I was to return to the factory, but it was impossible to get across Neva, since the bridges were ruined and the ice was too thin. I went to a collective farm field, hoping to find some cabbage remainders from the last harvest under the snow. But I was far from being the first food-seeker there. All I could find in the field were the bodies of starved-to-death people, and not a single frozen cabbage. Then I went to the nearby forest, hoping to find at least some snowball tree or mountain ash berries, and, nothing again.

But I wasn't going to give my life up so easily. The next day I dressed warmly, took a fishing net, and jumped into the ice-cold water of a small pond. I was hoping to catch some crustacean fish, but didn't have any luck. Long after changing into dry clothes at home, I had strong chills, so low my body temperature had become in the cold water.

The ice on the pond finally melted and I was able to use a bigger fishing net. This time my mother helped me cope with it. We pulled the net out and cried with happiness for there were half a bucket of crustacean fish in it. That meant our survival in the blockade.

Soon my mother was evacuated from Leningrad and I volunteered in the army to serve on the Leningrad front. On July 30, 1942, in the battle of Ligovo, our regiment was eliminated by the enemy. Out of 42 men, there were only two surviviors: soldier Obertyshev and I, both badly wounded.

After extensive treatment in six hospitals, in March, 1943, I was released from the Ufa hospital and directed to work at the Ufa Engine Factory, where, during wartime, great numbers of aviational engines were built. The work was very effort-consuming; we had to stay at the machines for 12-14 hours a day.

The most joyful day in my life was that of the Leningrad blockade's breakdown on January 18, 1943. I heard this wonderful news in the Ufa hospital. Nine hundred days of famine, bombing, and cold were over!

There is an official honorary recognition of the courage of Leningrad, its defenders, and inhabitants, issued by Franklin D. Roosevelt on May 17, 1944.

· · ·

HILDEGARD FELENKA OGLE
ROCKPORT, TEXAS

German Air Force

I was born in Bohemia (then Czechoslovakia) of German descent, a Czech citizen. Czechoslovakia was then a democratic society. In September 1938, the Germans declared war against my country. My step-father was drafted into the Czech Army. My mother and I tried to outrun the invaders, were in a freight train going deeper into the country to find my step-father's brother's place—they were supposed to take us in.

In 1939 they caught up with us. My mother's sister got us in trouble and the SS came and looked us up. With the Gestapo, you didn't have to be Jewish, just speak a different language and they would take you. Once they took you, you never saw anything again. But your own people, in order to make it better for themselves, would turn in other family members, friends, neighbors. For a little while we were left alone. Soon my mother volunteered my step-father as a volunteer in the German army. She was afraid they would put him in a camp. At that time everybody was afraid. These were harsh times and more to come.

Hidegard Felenka Ogle

In 1940 I was drafted into the Air Force, Luftwaffe, and sent to Holland to a high command. We worked in a bunker close to Arnheim, out in the country. Things were not so bad; air raid every day. The food was severely rationed. We had no trouble with the people; traded spirits (alcohol) for eggs or flour.

At that bunker where I worked, one day we were informed that Goering was coming and we were not to go about in the hallways. I did, anyway. I opened the door to the stairway and practically ran into him. He was short and fat, didn't have any medals on, no gun, no one else in hallway. He asked, "Do you work here?" Then I followed him upstairs to the command post; I was so busy looking around, had a lot of big maps on the walls. He asked for a glass of water; everybody panicked—no glass. They paid no attention to me, they were so busy concentrating on this man and worrying about how to get him a glass of water, so I just slipped out. I was lucky not to be in big trouble, just a young girl, telephone operator, no rank, nothing.

I went home occasionally. One time my mother had been taken to the Gestapo because she was really outspoken. At that time Germany was fighting in Russia and my mother made the statement that the Russians were going to win the war. A Czech person went to the Gestapo and told what my mother had said. I talked to those Gestapo people and sent two other family members in. We were all in the service, and I was young—guess that made an impression. Anyway, they let her go.

There was bombing going on day and night over the border in Germany. Holland didn't get too much. Then in 1944, after the Allies landed in France, the English paratroopers landed in a field close by the bunker where I worked, and all hell broke loose. The war was surely coming to an end. With all the bombing and very little food, at the beginning of 1945 all the female personnel were put on a bus and sent home; the men had to stay.

When I arrived in Pilsen my mother had died, so I didn't have anybody. My step-dad had been in service in Poland and then France, but we never heard anything. My kid brother was missing in Stalingrad. I was looking for some Czech people my mother knew. Someone pointed out that I was not German, so I was taken to prison. At that time partisans were out with guns looking for collaborators. You didn't even have to have done anything; they'd take you, anyway. Some were shot, had heads shaved, beaten, taken to prison. Here came the Americans marching, and in tanks, and yet all those German people were being marched off to jail.

After my prison stay (they didn't keep me very long), I was sent to a camp where anything possible could happen, anybody could rape us or do anything they wanted, with the military and Czech people in power. One time some of the women and I had to clear a wooded area full of unexploded bombs, a very frightening situation. They wanted to keep us there in Czechoslovakia for slave labor.

After five months or so, German prisoners were being taken back to Germany. Being Czech, I had no I.D., but my friend from Prague said, "Let's just go like we are from Germany." We did, they didn't ask us. Germany was no safe haven, either, no work; no food stamps, no place to stay; over-run with refugees.

All during the war we never knew what was going on; no news except English broadcasting, but there was always a lot of interference.

In late 1945 I got a job working for a hospital, TB patients, for only the food I should eat. These were very harsh years but youth is resilient.

Later when the Americans had taken over, I met my husband-to-be. Germans could not marry until the GI's time of enlistment was up, so in September, 1948, we married and in November came to the U.S.A. I have lived in Maine, Hawaii, Massachusetts, and Texas. My husband retired in 1960 from the service. In 1976 he died.

War is ugly, ugly, ugly! God was with me or I would never have gotten through all this alive.

• • •

DID YOU KNOW THAT...

In 1942, with a list of targets, eight German saboteurs who had lived in the U.S. and learned our ways, were divided into two teams and landed by submarine off the shores of Florida and New York. They buried dynamite and timing devices in the sand and threw their shovels in the water. Materials were discovered before any were used, the saboteurs captured, tried and convicted within a few days of their arrival. Six were sentenced to death; two received life sentences. 33

MAX G. PAPAZIAN

FORT WAYNE, INDIANA

Army, Pfc, Machine Gunner, 1943-46
32nd Infantry Div., 126th Regimental Combat Team
Basic Training: Camp Blanding, Florida
Duty in South Pacific

Aboard the USS Howze, crossing the Pacific took about 10-12 days. Those crossing the Equator for the first time were initiated and each "shellback" received a certificate.

On arrival at Goodenough Island, a replacement depot off the east coast of New Guinea, we were issued gear for the area, including a hammock with attached mosquito netting and weatherproof covering. Atabrine tablets (a substitute for quinine) were given out to control malaria. Intake of these was to be continued until returning home.

Max G. Papazian

In Aitape, New Guinea, we patrolled, never encountering the enemy directly but saw evidence of their presence each day. Other companies had met fierce resistance on the Drinimour River, units being almost isolated and surrounded by enemy troops.

We had to take precautions against typhus, which was prevalent in this jungle area.

In a convoy headed northeast of the New Guinea coast, naval guns started shelling as we neared our next objective; we were confined to our quarters. After a few hours we loaded on to landing crafts and rode to the beach of Morotai Island in the Dutch East Indies, currently referred to as the Moluccas. This island was the location of an important radar station.

When we hit the beaches, we experienced little resistance. Proceeding toward the radar station a few miles up the coast, we still had no enemy encounters or sightings. We quickly demolished any and all working electronic equipment, while at the same time picking up a few mementos for ourselves.

After being re-equipped and re-outfitted, we found ourselves on the way to the Philippines. When nearing our destination, the convoy was attacked by Japanese Zeros. All troops were confined to below decks while the Navy contended with the aircraft.

Some days later we made a beach landing on Leyte. We moved in and set up camp in the foothills of the mountain ranges, being kept in reserve temporarily. When sent in to bolster the fighting forces up in the mountains, we saw cave systems that the Japanese troops had dug into the mountainsides for cannons and tanks. Flame throwers were brought in to seal off the caves.

It was the rainy season and our foxholes filled up with the rain. After about a week of this we were to start an assault operation the next morning. We were all tired, wet and hungry, as we settled in for the night. I prayed to God to get me out of there, no matter how He did it, just as long as I could walk out on my own.

The next morning we started to move up the hill, with enemy tanks setting on the crest of it. The battle started in full force. While I was crawling up the hillside, I spotted a Japanese hand grenade sizzling about six or eight feet in front of me. As I turned to avoid the direct blast, it exploded, blowing my helmet off and my M-1 rifle out of my hands.

My right hand, arm, and neck had been hit with flying shrapnel fragments. I made my way downhill, found a medic who cleaned me up and bandaged my visible wounds, and continued on to the rear for transportation to a field hospital. Some of my buddies were not as fortunate. As I began to calm down I realized that God had heard and answered my prayer.

A Piper Cub plane was being used to transport the wounded back to the field hospital. This was to be my very first plane ride. I took off my combat boots for the first time in two weeks; that was a mistake. My feet puffed up and I couldn't get the boots back on when we landed. They had to place me on a litter and carry me to the field hospital.

While recuperating from the wounds, I was able to get rested and have some good hot food. Lew Ayres, the movie actor, visited and talked with us. He was doing his part in the war effort by encouraging the GIs. In 1993 I wrote him a letter, acknowledging his efforts and concern. By then he was 83 years old but graciously answered my letter and expressed his appreciation.

With only light bandages on my arm, I obtained permission to return to my unit, which was busy unloading material and supplies from incoming ships in preparation for the offensive action in Luzon.

In the Lingayen Gulf operation we were given the task of clearing and taking control of the Villa Verde Trail, a primary road stretching from Manila to Baguio, a resort community to the north. The entire area was heavily fortified by the Japanese.

With artillery support preceding us, we advanced through areas heavily shelled. It was not uncommon to walk past numerous dead enemy soldiers. Where there were extensive systems of caves built into hillsides, flame throwers sealed them off or cleared them out. We saw smoke coming out of other openings, from a quarter to half mile away.

While being in the rear area for a period of rest and relaxation, Company F was assigned to be personal security guards for General Douglas MacArthur and his staff. It was deemed an honor for us. However, it was all spit and polish; for those of us who had been in battle, it seemed a burden to have our uniforms clean and boots polished all the time. This special assignment lasted about two weeks, after which we moved back into the fighting.

One evening we began to settle in on a razor-backed ridge and I dug my foxhole deep enough that I could just see out; we were deep in hostile territory and weren't about to expose ourselves any more than we had to. We were supplied with whatever ammunition and hand grenades we wanted to see us through the night, hopefully. It was pitch black, no moon, which made the situation all the more tense. We all had turns standing guard. To communicate and to let one another know it was his turn to stand guard, we had string going from foxhole to foxhole.

Up the trail about one hundred yards from me was our light machine gun crews' installations. During the night we would hear the enemy soldiers rustling through the underbrush. Upon hearing the sounds I would pull the pin on a hand grenade and lob it over, letting it roll down the side of the hill. In spite of all the steps we had taken, some enemy soldiers managed to overrun a machine gun installation and put a saber through one of the guards. I can still hear him calling, "Sully, help me!" The security troops and backup machine gun crew opened fire and sprayed the area. At dawn we found our dead buddy along with numerous Japanese soldiers.

As we regrouped in the daylight, I was assigned the job of assistant gunner to fill the void in the machine gun crew. The enemy had retreated and we had no more direct contact with them, even though we continued to pursue them. I was issued a 45 caliber automatic revolver for personal firearm protection as a member of the machine gun crew.

Besides the 45, I carried a 30 caliber carbine rifle and a light machine gun, plus two cases of ammunition for it. Some of the new men, who came as replacements for those we had lost, complained about having to carry this additional ammunition for the crew.

After two or three more missions and my having some time out for a leg problem, General Yamashita, who was in charge of the Japanese forces, surrendered to one of our units out in the field. This was a few days after the atom bombs were dropped on Hiroshima and Nagasaki. We were assigned to go out and search for any stray Japanese soldiers. I, and many others, resented this assignment, but the news of Japan's surrender revived us. Things went really wild in camp with weapons being shot in the air.

We adopted a small monkey that came into our camp as our mascot; it ate whatever we gave it. We were waiting to see what was being arranged for our unit, with many of the older veterans looking forward to being sent home. One man was all set to leave for home after his patrol returned from what was to be their final mission; he never made it back.

Those of us left were assigned to go with the 32nd Infantry to Japan to serve as part of the occupation forces. We arrived at the southernmost island of Kyushu, where I thought it would have been extremely difficult to make a landing if we had carried through the invasion plans.

We landed at Sasebo and Fukuoka and moved into the city of Kokura, where we were billeted in former Japanese army barracks. I was given the responsibility of firing up the water heaters at least an hour and a half before reveille each morning. In return, I was excused from having to be in reveille formation exercises. We still drilled to maintain our infantry skills.

We served as Military Police for this area. I found a working sewing machine and started to alter, and/or modify our uniforms so that they appeared to have been freshly ironed all the time. I did this on my own time and made a little bit of extra money.

One unique feature of our quarters was the porcelainized open pit toilets. Japanese "honeydippers" came in on a regular basis to clean out the pits. They used the human waste for fertilizer.

When coming home we landed in Astoria, Oregon, after sailing up the Columbia River, which was a beautiful sight. What a pleasure and delight it was to be back in the U.S! As we disembarked we were met by USO volunteers providing us with refreshments. The first thing I asked for was a large glass of fresh milk.

Malarial attacks continued for the next two years, occurring about two or three times a year.

• • •

DID YOU KNOW THAT...

In 1929 when 47 nations met in Geneva, Switzerland, to set rules for POWs, Japan objected because their code does not allow a soldier to become a prisoner; he should commit suicide. Surrender was a punishable offense. It was common for a superior to beat or strike an entire squad if responsibility could not be placed on one. Even so, they signed the agreement!

Prisoners of the Japanese very seldom tried escape because it meant death, if caught, and also to several additional men. 34

WILLIAM STEWARD
VIVIAN, LOUISIANA

Army, Pfc., Infantry Rifleman, 1941-54
Basic Training: Ft. Warren, Wyoming
Duty in Europe

March, 1945: My unit was fighting Germans just east of the Rhine River in Germany. It had taken the bridge at Remagen, the only bridge still standing over the Rhine. The Germans, of course, wanted that bridge back.

We were engaged in heavy fighting, taking many casualties, while moving to knock out a section of the Reich Autobaun. Our runner went down with a bullet to the left side of his face, leaving him alive but out of action. I became the new runner.

We moved from one German village to another, which we called "village hopping." As soon as we took a village, we moved quickly to hit the next one before the enemy could mount a proper defense.

One morning we were moving in tactical formation on a small trail that led up a gradual incline. Sometimes when we moved on a village we could see white flags hanging out windows of the houses, telling us the village wished to surrender, but not this village. We all knew they were ready to put up a fight.

Suddenly an enemy machine gun opened up on us from the left flank and we scrambled for cover. The first nine men moved forward and took cover behind some bushes while the rest of us scrambled back behind, just over a small rise. This left the platoon split into two groups, with the nine of us exposed and in trouble.

I felt something slam into the left side of my helmet, ripping it off my head. I was holding my "walkie-talkie" radio to my left ear, trying to contact the command post. The radio all but exploded in my left hand. I was sure that whatever had happened had ripped open my left ear drum. I rolled over on my right side, holding my left ear in pain. When I opened my eyes I could see my helmet a few feet from me with a nasty-looking scar down the left side. My radio was little more than a mass of wires and tubes.

Then the dirt kicked up just inches from my face. A sniper had fired at my head and the bullet grazed my helmet and smashed my radio; the second shot missed me by less than six inches.

Following the two shots from the sniper, everything suddenly became quiet. Then a German soldier walked out front waving a white flag. Dumb old me, I thought the Germans wanted to surrender. How wrong I was! The man yelled at us in perfect English, "Come out with your hands up! We have you covered from your left flank with a machine gun and from the front with another. There's twenty rifles pointed at all of you. Right now! Come out with your hands up!"

If there was anything that frightened me more than a sniper, it had to be the thought of surrendering to an enemy who excelled in making prisoners talk. I could just see them pulling out my fingernails with pliers, or hanging me up by my thumbs and whipping the flesh off my back.

I began shucking some of my gear, keeping my "tommy" and two extra clips. I was about to leap up and make a dash toward the rear and the safety of the rest of the men down below the small rise when the lieutenant called to me, "What are you doing, Steward?"

"I won't let them take me prisoner, sir! If you object to me trying to save myself, say so now! I'm gettin' the hell out of here!"

"You'll never make it!" the lieutenant said. "That machine gun will cut you to pieces!"

"Maybe so, but that's better than being tortured to death! I'll take my chances!"

"If you're determined to go, and you make it, get the platoon sergeant's radio and have the mortar section drop smoke between our position and the Krauts!"

When the German with the white flag saw he was getting no response to his demands, he turned and began walking back up the hill toward the village. That's when I leaped to my feet and started my run. I was a track champion in high school and I could move. I could hear the machine gun chatter to my right as I turned on the speed. I saw something in the dim little trail in front of me and, as I tried to jump it, I could see that it was the body of the replacement who had joined our platoon just 24 hours before. The back of the man's field jacket was covered with blood. The burst of machine gun fire from the gun on our left flank hit him in the side and back.

As I attempted to jump the dead replacement, I fell sprawling. The two extra clips I was carrying for my tommy went flying in the air. I leaped back to my feet and continued my run. Finally, I slid over the small rise in the terrain to join the rest of the men.

"Give me the radio, Sarge!" I yelled at the platoon sergeant. "Give me the radio!" I shouted, almost in a panic.

"Calm down!" the sergeant said. "What's going on?"

"Call the mortar section, quick! The lieutenant and the others are in trouble! Get some smoke between them and the Krauts to cover their withdrawal! For God's sake, Sarge, hurry! Hurry!"

"Okay, you just calm down! You get back up there and tell them to sit tight. I'll get some smoke up there."

"Go back up there? You gotta be out of your mind! I almost got killed getting down here! That machine gun will get me for sure!"

"Well, you're the runner, aren't you?"

"So?"

"Then do your job!"

The sergeant's statement hit me like a shot. He was right; it was my job. Even though I hated the thought of going back up in the trap, I started my run. To my surprise, the German gunner didn't fire on me. Perhaps he thought if I was dumb enough to go back, he would just let me go.

When the smoke began to cover the area from our bursting mortar rounds, the lieutenant led us right up under the German guns, over a small rise to our right flank, then to safety. We called in artillery fire on the village and levelled it to a pile of ashes.

I reported the dead replacement's position to the C.P. over the platoon sergeant's radio after I had reported his death to the lieutenant. After that I took stock of myself. I had no wounds other than a skinned hand and elbow. I had two bullet holes in the tail of my battle jacket. I never saw my scarred-up helmet again, nor what was left of my radio. That evening as the men of the platoon dug in, the lieutenant came to me.

"I'm going to recommend you for the Silver Star, Steward."

"But, sir, I want you to understand that I was..." I stuttered, trying to explain that I was just trying to save myself from capture.

"I don't want to hear it!" the lieutenant said. "I know what you are about to say. That has nothing to do with anything. Besides, you came back up, didn't you?"

"Well, I..."

"The recommendation stands!" the lieutenant interrupted again.

The recommendation went to regiment. In WW II the Silver Star Medal was passed out very stingily. I was awarded the Bronze Star instead. I am very grateful to my lieutenant for that recommendation.

• • •

DID YOU KNOW THAT...

Although the first jet aircraft battle occurred in Korea in November, 1950, the Germans were using jet planes in September, 1944. Their speed and maneuverability were reported to be much better than anything the Allies had. Requests were sent from the European Theater to Gen. Arnold for large numbers of the new American jet fighter, the Lockheed P-80. However, only two models reached the American pilots before Germany's surrender; neither of those was used in combat. 35

MILO B. TESAR

EAST LANSING, MICHIGAN

Army, Field Artillery, 2nd Lt. - Major
Basic Training: Fort Sill, Oklahoma
Duty in Pacific

On Oahu, Hawaii, in May, 1942, the 13th FA Bn had three batteries of four 105s in camouflaged field positions in cane or pineapple fields or gulches. The three 105 battalions in the division had 35 guns. A fourth Bn had four 155-mm (6-inch) guns for a division total of 48 guns. Batteries were about two miles apart and two to three miles from the beach.

Each battery had an observation post (OP) on a bluff so any Japs attacking in boats could be spotted several miles out on the Pacific. Communication to the batteries and the Bn fire direction center was by telephones (as Radar uses in the TV show MASH) and radio. Each battery had its own OP; ours was on the edge of a sugar cane field high above what is now Sunset Beach, a world-famous surfing area. We manned the OP 24 hours a day, our job being to spot Japanese boats/soldiers early to deliver massed artillery fire from 4 to 48 guns.

Our main force against expected attacking Japanese troops after landing would have been the approximate 8,500 infantry. With our 2500 artillerymen and 3000 service personnel, the division had about 14,000 men defending the north shore of Oahu. Another division was on the south shore including Honolulu. Fortunately, the Japanese never attacked after the Pearl Harbor air raid on our ships.

The U.S. would have had a hard time defending the island of Oahu if Japan had attacked right after Pearl Harbor with six to eight divisions and planes from the carriers 200 miles north of Oahu. The Zero fighters were better than our planes in 1941. Our carriers were on maneuvers (not expecting any attack) far away in the Pacific. Eighteen of our ships, including five battleships, were sunk at Pearl Harbor and there was extensive damage to many ships.

Rolled barbed-wire was on all the landing beaches. Houses, buildings, restaurants, and our shacks were blacked out at night. Civilian and military vehicles had cats-eye lights.

Barbed wire on Waikiki Beach, Honolulu, HI, 1942

After leaving Oahu, we had more training in Australia, and then I landed in Hollandia, New Guinea, with the infantry second wave on Red Beach. That meant using the rope ladder from our Dutch troopship to get into the 40-man landing boat. Resistance was light. Infantry moved forward rapidly around a swamp and made enemy contact.

Our guns were towed by D-7 Caterpillar bulldozers also used for clearing the jungle and improving dirt trails for 4-wheel-drive jeeps.

Just after landing at Hollandia I looked up at a noise above me, just in time to see a Jap sniper in the treetop aiming at me. Luckily, I got him first with my carbine. He didn't fall out of the tree; he had tied himself in.

In the battle of Leyte Gulf the U.S. had 282 ships, hundreds of airplanes, and 187,000 sailors in an all-out effort to defeat Japan's navy. Leyte marked the end of Japanese naval strength, badly weakened in June, 1942, in the Battle of Midway. It marked the start of Japan's Kamikaze corps where suicidal bomber pilots hit several of our ships in Leyte Gulf and damaged many others. It was terrifying to be on a ship in the Gulf and see a Kamikaze plane diving toward you, hoping it would miss.

Milo B. Tesar — Mindanao, Philippines with
captured flag and sword, 1945

Japan had about 80,000 men in well-defended positions, caves and pillboxes in Leyte. Our six divisions (85,000 men) mounted an all-out attack, starting near Tacloban on the east coast of Leyte. The Japs were ready for us. They knew they had to hold the island or else it would only be a question of when U.S. troops would attack the Japanese mainland.

The land battle on Leyte was difficult and bloody for us and the Japs. It was a "dig-em-out" campaign by the infantry, using rifles, grenades and flame throwers with some hand-to-hand bayonet fighting after artillery fire to neutralized strong points. Our army destroyed, neutralized, or captured all

Japanese divisions by early December, 1944. But it wasn't a cheap victory. Our six divisions lost over 2700 killed and 11,000 wounded.

Our artillery was much more mobile than theirs. As in New Guinea, our artillery had D-7 dozers to tow guns, ammunition and supplies, and to clear jungle trails into passable roads for 4-wheel drive jeeps and light personnel carriers in the jungle with its daily rains.

The major advance in artillery since the mid '30s was to mass many guns on one target. Our Fire Direction Center in a tent about a mile behind the front lines was the hub of massing the fire, all at one time, of 4 to 12 guns in a battalion, on a target, or 48 guns in the division on major targets. One visible tracer (shell burst) would be used to adjust the other guns on the same target. Maps were then made in the fire direction center to mass the fire in the same or adjacent area. This was particularly effective on troops in an open area using the radio controlled fuzes (VT) for air bursts. Fortunately for us, the Japanese didn't have this capability.

The V-T fuze was an important advance early in WW II. Shells with the V-T fuze would burst on impact, or could be set for shell burst in the air above enemy troops in the open, with devastating effect. We used the air burst a lot in semi-open jungle/grass areas.

Our infantry had better automatic and semi-automatic rifles, machine guns and flame throwers used for routing Japs out of caves and pill boxes. One wounded Japanese prisoner said, when interrogated, that our flame throwers were very good, our troops had cleaner rifles, and could throw grenades farther and more accurately than they could. He said there was no place to hide if our artillery air bursts got them in the open, where he was wounded.

Japanese infantry didn't fight only during daylight as was common in European wars. They sometimes breached our perimeters at night and crawled to an individual sentry on guard and killed him with a knife or threw a grenade into several GIs, generally sacrificing their own life. They wore rubberized cotton slip-on shoes with the big toe separated from the other four toes. It was a great shoe for them in the wet jungles and when crossing rivers.

Combat on Leyte ended in early December, 1944.

On Mindoro Island resistance was light; the Japs had fled into the hills after a 5A.M. shelling of the beach by a battleship and cruiser. Our mission was to secure the airport for P-38 fighters and light bombers against Luzon, the next target.

At Mindanao Island we landed on the west side and marched and fought for 140 miles to Davao, with guns held over our heads as we crossed rivers. We fought Japanese infantry and Moros (Muslems), Filipinos sympathetic to Japan. One battalion of the 19th Infantry encountered heavy resistance and had to move at night to secure the Taloma River bridge. I directed artillery fire on the Japanese troops all night to keep them from dynamiting the bridge. Our artillery barrages with twelve 105s forced the Japanese to withdraw to the high ground above Davao.

When we got to Davao, population 35,000, it was nearly deserted after U.S. bombing in late April. The Filipinos, sympathizers of Japanese who seized the island in 1942, had fled into the hills. But Japanese soldiers in caves infiltrated our lines with severe damage until our artillery and infantry forced them north. Small enemy groups came back to man big guns guarding Davao. Using a captured Japanese telescope, I was able to spot their gun positions. We destroyed one gun with directed fire (just like a rifle) at 2000 yards. We had moved one 105 gun over a river on a pontoon and up a bluff. We could see when one of their guns, 2000 yards across a gulch, fired. Our gunnery crew adjusted on that gun and destroyed it. Later we used all guns of one of our batteries to destroy the other ten of their guns. The enemy again retreated north. For my part in the march, artillery support across Mindanao, and elimination of Japanese artillery defending Davao, I was awarded the Bronze Star.

In mid June I became fire direction center officer, to direct massed artillery fire on remaining Japanese troops north of Davao. In early August I and a battalion Piper Cub pilot made a reconnaissance flight over enemy territory. I spotted Japanese troops near a hill near Licinan air drome and started adjusting our guns. Our plane came under severe anti-aircraft and machine gun fire from the air drome. We flew lower to get a better view of the target. After a short time we were forced to leave because the danger of being shot down was too great, but not before completing our mission and neutralizing the troops. For this action I was awarded the Silver Star.

After the atom bombs were dropped on Hiroshima and Nagasaki, Gen. MacArthur accepted the Japanese surrender aboard the USS Missouri on September 2, 1945. I was among the 12 officers and 20 men who were the first U.S. personnel in the army of occupation in Hiroshima, Honshu Island. We had our carbines and pistols ready when we landed from the destroyer as a token response if the Japanese army decided to eliminate or imprison us. Fortunately, the Emperor had given the word of surrender to all Japanese military and civilians and there was no engagement between us. We destroyed all cannons, rifles, pistols, swords and military equipment in the area.

In the Honshu POW camp, when the Japanese surrendered, the American captives there tore down the Japanese flag and hoisted the Stars and Stripes. One POW had managed to conceal the flag from the time of his capture at Corregidor, through the horrendous Bataan Death March and the following trying days of imprisonment.

• • •

DID YOU KNOW THAT...

Four months after Pearl Harbor, when American morale was very low because of all the defeats in the Pacific, Jimmy Doolittle's Raiders bombed Tokyo. Since there were no land bases close enough to fly to Japan, on April 18, 1942, sixteen B-25 Mitchell bombers took off from the carrier Hornet, something never before done. After dropping 500-pound bombs, the bombers flew to various points in China. Besides lifting the morale of the Allies, the successful raid was a psychological shock for Japan.[36]

AMERICAN LAND BOMBED AND INVADED

JUNE 7, 1942

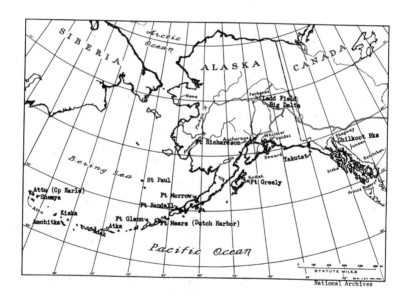

National Archives

WHERE ARE THE ALEUTIAN ISLANDS?

The Aleutian Island Chain, part of Alaska, extends 1,100 miles southwest of Anchorage, between the Pacific Ocean and the Bering Sea. Since Alaska and the Islands were acquired by the U.S. in 1867, the area and its people were pretty much ignored. However, after the attack on Pearl Harbor, the Islands were viewed as an essential point of defense. For the Japanese, they would be a steppingstone to Canada and the U.S. mainland.

Gen. Billy Mitchell told Congress in 1935 that "Japan is our dangerous enemy in the Pacific....I believe in the future, he who holds Alaska will hold the world, and I think it is the most important strategic place in the world." 37

While only 21,945 Army troops, scattered hundreds of thousands of miles apart, were stationed in Alaska previous to December 7, 1941, things changed quickly. An air base was located at Kodiak, 600 miles from Dutch Harbor, and PBYs were flying from there; they moved to Cold Bay, 180 miles away from Dutch Harbor; and finally were based at Dutch Harbor. Dutch Harbor is in a natural, protected area from the Bering Sea, the best harbor in the Aleutians. It is connected to Unalaska by bridge.

Dutch Harbor — courtesy Rita Byrer

Because of the rugged terrain at Dutch Harbor, Fort Glenn air field was built on Umnak Island, 70 miles west of Dutch Harbor. Steel matting was used on runways because of the mud. The PBYs were flying boats, being able to land on water or land. They were sturdy, could withstand bad weather, and could hold 1750 gallons of gas. Their primary purpose was reconnaissance, but they could carry and use bombs, torpedoes and depth charges.

Weather conditions in the Aleutians are among the worst in the world. Violent winds (williwaws) blow daily, up to 170 miles per hour, sweeping away buildings not anchored down with steel cable. Rain, and some snow, falls on an average of 200 days a year, with fog and heavy clouds being very common. Temperatures do not go as low as in other parts of Alaska because the islands are a little farther south.

Surrounding waters are ice free because of the Japanese Current. Average temperature, however, in August, the warmest month, is only 56 degrees.

Even though cold was not a problem on ground level, planes that tried to get above the wind got in cold air and wings started freezing up.

Jokes about the weather were prolific, one among the pilots being: "Stick your hand out. If it touches a ship's mast, you're flying too low." [38]

Pilots also had trouble with their compasses. Because of so many minerals being in Alaska, the compasses would not operate properly.

BOMBING OF DUTCH HARBOR/UNALASKA

During the night of June 2, 1942, Japanese carriers sneaked in within 200 miles of Dutch Harbor. With them were 82 attack planes, six cruisers, twelve destroyers, three transports with 2500 troops aboard, and eight submarines, plus other vessels. [39]

On the morning of June 3, the PBY crew was heading back in toward Dutch Harbor after an all-night search. Suddenly the radioman picked up a message from a tender that Dutch Harbor was under attack.

Even though the American planes were ready, because of wind, unstable air, and poor communication equipment, the message did not get through to Fort Glenn, and Cold Bay pilots had so far to come that the Japanese pilots had the sky to themselves. The 6,282 soldiers on the island were waiting in trenches and shelters in the hills.

Bunkers, Dutch Harbor — courtesy Rita Byrer

The attack came at almost the same time as the one on Midway. Fourteen-sixteen (sources differ) bombs were released by four Jap bombers, as antiaircraft guns blasted away at them. Several buildings were damaged; 25 men were killed and 25 wounded.

Track of coastal gun, Unalaska — courtesy Rita Byrer

Admiral Nimitz was expecting this attack. Our Intelligence teams had broken the Japanese Naval Code and knew that the Japanese intended to bomb Dutch Harbor the day before Midway was attacked, creating a diversion, drawing attention away from Midway. Having this information, Nimitz sent five cruisers and four destroyers, all he could spare from the expected Midway battle, to Kodiak Island, headquarters of the Alaska Naval Sector.

On the evening of June 4, there was another attack on Dutch Harbor, this time by three flights of bombers. New fuel oil tanks and contents of 22,000 barrels of fuel were destroyed, plus some damage to buildings.

The first Zero captured by the Allies was not far from Dutch Harbor. With U.S. having no planes to compare with the Zero, engineers studied it and designed the Navy's F6F Hellcat, closely following the principles of the Zero. The Hellcats, in less than eighteen months, ruled the Pacific skies.40

JAPANESE FORCES INVADE

On June 7, 1942, three days after the attacks on Dutch Harbor, the Japanese landed 2500 combat troops on Kiska and Attu. Attu is approximately one thousand miles west of Dutch Harbor and 350 miles west of Kiska.

At Kiska, with machine guns riddling their cabin, nine American sailors surrendered along with 41 Aleuts. The tenth man evaded the Japanese and managed for fifty days to survive in the hills before surrendering because of lack of food.

At Attu 42 Aleuts, along with an American female teacher, were captured, held three months on the island, and then sent to Japan, where they were kept until after the war. The woman's husband, Foster Jones, from St. Paris, Ohio, was shot.

The June 7 invasion of Kiska and Attu was not known by the American military officials until June 10. American pilots were in the air for over one hundred hours searching for the Japanese task force, taking turns sleeping in the planes, but rain, fog, and clouds were so heavy that nothing could be seen. Finally, one of the pilots found a hole in the clouds, went down to take a look and was fired upon. Americans had been suspicious because no messages had been coming from the station in Kiska.

Japanese officials were anxious to capture Kiska and Attu to avoid having the Americans use it as a jumping-off place for the bombing of Japan. They were aware that the B-29, capable of longer flights, would be in operation before long. On April 18, 1942, Lt. James Doolittle had led sixteen B-25 Mitchell bombers to an attack on Tokyo. While the bombers were launched from the carrier Hornet, Japan thought they might have come from one of the Aleutian Islands. Never before had land-based bombers been flown from an aircraft carrier.

Besides averting these air strikes on Japan, bases in the North would provide a gateway for them to Canada and the United States for future bombing raids.

Japan had also planned for the bombing attacks and invasion to be a diversion from their planned action at Midway. Because Admiral Nimitz became aware of their intentions, Midway was not the great success that Japan had expected; half of its carriers were lost. This strength was never regained, thus Midway became the turning point of the war.

American bomb runs were made almost continuously when the weather was fit. Aircraft refueled, rearmed, and took off again. Almost the entire task fell on the Navy's PBYs stationed at Dutch Harbor because Kiska was too far away for the Army's B-17s at Fort Glenn.41

A PBY squadron from British Columbia started the Kiska Blitz, day and night bombing. The Canadians and Americans were directed by Adm. Nimitz to keep pressure on the Japanese, to attack the enemy in Kiska continuously with bombs and torpedoes, day and night, until the supply of bombs and aviation gasoline were gone.

This pressure did not accomplish much; the Japanese were getting settled in more efficiently. Our planes were being shot up, or shot down, and the engines needed overhauls which could not be done any closer than in Seattle. To top that off, the supply of fuel, ammunition, and bombs was exhausted.

"School pencils were donated to stuff bullet holes in the pontoons of riddled seaplanes damaged by heavy anti-aircraft fire over Kiska." 42

Because planes had to fly such long distances and in such terrible weather conditions to bomb Attu and Kiska, an airfield was built on Adak, which cut the distance from 600 miles to around 250 miles (one way) to Kiska. However, P-39 fighters still had difficulty sometimes getting in the air because the runway was covered with water, looking like a lake. But Adak became a major base for 90,000 men on their way to Attu and Kiska.

Later came an airfield at Atka, 60 miles east of Adak. Shortly thereafter, U.S. forces landed on Amchitka, and an airfield there, 75 miles from Kiska, made bombing runs routine.

When reports were received that the Japanese might be planning an attack on Nome in the Bering Sea, quick action began. The War Dept. (Ferrying Command) commandeered eleven scheduled airliners. As other airlines joined in, forty-six commercial planes, plus other available planes, within 24 hours carried "2272 men, 20 antiaircraft guns, and tons of equipment..." to Nome, 600 miles north of Anchorage.43

Getting planes to this northern outpost was quite hazardous. With so few air bases between, many ran short of fuel. And, because of lack of radio transmitters, it was impossible to communicate with some of the fields. Some landed on frozen lakes and farm fields; some never made it. Colonel Simon Bolivar Buckner, Jr., commander of Alaskan troops, had tried to convince officials who didn't know the situation that "Planes cannot be *rushed* to Alaska."44

Before the airlift was scrubbed, it had taken almost 900,000 pounds of men and equipment into Nome.

While these attacks, invasions, and airlifts were taking place, there was almost a complete news blackout. The Government did not want American citizens worrying about an invasion of the lower states; their morale was low already. Not until two weeks after Kiska and Attu were occupied by the Japanese was it announced by the Navy, making it sound very minor. When veterans from Alaska returned home, citizens refused to believe their stories.

ALTERNATE TRANSPORTATION NEEDED

Besides dealing with the weather in this northern territory, transportation was a big problem. Everything had to be shipped in, and it was approximately 2,000 miles from Seattle. Ships, even old ones, were scarce. There was never enough of anything. Men's resistance was down; they were prone to sickness; depression was common. After being there a few months, they developed the Alaskan Stare, a blank look, staring into space. Living in tents, sloshing through mud and muck, fighting giant mosquitoes, not always having much or the right kind of food, no entertainment to break the monotony, all took its toll. Men brought in many dogs to keep them company. With no trees being in the Aleutians, some pilots flew one in for the use of the Colonel's dog.

The weather rusted and shook planes apart and, not being able to keep enough spare parts, mechanics had to use those from wrecked planes or forge their own.

Alaska needed to be connected with the U.S. by a highway and/or railroad. In March, 1942, engineers began cutting their way through the mountains and forest in sub-zero weather for the approximate 1645-mile Alcan Highway.

Since much of the road would be going through Canadian

territory, the cooperation of Canada was required. It had been agreed earlier that the two countries would cooperate in defending the Pacific Coast and Alaska. After learning of the Japanese plan to attack the Aleutians, the Canadian Air Force patrolled the western coast of British Columbia; they also went to various bases in Alaska and flew with our men, under U.S. command.

More than 11,000 troops worked on the road in snow and rain; with insects, muskeg, permafrost, and winter temperatures falling to 50 degrees below zero.

The Alcan Highway, connecting Alaska with the other states, was built by 46,000 soldiers and civilian contractors. It was finished on November 20, 1942, just eight months and eleven days after starting.

The road would also shorten the Lend-Lease route to the USSR from 13,000 miles to 1,900 miles. Lend-Lease planes were delivered by the Ferry Groups of the U.S. Army Air Force Air Transport Command via the Northwest Staging Route: from the factory to Great Falls, MT; by another pilot to Ladd Field in Fairbanks; then by a Russian pilot to Russia. Approximately 1,000 women were trained as WASPs (Women Airforce Service Pilots) and most were assigned to the domestic ferry groups of the Air Transport Command. Although WASPs were under Air Force rules and regulations, they were Civil Service employees.[45]

An alternative method of hauling fuel was also needed to supply gasoline for the building of the highway and for the Northwest Staging Route. The U.S. Government, with Canada's permission, decided on the project called "CANOL." This included building a pipeline from Norman Wells in the Northwest Territories of Canada, to Whitehorse, Yukon, approximately 500 miles; and another to supply points as far as Fairbanks, Skagway, and Watson Lake. There was a small oilfield and refinery in Norman Wells, and 30 new wells were drilled, with production soaring to 20,000 barrels a day.

Skagway played a large role in transportation of men, goods and supplies between there and Whitehorse. Their railroad was built during the Gold Rush of 1897 and was in bad shape. The U.S. Army took over the operation. Locomotives and freight cars were confiscated from wherever they could find them. Some of the decrepit passenger cars left over from Gold Rush days were kept in service.

Other railroad projects kept supplies going to Anchorage and Fairbanks. One train, running between Terrace and Prince Rupert, British Columbia, was armed with 75 mm and 45 mm guns, a search-light, and infantry. The Japanese had fished around the area for years before the war, and it was feared they might blow up a tunnel or bridge.

AMERICANS REGAIN ATTU AND KISKA

American strategists said that if the line of supplies coming to Kiska and Attu could be blocked, the Japanese would soon have to surrender. Accordingly, a blockade was initiated close to the Russian Komandorski Islands and the Kurile Islands of Japan.

While Allies were enforcing the blockade, a Japanese naval task force went out to break it up. Even though the American vessels were smaller, older, slower, and outnumbered, after a 3½ hour battle, with no air power on either side, the Japanese suddenly retreated. They mistakenly thought a large group of American bombers was on its way.

After a year, the Japanese still held Kiska and Attu. Those Americans in charge felt some action should be taken toward clearing the Japanese out. Therefore, the plan was made to invade Attu, which, according to reconnaissance pictures, had about 2600 soldiers. The American invasion force was to have 10,000.

In order to mislead the Japanese, Kiska, as well as Attu, was bombed before the invasion.

D-Day was planned for May 7, 1943, but because of bad weather, it was delayed until May 11. Landings were to be at three different points, all pressing toward a mountain pass, hopefully trapping the Japanese in the valley.

"All together, it was the largest American force to be assembled in the Pacific since the invasion of Guadalcanal eight months before." 46

When landing, there was no enemy gunfire and not an enemy seen. The Japanese had moved to the high ground where they could see every move made.

Wind and waves made landing, in the fog, so bad that the ships could not stay in close to the beach. Heavy equipment got stuck in the muck and mire; men had to be taken from combat lines to carry food, supplies, and ammunition, over the steep trails from the beaches. Heavy artillery was dragged from place to place, could not be moved because of the muskeg.

It was hard going for the American soldiers, over tough terrain, and fierce fighting was necessary once they were on high ground, to displace the well-entrenched enemy. The cold was so severe that after awhile men were limping around on frozen feet, some developing gangrene. Some became feverish and were vomiting. Many were wounded. Men stripped caps, hoods, waterproof boots from dead Japanese. And, being hungry, they tried to use grenades to get fish. The supply plane flew over but fog was so thick men couldn't be located to drop supplies until the fourth day.

Additional forces were requested, but planes were grounded. Later the weather broke and P-38s arrived. Battleships had used up their ammunition. By May 18 "Ninety (American) craft had gone down. Victims of Attu shoals, reefs, williwaws, and surf."[47]

But, as the Americans' fortitude started paying off, and the chances of victory were looking quite slim for the Japanese, the Japanese general burned his records and talked to his men. The last entry in the lieutenant's diary was: "The last assault is to be carried out. All patients in the hospital are to commit suicide....Gave four hundred shots of morphine to severely wounded, and killed them....finished all the patients with grenades...."[48]

"Early in the day five hundred men, the bulk of his (Yamasaki) force, committed mass suicide by pulling the pins of their grenades and holding them against their chests."[49]

The battle of Attu ended May 30, 1943; Attu was back in American hands.

After capturing Attu, effort was concentrated on Kiska. From May 24 to August 15 it "...received a total of 600 tons of explosives as a result of surface bombardment, while 1310 tons were dropped from the air....much strafing was done."[50]

Along with the bombing of Kiska, Paramushiro of Japan's

Kurile Islands, was bombed. They were the first bombs to be dropped on the Japanese homeland since Doolittle's B-25s bombed it more than a year earlier.

As American air and naval power gained the upper hand, it became difficult for the Japanese to resupply Kiska except by submarine. It was looking hopeless for them by the middle of 1943. They decided to have a fleet of destroyers come toward the island, wait for fog, and then dash in, pick up the men and get out quickly. On July 28 nine destroyers carried out a similar plan.

In the meantime, the Americans, while suspicious, did not know this had actually happened and went ahead with invasion plans.

The Allied landing force at Kiska August 15, 1943, consisted of: "34,426 troops, 5,300 of whom were Canadian. Three battleships, one heavy cruiser, one light cruiser, 19 destroyers, 5 attack transports, one attack cargo vessel, 10 transports, 3 cargo vessels, one fast transport, fourteen LSTs, nine LCI (L)s, 19 LCT (5)s, 12 light minelayers, 3 fast minesweepers, 2 tugs, one harbor tug, and one surveying ship. Air support: ...24 heavy bombers, 44 medium bombers, 28 dive bombers, 60 fighters, 12 patrol bombers."[51]

Position by position was found abandoned. When realizing the Japanese were actually gone, it was a little embarrassing, but officials thought it had been a good drill for future use. And it ended the Aleutian campaign after 439 days, nearly 15 months. In those 15 months the Air Force dropped a total of 1,500,000 pounds of bombs. Half a million servicemen served in the Aleutians during WW II.[52]

After the Japanese occupation had ended, the Aleutians continued to be a base for bombing and harassing the Kuriles (750 miles), keeping Japanese planes and ground troops on the alert; and our troops in the South Pacific had to fight that many fewer Japanese. Those in charge felt those bases in the Aleutians served a great purpose, teaching lessons that helped win the war in the Pacific.

In 1947 the Dutch Harbor naval base was decommissioned. Some buildings were sold; some were renovated for civilian use. Others deteriorated. In 1985 the base became a national historic landmark, one of eight World War II national landmarks in Alaska.

EVACUATION OF ALEUTS

With the prospect of Dutch Harbor being attacked, there was no concensus as to what should be done in preparation. Military dependents and women, except Aleuts, were removed from Unalaska. Alaska was declared a combat zone and certain areas were restricted. Travel in and out of Alaska was also restricted.

Government and civilian groups could not decide whether to evacuate Aleuts, how and when, what responsibilities were included, and how to fund the operations. With this reluctance to act, too much time passed and then the Aleuts had to be moved hurriedly, with no decisions actually having been made as to destinations, even as the ships pulled out.

With no opportunity to express their own wishes, 881 Aleuts were taken from their homes and shipped to unknown destinations, supposedly to protect them from attack. Given as little as five hours' notice and in most cases being allowed only to take one suitcase and some blankets, family pictures and valuable heirlooms could not be packed for safekeeping. Furniture, clothing, guns, boats, fishing equipment, all had to be left as was. Atka evacuees watched their houses being burned by the military, leaving nothing for the Japanese to use.

The ships left for southeast Alaska carrying the Aleuts to unused canneries, deserted gold mining camps, and an abandoned CCC camp, the only place constructed for year-round use. In most cases drinking water had to be taken from streams, and the few toilets were on pilings, depending on the tide to carry out the waste; dishwashing, bathing, and laundry facilities were poor or non-existent. Privacy was at a premium, with some families having to hang blankets to divide their section from that of others; germs and sickness were common, with ten percent of the Aleuts dying in the camps.

With little help from the government, they improved the buildings and enhanced their minimal food supply by working, when possible, at neighboring sawmills or canneries.

Kohlhoff, in *When the Wind Was a River*, quotes what Alaska's Attorney General wrote to the Governor about the situation: "'I have no language at my command which can adequately describe what I saw; if I had I am confident you would not believe my statements.'"[53]

Attu, the most westerly island, only 650 miles from the Japanese Kurile Islands, was never evacuated. The natives were left to be captured when the island was invaded, three days after the bombing of Dutch Harbor.

Not until two (or for some, three) years later were evacuees returned home. Marilyn George, in *Senior Voice*, quotes The Commission on Wartime Relocation and Internment of Civilians: "'Aleuts were required to remain in these camps long after any danger existed to them from wartime operations. Failure to rehabilitate the villages in 1944 contributed to substantial losses to the villagers.'"[54]

When returning to their villages, the Aleuts found their homes and churches weather-worn and dilapidated from neglect, possessions vandalized and ransacked by souvenir-hunters. Guns, boats, and engines that they depended on for their livelihood were gone.

Those from Attu were never allowed to return to their island but were resettled instead in Atka, a village of ancient rivalry, officials refusing to fund restoration. According to Kohlhoff, the military gave clearance for Attu's resettlement and suggested that they be settled on the site where they were before. But apparently, because it would be easier and less expensive, they were all taken to Atka.[55]

Marilyn George also quotes this statement of the Commission: "'It was simply convenient to separate them, limit their freedom, and manage them as a herd of animals would be managed. They suffered from lack of adequate shelter, medical care, proper sanitary facilities and adequate water supplies. The resulting deaths were inexcusable.'"[56]

On August 10, 1988, 43 years after Aleut evacuation, President Reagan signed Public Law 100-383 giving the Aleuts "...financial restitution and an apology from Congress and the President on behalf of the people of the U.S.'"[57]

THE TUNDRA ARMY OR ALASKA TERRITORIAL GUARD

According to the natives, Japanese had been "snooping around" the islands for years, drawing maps and making scientific studies.

Major "Muktuk" Marston emphasized that the Eskimos had a "...complete and exact knowledge of our vulnerable coastline. They could become our first line of defense—eyes and ears for our Army." 58 They could be "...lookouts or scouts along our 5000 miles of irregular Bering Sea and Arctic Ocean coastline and up the many meandering rivers; be an invaluable aid to our airmen in case of crash or forced landings, etc." 59

With Ernest Gruening, U.S. Senator from Alaska, agreeing, Major Marvin R. Marston set out by dog team to organize whites, Indians, Eskimos, and Aleuts on all of the Alaska coastline and all the islands of the Bering Sea and Arctic Ocean. He asked the villagers to help to repel the Japanese when they came. As members of the Territorial Guard, our government would supply them with rifles and ammunition.

Age wasn't important; they knew the country and how to survive in it, were good citizens and did whatever was asked of them, without complaints: constructing buildings, building an airstrip or a road. At one time they were kept busy during the hunting season. When the job was done, they had no skins, meat or fish for the winter. "Muktuk" appealed to the governor, who made promises that something would be done. Promises were not kept; the people had to kill some of their valued sled dogs to eat. 60

Up until 1945, Eskimos, Indians, and Aleuts were treated as second-class citizens, but then the Non-Discrimination Act was passed and they were recognized as being equal and were encouraged to be participating citizens.

These Territorial Guards "shot down and/or recovered eighteen or more enemy balloons carrying bombs, radar...." 61

The Territorial Guard included 2700 armed members; with 20,000 others, including women and children, providing helpful services. In 1947 the Guard was disbanded with members becoming part of the National Guard when it was established in 1949, not without dissent, however. At an awards ceremony, all 300 Eskimos received a marksmanship award, an unprecedented accomplishment.

Today the scouts, with modern equipment and arms, patrol these remote areas. When using the radio, secrecy is maintained by talking in the Eskimo language.

. . .

GLENN REID
PETERSBURG, ALASKA

Army Transportation Corps, Tech. Sgt., 1942-45

STANLEY REID
PETERSBURG, ALASKA

Army Air Corps, Sgt., 1942-45

PETER THYNES
PETERSBURG, ALASKA

Army Air Corps, Tech. Sgt., 1942-45

With "...some of the roughest waters and worst weather conditions in any theater of war," and "with weather conditions...far different than the pilots in command were accustomed to..."62 men were recruited from Alaska, who had previous experience on the coastal waters, for rescue and other such missions. Glenn, Stanley, and Peter were three of these men.

Glenn Reid

Power Barge

Glenn was in the Army Transportation Corps, being the skipper of an 85 ft. self-propelled Power Barge, all wood, 3 or 4 inches thick, flat bottom, powered by two 125 horse Caterpillar engines. With a crew of nine, the boat hauled supplies to radar stations from Amchitka to Dutch Harbor, the Pacific side. There was no radar on the boat; they found their way by "Dead Reckoning." The big Navy boats had radar, but at that time the smaller ones did not.

Pribilof Islands, 1943

There was a 20 mm gun on the boat, but somebody shot it one time and about shook it loose.

Harbor of Chernofski, Unalaska

The crew of nine lived on the boat for three years, having an oil cooking stove and heater, a generator, and a powered radio. They felt they were better off than the fellows on the islands because they were not living in, or tramping through, mud and muck. And there weren't any luxuries on the islands. Glenn told us that boredom was the main problem, and that after awhile, on the boats or the islands, guys acquired the Aleutian Stare (staring off into space).

One time at Amchitka, Glenn said that the skipper of another boat swung in too close and jammed his rudder; banged it up pretty bad. "Some of those guys didn't know from nothin'."

Stanley and Pete were sailors in the Army Air Corps. They were among the 12-16 crew members on a 104 ft. crash boat, which was similar to a PT boat. It had wooden hulls one and a fourth inches thick, had 1500 horsepower, and used 140 octane gasoline. These boats were built particularly for rescuing pilots, but usually by the time the crash boat arrived, it was too late. They picked up guys who had some kind of accident, maybe broken an arm or leg, or had appendicitis, and took them where they could get medical attention. There was a medic on board. Civilians from distant outposts were also rescued and taken in, when necessary.

There was no radar on these boats, and they also used "Dead Reckoning" to set the course. They ran into no ice except up in the Pribilofs. In the Aleutians, wind, rain, and fog caused most of the problems.

Stanley Reid

P-750, Adak, flag half-mast because of Pres. Roosevelt's death

In 1943 a troopship was tied up beside them at Adak, headed for Attu. Those kids had just come right out of desert training, were wearing summer clothes and were sliding up and down the masts. They ended up with frostbite. Stanley and Pete emphasized that you can get in trouble up there if you're not prepared.

Stanley related a story about an FS (freight and service) boat breaking loose and taking off all the long approach to the dock at Amchitka. A Navy ship, tied to the dock, put some guys out to cut their lines loose. They cut the lines, but the Navy ship took off and left them there. They couldn't get back on the beach and could do nothing but sit on the end of the dock. A storm was blowing, about 85-90 knots an hour. Waves started breaking over the top of the dock. The men on the crash boat tried taking the guys off in the morning, and as one guy jumped on board, he broke his ankle. They waited until about 4 o'clock in the afternoon, thought it was going to quiet down a little, but it never did. So they picked the guys up, one at a time, as the boat came up on top of the waves. The Navy men stayed on the crash boat until the next day when the boat could finally get ashore.

Pete said that many of the guys who were skippers or captains of the boats had never seen ice or saltwater. It seemed that the ones with experience in Alaskan waters were made deckhands.

On these crash boats they cooked with electricity, had gas generators, hot water heat. They ate well, Stanley remembered, except for one short period when the water was so rough that they couldn't get up to the dock to get supplies.

There was one 20 mm and two 50 caliber machine guns on board; no depth charges. One colonel didn't think we had enough armament and wanted to put one more 50 caliber on each side amidship. The first time those things were fired the whole deck shook. They had to give up on those!

Pete's crew set out crab pots, with mutton for bait—good results. The supply depot gave the crew so much grub for so long a time; they had to take it. Once there was a whole quarter of mutton in the rations, terrible stuff! So they used it for crab pot bait.

They fished for halibut; did ptarmigan hunting.

A fellow that had been flying from England to Germany couldn't fly any more, so came on Pete's boat. Every time they anchored, he had his fishing pole out immediately, loved fishing. But after the first couple of storms, he said, "I felt much safer in that bomber than on this boat!"

None of the three felt they were ever in any danger. One time Pete said they had a Japanese plane fly over the north end of Amchitka Island and they were on alert for about six hours.

Glenn added that he was on Amchitka about two weeks after that Japanese plane flew over—guessed they knew he was coming and shagged off.

Glenn also told us that most of the PBY crashes were caused by weather. At Amchitka, though, there were fighter planes scattered all along the runway, such a small strip of land.

Two Japanese freighters had sunk in Kiska Harbor. After the Japanese had left, Pete went aboard and looked them over. The guys opened up a big crate and inside was an armature for an electric motor—had GE on it.

About one third of one ship was out of the water. There was a big hole in the side; all the metal was turned out like a bomb went right down the smokestack into the engine room.

There were a half dozen or so one-or-two-man submarines, looked like long torpedo tubes, left on the beach. According to Stanley, they were their one-way ticket to heaven, or hell!

Shortly after the end of the war, some of the guys were discharged. Stanley had enough points to get out, but they didn't let him go. He felt very fortunate that they had kept him after learning that the plane with the other guys on it had crashed at Anchorage and all were killed.

Pete and Stanley both agreed with Glenn that, next to the weather, boredom was the biggest problem.

With over five hundred men (half being from Alaska) operating thirty-one boats that performed over one hundred missions, never a man or boat was lost.63

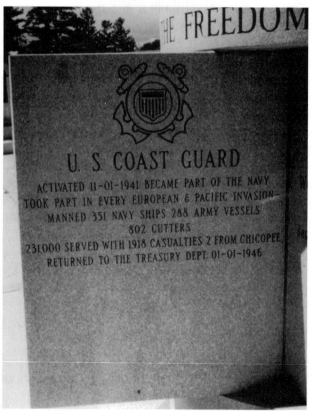

One of ten panels on monument, Chicopee, MA.
Courtesy Delfo Barabani

ROBERT L. INSKEEP

BELLEFONTAINE, OHIO

U.S. Coast Guard, EM 2/C 1942-46,
Boot Camp: Alameda, California
Duty in Pacific

Sworn in on July 4, 1942, in Cleveland Stadium in front of 90,000 people (for citizen morale building—had already been through that).

After three weeks of Boot Camp, we were lined up on the parade grounds. I heard one of the leaders tell a friend of his, who was in our group, "When they ask half of you to step forward, stand still." So when the order came, I stood still; the ones who stepped forward were shipped out the next day.

I was put on duty patrolling the San Francisco Bay in small patrol boats that were confiscated from rum runners. They, of course, were fast.

Robert L. Inskeep

Then I was assigned to the USS Daphne, a cutter that patrolled about eight miles outside the Golden Gate Bridge because of enemy subs. We were out for a week and in for a week. When getting a blip on our sonar, which meant a sub was nearby, we went to general quarters and ahead full steam, following the sonar to the sub and started dropping depth charges. These charges are like an oil drum, only somewhat smaller and can be set to the depth you want them to explode. They can be rolled off the stern of the ship or propelled from the side of the ship by a type of cannon that shoots them up and out from the ship. We dropped about ten of them but saw no sign of a hit. Being the electrician, I was at the control panel in the engine room and, when the charges went off, they jolted me up in the air. Some of the switches were thrown out, and I had to put them back each time the charges went off.

One time while on patrol one of the yardarm lights was on, and I was told to put it out. I couldn't turn it off, so the Warrant Officer told me to climb the mast and put it out one way or another. So up I went and had to take the bulb out. The ship was listing at about 15 to 20 degrees, and I had to hold on tight. As I started down, I dropped my screwdriver and it never hit the deck. Because of the list, it went right into the drink.

About this time I had to have my tonsils out at the base hospital on Governors Island. Gig Young, the movie star, was the hospital corpsman who took care of me. For a movie star, he was all right.

One of the doctors that was in charge of the blood bank came around to get patients that weren't in bad shape to give blood, promising a couple of shots of whiskey afterwards. He got all the blood he needed!

The people of North Platte, Nebraska, treated the servicemen when the train stopped ten minutes for water. The ladies there were the very best and served the whole trainload of servicemen in those ten minutes. I now live in Bellefontaine, Ohio, which, at that time, was also one of the best places to stop.

This receiving station had excellent cooks and the meals were wonderful. They had a policy of letting you bring guests on Sunday noon. The meals were served family style, but they had to stop doing it because too many people were coming.

I became part of a Construction Detachment (CD), which in the Navy is called a Construction Battalion (CB), to build

Loran stations (aid to navigation) in the South Pacific. On arrival in Honolulu, girls gave us the traditional welcome by putting a lei around our necks.

After a short time we headed southwest for Canton Island on the USS Haleakala. Crossing the equator was initiation time. The crew, which was all Hawaiian, had us strip and then put paint on us; made us kneel before Neptune, eat an awful-tasting pie and chase it down with saltwater. The custom is, if you can gain control of the crew, you don't have to get initiated. So we grabbed the firehoses and began a battle for supremacy. We lost and then became Shellbacks in the realm of Neptune, the ruler of the sea. (See pictures pages 274-275.)

Canton Island was small and was used as a refueling station for Pan Am and also as a landing place for seaplanes. The coral grows pretty fast in the little harbor and I watched them blasting it out for the seaplanes, which they have to do quite often.

The Bob Hope Show stopped there for fuel and agreed to put on a show for us. Army, Navy, and Coast Guard members got to see Frances Langford, Jerry Colona, and, of course, Bob Hope. There was one palm tree on this island and Bob said the dogs had to line up since it was the only tree.

The water was so clear we built squares out of wood and glued glass on the bottom side. Holding it on top of the water, we could see to the bottom and watched all the beautiful fish and coral. When you dive under water with goggles on, you enter a different world; the colors of the fish, coral, and plants are truly the rapture of the deep. A piece of steel rod and pipe made a fishing spear with a strip of innertube, holding the strip of tube around the pipe and over the end. The steel rod was inserted in the pipe; then you could pull back on the rubber tube and let it fly. Proved to be pretty accurate.

A Catholic priest on the island needed a bodyguard to transport a bagful of money, so they sent me over. I went to the armory in a quonset hut to get a .45 automatic. The man in charge picked one up and pulled the trigger to check it out; the gun went off, missing my head by about an inch. After helping the priest I was almost afraid to take the gun back.

After arriving at Ataful in the Tokelau Group, and waiting for high tide to let the barge wash ashore, we unloaded. Then clearing the palm trees and bulldozing the stumps began. A tower was erected, 3 huts with one for the Loran equipment, one for storage and mess hall and one for sleeping quarters. All of this took about 4 months, and we had time to get to know the islanders. A crew of 10 men was left to run the station.

The islanders believed that having more than one friend meant trouble, so each of us had only one native family as friends. The things they used and ate came from the sea and the palm trees. The coconut shells were bowls; they ate the meat; drank the juice; used the leaves to wrap fish in to cook. They ate the heart of the palm tree; used the leaves to weave baskets and thatch the roof on their huts. The sea supplied seafood. They also had a few chickens and pigs for a feast once in a while.

When we first arrived, the officers chose the place for our tents, and at the first high tide we had a foot of water in the tents.

LST 770

When we got back to Oahu, I was reassigned, as an electrician's mate, to the LST 770. The LST is 327 feet long with a 50 foot beam; draws 7 feet of water at the bow and 13 feet of water at the stern; top speed of 10.8 knots—nickname, Large Slow Target. The tank deck is 248 feet long, 30 feet wide, 20 feet high for cargo purposes. We carried 16 amphibious tractors in the tank deck with a LCT on the top deck, for launching later. LST means Landing Ship Tank; LCT means Landing Craft Tank.

On one occasion we were alongside a ship taking on sup-plies when our crane operator dropped two or three crates of oranges on the deck (on purpose) and the oranges rolled over the deck, causing a scramble for them. Most of us got one. It was the only way to get one as they were going to the officers' mess.

We had a lot of 77th division on board and were running out of flour. The officers ordered that only the crew could have bread. This made the Chief Petty Officer mad and he gave them bread, anyway. He was in charge of the galley, and, he was reprimanded and 25 years of good conduct ended.

At Aka Shima the LCT 1266 was launched. This was done by emptying the ballast tanks on the port side and filling the ones on the starboard side, making the ship list to the starboard; the LCT slid off the deck and into the water.

The island, Ie Shima, where Ernie Pyle (war correspondent) was killed, was thought, because of information received and flyovers, to be deserted. However, it took the 77th Division, after three days of bombardment, five days to secure the island.
During this time Buckner Bay was full of ships and there were Kamikaze attacks daily. The outer defense of Okinawa con-sisted of aircraft carriers; their pilots were bringing down about 150 planes a day, but a lot still got through and did damage to our ships.

General Simon Bolivar Buckner, for whom Buckner Bay was named, was at an observation post during the final push when it was hit by Japanese artillery shells. The explosion hurled a block of coral at him; he died within a few minutes. He was only two miles and four days short of his goal in capturing Okinawa.

There were nine bunks in each compartment down the side of the ship. My bunk was the top one of three and a hatch was right above my head, so I could open it and watch the stars and feel the gentle South Pacific breeze.

When beaching an LST to unload cargo, you fill the forward ballast tanks and empty the after tanks, hit the beach at a good speed, and drive the bow right into the sand. When leav-ing, we fill the after tanks and empty the forward ones. The bow lifts up and with full speed backwards, it pulls off the beach.

On one of the trips to Japan there was a large warehouse filled with rifles that had been taken away from the Japs. There were rows of them stacked about 4 ft. high and the guys would sneak ashore at night to steal a few for souvenirs. The captain in charge got tired of being called out at night by his sentries reporting us in the warehouse, so he had a whole truckload sent over to us with his compliments and that ended the sorties.

When we arrived back at Pearl Harbor our pennant from the mast was dragging in the water, a custom on returning to show how long we were out—the pennant gets longer for every day or month out. It was also the custom for submarines to hoist a broomstick to show they had a clean sweep. The crews of these ships received a salute from those in the harbor.

• • •

DID YOU KNOW THAT...

Originally the helicopter was developed by the Coast Guard for anti-sub warfare. By late 1942 the U-boats were not as much of a threat, and the helicopter's focus was shifted to search and rescue. The Coast Guard trained all American, British, Canadian, Australian, and civilian helicopter pilots during the war.[64]

US KEEP FO

U. S. MARINE CORPS
MAJOR EVENTS

PEARL HARBOR WAKE ISLAND BATAAN CORREGIDOR
GUADALCANAL MAKIN RAID NEW GEORGIA CHOISEUL RAID
BOUGAINVILLE TARAWA CAPE GLOUCESTER ROI NAMUR
ENIWETOK TALASEA EMIRAU SAIPAN GUAM TINIAN
PELELIU PHILIPPINES IWO JIMA OKINAWA
OCCUPIED JAPAN 08-30-1945 & CHINA 09-30-1945
SERVED 475,604 LOST 24,511 8 FROM CHICOPEE

One of ten panels on monument, Chicopee, MA.
Courtesy Delfo Barabani

RAYMOND G. DAVIS

STOCKBRIDGE, GA

General, U.S. Marine Corps, 1938-72

When entering The Basic School, June, 1938, my class included one "Pappy" Boyington. "Pappy" was the top character of all time as far as I am concerned and I'll believe any tale anybody has about him. He was a great flier, even in those days. I would always get into Pappy's plane because he was obviously a skilled flier.

I was especially fortunate in that my company commander was Chesty Puller, one of the most magic names in Marine Corps history....He would describe the kind of things that make or break people in combat and what works and what doesn't.

As a new second Lieutenant fresh from The Basic School, I reported in May, 1939, for duty aboard the USS Portland, a heavy cruiser....My Battle Station (during General Quarters) was high in the mast in the fire control director which provided data to control the 5"-25 caliber Anti-Aircraft (AA) dual purpose guns. Our 40-man Marine Detachment manned four of these guns.

Going to sea was a new experience for me....It took me awhile to get my sea legs.

We soon went to sea to conduct battle drills out on the gunnery ranges, and then on out to fleet exercises. Two of our battle drills were conducted in heavy seas with my battle station high in the foremast where the gun directors were. I was cramped inside one of these directors to control the guns with assigned dials to watch and knobs to turn. The pitch and roll of the ship was greatly multiplied for those of us high up on the mast. I barely made it through the first drill. I was sick in my stateroom afterward and missed dinner.

Marine Detachment First Sergeant Wheeler took me in tow from the very first day that I inspected the troops with him. He knew each Marine, his qualifications, his interests, his home, his family, his problems—all about him. Afterwards, I asked him for a copy of his notes on them, but he had it all in his head! I learned an important lesson right then and there: to know all Marines in my charge and look out for them.

Gen. Ray Davis

Upon our arrival at Pearl Harbor....It turned out that our main duty was to keep the sailors and Marines in single lines at houses in the red light district.

At the same time that I was serving aboard USS Portland, Captain Chesty Puller was Commander of the Marine Detachment on a nearby battleship. Fortunately, I met him ashore on liberty on more than one occasion, where my mentor provided me with further professional guidance. Once he said: "It's been years since we've had a war. Might be years before another, so you are being judged in your peacetime roles—perfection in drill, in dress, in bearing, in demeanor, shooting, self-improvement. But more than anything else, *by the performance of your Marines.*" Those words formed another key lesson for me, that whatever success I might have in the Corps would be totally dependent on how well I could motivate and lead the men who served with me. I would suggest this as a great lesson no matter what walk of life one may follow. Puller summed it up for me thusly: "Every waking hour Marines are to be schooled and trained, challenged and tested, corrected and encouraged, with perfection as the goal!" Then and there, perfection in every United States Marine Corps task became my goal!

Later in Australia, (after Guadalcanal) we received gigantic search radars. Five corporals and privates first class came with them to fill the billets of senior noncommissioned officers. In those days we could promote to fill "Table of Organization" requirements so that when this crew got the radar set up, tested and working, these bright, young Marines became senior specialist non-commissioned officers. Their performance was such that I never regretted the decision to promote them. In the same vein, some of our finest officers had been young corporals and sergeants who won battlefield commissions.

We started moving out for the Pacific...but we had no idea that our destination was Guadalcanal. We were being equipped with new types of antiaircraft guns because of concern about Japanese air power. It was decided at the last minute that we would keep all of our .50 caliber heavy machine guns and take along a bunch of 20 mm plus 40 mm automatic guns received in crates from the factories in Sweden. Consequently we went in equipped with three complete sets of weapons for the anti-aircraft. The anti-tank halftracks were also just arriving. In the process of getting reequipped, while we were moving out, we were told to pack up everything. The word was passed that "Where you are going, you'll need every stick of lumber you can take," so we made boxes out of old scrap lumber, and filled empty boxes with more old scrap lumber, and shipped it all out.

We were aboard a converted passenger liner, the ERICS-SON, for one month. I got detailed as the Transport

Quartermaster for our battalion to combat load ships, so when we got to our eventual destination, Guadalcanal, we could have the supplies and equipment in the proper order for combat unloading, as needed to fight the war.

It rained constantly and all the cardboard packing boxes and all paper items on the dock got wet, melted down and trampled over—remember that the ships had to be unloaded and then reloaded.

I landed on Guadalcanal D-Day, August 1942, an hour and a half after the first wave of assault troops. Essentially, it became an "administrative landing" in that the Japanese did not defend at the beaches, but chose to fight the attacking troops inland. However, as we loaded into boats and were heading for shore, a formation of Japanese torpedo bombers attacked us. This was the first engagement for these American ships, and shot and shell were flying—it seemed like everybody was shooting at everything and everybody. The sky was full—just full of bullets. I felt very uneasy out there with the Japanese aircraft strafing and bombing, and our own ships firing machine guns and AA guns—every ship seemed to be firing. Indeed, I was happy to get ashore.

By nightfall, the 1st Marine Division had captured the Japanese airstrip there, which became Henderson Field. It was to become the target of Japanese land, sea and air forces for the remainder of the campaign.

My primary mission was antiaircraft defense of Henderson Field. My command post was alongside the upper end of the airstrip, in a coconut grove. Remember that this strip was the main target of the Japanese for the next six months. As I recall, we were the first American troops in history to ever be heavily shelled by enemy battleships. During the month of October, there were 31 consecutive days during which we were bombed from overhead with the "Betty" bombers every day at noon. Also, we were shelled every night from the battleships, cruisers and destroyers offshore.

My Marines, when enemy fire was incoming, were in small holes—no more than two men per foxhole. My hole was a deep slit, covered with crisscross coconut logs to stop the instant fuze bombs. We could see the enemy bomb bays open and hear the clicks of the bomb release before we jumped into the holes. At night we absorbed fire from ships of the Japanese

Navy. They were out of range of my guns, but we watched carefully to see the ships' gun flashes because they would signal the time to go for the holes. Late one night after the first flash, I dived into my hole to come face-to-face with a large screaming bat. I told him, as I recovered from the terror and shock: "Buddy—yell all you want—I'm staying!"...

....Every day at noon the Japanese would come over and drop bombs. The scheme of the fighter squadron was to climb to maximum altitude just before noon to wait for the "Betty" bombers, and as the bombers came by, the Marine fighters would dive through the formation. Because the Marines were few in number, they always targeted the bomber on the left wing of the formation. Every day, day after day after day, they would shoot down the guy on the left wing of the bomber formation. The result was that the guy on the left wing would get so nervous coming in that he'd fly erratically and maybe peel off to hide among the other bombers, causing the whole formation to be rattled.

As this bombardment continued, we kept digging our holes deeper and deeper in the ground. In a deep, narrow foxhole there would be two guys, so a direct hit would never get more than two Marines. This tactic really paid off.

Shortly after coming ashore: One night the Password was something or other, and the Response (from the incoming man) was "Hallelujah!" To be sure that he was heard by the defending Marine, the man returning to the lines shouted loud and clear so as not to be fired on. The result of that, of course, was that the entire night was filled with endless shooting and shouts of Hallelujah; it sounded like a Holy Roller meeting on the 4th of July! The wild random firing at night got so intense that I parked three trucks to shine their headlights on my command post to let folks know that we were friendlies!

One of my drivers killed three cows which he claimed was a squad of Japs moving towards his night position. After struggling to bury them—this was his punishment—he decided to burn them. Result? A major grass fire threatened a key ammo dump.

The Division Commander soon stopped the night firing by requiring that weapons be unloaded and bayonets fixed at nightfall. This became a pattern in the subsequent landings in which I participated.

There were many problems other than that of live firing. For example, I was sent for by the Division Supply/Logistics Officer. He was upset and accused my outfit of "stealing" jeeps. I wasn't aware of this, so I went back to investigate. It seems that my troops had become so hardened to the bombers' air raids that after awhile when others abandoned jeeps in the area in response to early warning and got into holes, my men would get the abandoned jeeps and haul them off to nearby woods, where they would paint out the numbers and unit symbols. Not surprisingly we did have extra jeeps, but I noted that they were always Army jeeps; Marines would not "steal" from brother Marines. The variations in paint made it easy to spot the four extras and send them back to the Army.

Then there were problems with chow and health: After the Japs drove our Navy off, we had few rations and Japanese rice with raisins (to camouflage the bugs!) became the staple diet at times. Finally some brave California fishing boats brought some supplies in to us. As a Division, our health deteriorated mostly from malaria and dysentery—our medical supply ship had been lost. Later, we found the Japanese quinine supplies which helped to keep malaria under control. Hundreds of enemy corpses multiplied the fly population, even though we soon learned to bury them quickly.

It became obvious that the biggest problem for the entire force of Marines was malaria. I think everybody had it. With inadequate protection and an unbelievable mosquito population, the situation simply got out of hand.

Early in 1943, the First Marine Division moved to Australia to prepare for its next fight. Initially, it was estimated that it would take us eight weeks to get up to strength, reequipping and retrained to go back into combat. Unfortunately the malaria reoccurrence was such that the troops would be in the hospital for two or three weeks to recover from an attack. They would get out of the hospital, spend time in the pubs and on the town in Melbourne, and in two weeks' time be back in the hospital. The "rotation" was about 5,000 troops; that is, 5,000 in the hospital and another 5,000 out. In two weeks' time another 5,000 out would go back in and replace that 5,000. Result was that at the end we were there for eight months instead of eight weeks recovering from both malaria and dysentery.

I liked Australia, but the schedule was uncertain. Also, the training area was very limited. We really had no opportunity to get ourselves fully equipped with new weapons. Up until then we did not have the big radars that were supposed to go with the automatic antiaircraft guns (Bofors 40 mm). The radars were so big that they had not been sent to Guadalcanal but were finally shipped to us in Australia. We had no trained personnel to serve as instructors. We did receive a few Marines just out of school who knew how to work the things, but it took an all-out effort at technical and other kinds of training to get these complex weapons in hand.

Although I don't recall having a formal rifle range, they did have a place to fire small weapons. By the time 1st Marine Division left Australia in September, 1943, my men were in good physical condition and well trained. We were mounted out in converted Liberty ships, which was another time that we used commercial loading, where all the space around the vehicles, and inside them, was filled; then this was leveled off, and another layer, with more vehicles and gear on top of that, up to the top of the ship. There was no interior deck space, so the vehicles were buried in the supplies. I was in charge of loading one of those ships, which kept me on the dock 24 hours a day for a few days.

We went to Milne Bay, New Guinea, where we finally mounted out for Cape Gloucester. D-Day was 26 December 43. Then I became Chesty Puller's first battalion commander and on 24 April 1944, I took off with the 1st Marine Regiment for Pavuvu. There I would reequip and train my infantry battalion, First Regiment's 1st Battalion, for one of the bloodiest battles in Marine Corps history: PELELIU!

My battalion, landed in reserve, which was meaningless, because the Japanese defenses were so thick and so sturdy that when I got off the amphibian tractor on the beach, my run for cover was not quick enough, and I got a fragment from a mortar shell through my left knee. Machine gun bullets were flying from two directions.

It became the most hotly contested and brutal campaign of World War II in many respects. A figure I'm not proud of is the fact that my battalion had 71 percent casualties including me, and the whole regiment was almost as bad. The enemy had tunneled back under the coral ridge lines, sometimes 100 to 200 feet, and they would lay a machine gun to shoot out of a distant hole, with deadly crossfire from well dug-in and fight-to-the-death defensive positions. We were withdrawn within three weeks, because we had just been expended.

To show you how bad it was, even though we came ashore "in reserve"…the second day ashore I was assigned a mission of the central thrust up to the north of the island, in the worst of the defended territory, and we went to work on it. One historian said we expended more eleven inch battleship shells in one night than ever were expended before, trying to break up this enemy defensive system and keep them off us during the night. After three days of this deadly fighting, we had enough success to please Chesty Puller as he came forward. He then recommended me for the Navy Cross.

Let me offer a little glance into the Japanese character: We had just been assigned a couple of war dogs, with their handlers, as we captured a large enemy shop area near the airfield. I used one of these heavily reinforced concrete buildings for my communications center and sick bay. My command post was outside in some holes in the ground. That night, one of the dogs yelped, a couple of shots were fired, somebody yelled, and I went to investigate. An enemy soldier, wearing nothing but a loin cloth, armed only with a bayonet, had been sent to toss a grenade into the aid station. Seems that the dog fell asleep, was frightened by the shots when his handler shot the Japanese, so he yelped. As happened more than once, the lone enemy soldier, if not shot to death, would try to stick himself with the bayonet, after he had tossed the grenade into the group of wounded Marines. He'd commit suicide after accomplishing this mission—and that was characteristic of the people we were fighting against.

Peleliu was tough because we never found a way to get the enemy out of his defensive situation.…Captured documents had given all of us an indication of the heavy fortifications we would face at Peleliu.…

Harry Gailey, in his book, "Peleliu 1944" noted that: "In terms of sheer heroism, every man who fought at Peleliu deserved the highest awards his country could bestow."

A CHALLENGE TO ALL VETERANS

Veterans are a National Treasure! ...I find more and more that people appreciate the one common golden thread that runs through all our experience—The service of Veterans in the noble cause of freedom....

They are a major active force for good—indeed a National Treasure for America—*but Veterans must do more*! Veterans are in such great numbers that they could, if unified, turn our Nation toward greater goals and, in turn, better control the destiny of Veterans in the future. With a Veteran population of near 35 million plus 2 family members, 100 million votes could be generated.

The big challenge would seem to be development of a common national goal which would seem to be the maintenance of the *readiness of our Armed Forces.*

In the past, our Nation has failed those who would defend it. Hundreds of acres of white crosses in National cemeteries, in large measure, came about through our lack of readiness. In my frequent visits to National cemeteries, I have become more aware of the real cost of war, but more important to me is the great additional cost when we are ill prepared.

During WW II our initial units drilled with broomsticks because we had no rifles. The Marine Corps, for example, was built from 17,000 to near 500,000....

We demobilized after WW II. Forces were stripped down to the bone with the Marine Corps going from 500,000 to 70,000. This brought on the Korean War. Kim Il Sung took most of Korea in just 5 days. Only the immediate response of War Veteran Harry Truman saved South Korea, now our strong ally. Casualties in our unready units were unnecessarily high.

In Viet Nam our inept leadership in Washington counted for many of the 52,000 lives lost.

In the Persian Gulf War we were prepared, fully committed, and well led. Arrayed against a massive, experienced and fully equipped enemy our losses were minimum—less than on our streets here at home during that period. In short, readiness saves lives—many, many lives. Readiness will be maintained only if we have competent leadership in Washington.

The key to success is for all Veterans to adopt this single goal as a primary consideration in the election of officials—local, state and national. With leaders in office who are committed to this goal, our other needs will be more readily met.

Ray Davis, General, U.S. Marine Corps, (Retired)
WW II, Korea, Vietnam
Medal of Honor, Navy Cross, Purple Heart, 2 Distinguished Service Medals, 2 Silver Stars, 2 Legions of Merit, Bronze Star

Reprinted with permission from the book, *The Story of Ray Davis* by Ray Davis (Research Triangle Publishing, 1995. Copyright 1995 by Marine Books). 65

Gen. Davis, Pres. Clinton, and South Korean Pres. Kim Young-Sam at dedication of Korean Veterans' Memorial, 7/27/95 — courtesy Gen. Davis.

SHELDON O. HALL
RUSSELLS POINT, OHIO

Marine Corps, Captain, Fighter Pilot, 1941-46
Basic Training: Corpus Christi, Texas
Duty in South Pacific

Our fighter squadron was flying out of a fighter strip north of Henderson Field, Guadalcanal. We had been having all kinds of combat action with the Japanese coming down from the north in the Solomon Islands. We were the first squadron to have the Corsair fighter plane. We started with the Grauman F4F fighter, but then they gave us 24 Corsairs. We had to go out to a converted aircraft carrier and they catapulted us off.

Sheldon O. Hall

On July 18, we plannned to go from Guadalcanal to the northern most island, Bougainville, to strike a big Japanese air-base and seaport. We were to escort all the army bombers.

Had a terrific battle, Kahili Atoll, their airport and seaport. I had led my squadron into combat and we were escorting these bombers and the Japanese attacked us. That day I got two Japanese Zeroes and a ship; I didn't get any credit for them because that's the day I got shot down and you had to have verification of somebody seeing you get these planes or have it on a camera, which was carried on the wing of the plane. Of course, the plane was on the bottom of the ocean.

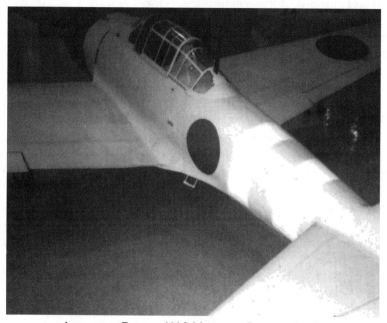

Japanese Zero — NAS Museum, Pensacola, FL

After the battle at Kahili, I headed home and was below a cloud and thought everything was fine. On the left side of the plane is the throttle control, your gasoline mixture control, your propeller control, and all of a sudden a 20 mm shell went right through that and came out the other side of the plane, took everything out. I had the option of bailing out of the plane or trying to land it in the ocean. The Japanese at that time were shooting the pilots in parachutes, so I landed in the ocean. I landed tail first and then the nose came down and hit the water, and it was just like hitting a wall. It busted my shoulder strap, my head went up against the dashboard, busted my jaw, broke my nose, knocked my teeth out, and a few other things, shrapnel wounds in my hand and leg. In a numbed state, I knew from the briefings we'd had with our intelligence officers to get out of the plane and inflate the rubber boat. When I came to, I was standing on the wing of the plane—it hadn't sunk—and I was inflating the rubber boat. I got into the thing, little rubber raft. The plane sank and the Japanese made two passes, strafing at me. They were lousy shots.

That was interesting because in the raft we had about a 30-ft. tow rope. I could see these planes making these passes at me so I got out of the raft into the ocean, and got as far away from the raft as I could. Every time they'd make a pass, I thought I'd duck under the water as far as I could. Well, I had my Mae West on and it was inflated, so I couldn't get under water. I was kind of like an ostrich; I buried my head under the water. I was in the water for 36 hours, a long 36 hours! In my jungle pack we had those candy bars, chocolate, so I nibbled on one of those. Couldn't really eat very well, anyway, with no front teeth.

We had a little metal mirror in the pack and I surveyed the damage. My nose was laying off to the side, so I straightened it up. It's still crooked, but I could at least breathe through it.

At that time that plane cost about $150,000—probably couldn't buy one now for a million and a half. No one saw me go down because there was a cloud cover. At first I paddled like mad with those little rubber oar-like things that go on your hands. Finally, I got to thinking that the intelligence officer had told us that the tide ebbs and flows twice every 24 hours. I could see land in the distance and knew just about where I was, so I just finally let the tide take me in to land. I'm glad it did—it could have taken me the other way!

So I got on the island of Choiseul. The northern half of the island was occupied by natives; the southern part by the Japanese. On this island were coconut plantations run by Australians. Melanesian natives worked for them and had originally been headhunters; however, there was a Methodist missionary from the U.S. and a Catholic missionary from France on the island, and they had converted these natives to Christianity. I roamed around that island for three days by myself, no life, just jungle. I roamed south too far one time and got right in the middle of a Japanese camp. I got down on my hands and knees and crawled out of there. I don't know how they missed me, but they didn't see me. Every once in awhile I'd go into the jungle and get some bananas or something. We carried a knife, a gun, a jungle pack. We wore the hunting knife and a .45 pistol all the time. In the jungle pack we just had survival.

I was sleeping in the little shacks that had been deserted by the natives who had been working the coconut plantations. The third morning I walked around the corner of the little shack where I had been sleeping and there stood three natives. I hollered, "Me American." One native said, "We know. You've got red hair." He was the chief and the only one who spoke English, so that I could understand it. His name was Harry.

Those three natives immediately took me up into the mountains. And I mean they moved! And when we'd get hungry, they'd go off and come back with the most beautiful bananas you ever saw. We spent one night with a native man and his wife, about halfway up the mountain. They were very interesting people—lived in a little dugout, a cave; very religious people. They had been taught.

From there we went on up into the mountains to a native village; there's nothing there. All the buildings were built off the ground to get away from the insects and stuff, wild animals. Every morning at sunrise they'd have a church service and every night at sunset. They'd just get together and sing a few songs, have a prayer, and go about their business. The missionaries had taken songbooks to them and all the hymns are the same ones we sing except they were in their native tongue. They took me clear to the top of the mountain to a Coast Watcher. He was of the Royal Australian Navy. He had a short wave radio system and he would radio back to Guadalcanal that he had found survivors. I was the 21st pilot they picked up on that island. I found out from him that they saw me come ashore and had been watching me every day. They wanted to make sure I wasn't a spy or whatever. I lived with this Coast Watcher for two days and then he got a contingent of navy, and they took me across the island, opposite side from where I landed. And they made arrangements for PBYs from Henderson Field, escort of fighter planes, to pick me up.

Their little native village was really something. No streets, just paths. They made sure that I went to church every morning and every night—that was ritual. I was talking to Harry, the chief, and said, "Do you have any problems of theft, or fellows messing around with women, or anything like that?"

He said, "If we find somebody doing something wrong, they just disappear."

So they took me over to the east side of the island, the PBY came in, escorted by army P40s from Henderson Field. That's one of the few times the army and navy worked together, and picked up a Marine.

The natives had 20 or 30 outrigger boats. They all headed out to that PBY that landed out there in the bay. They rode me out there. It was a big day for them; they loved it. The navy always rewarded the natives for picking up a pilot, so it was $100 cash or 100 lbs. of rice. They took the sack of rice, so I always tell people that I'm worth a 100-lb. sack of rice. They were as happy as could be.

The PBY is called the Flying Coffin because every time you landed those things, the rivets would pop, so they'd go around plugging the holes with lead pencils.

They took me back to the island of Tulagi because I had blood poison in my hand and wrist. Took me to the navy hospital, where I stayed three days and then was transported back to Guadalcanal.

I had wondered about my belongings. Well, when I got there, everything had been ransacked. People go through your stuff and take what they want. All that I had that I really wanted was gone. I was Missing in Action sixteen days. That was the telegram that my folks received and it was on their wedding anniversary. They sent the first one, bad news, to my dad; they sent the second one, the good one, to my mother. The crash was on the 18th. The telegram was dated the 22nd.

During that eighteen days in July we had really been flying. I logged 94 combat hours in 18 days. All those in the fighter squadron were getting that many combat hours.

No trouble with food, 1943. Always had Spam! They had butter, don't know what they preserved it with, but it would set out there in 110 degrees and never melt! The food wasn't the best, but it wasn't anything you'd starve on. There was a contingent of Seabees on the base and if you were short of something, we'd contact them with some kind of little incentive, and they'd get whatever it was.

Every night at the fighter strip Washing Machine Charlie would come at 9:00. We'd hear this single airplane droning up above us and know he was going to drop two bombs—never hit anything! I think their tactic was to keep us awake, keep us tired. Then Tokyo Rose was always on the radio talking to the American boys, saying "Wouldn't you like to have a nice Thanksgiving dinner? Wouldn't you like to spend Christmas at home?"

I was sent by hospital ship to the the naval hospital in Oakland, California. Eventually I ended up in Florida at a navy auxiliary base as fighter pilot instructor, just south of Jacksonville. I met my wife there—she was a control tower operator, a Navy WAVE. I gave some ground school instruction and then we'd fly. Students had their planes and I had mine—all Corsairs. I had a flight of four. We had some wild classes! Some good pilots, too!

In the Pacific we could'nt keep up with the Zeroes in speed. We could out-maneuver them, had more fire power, had armor plate. The armor plate consisted of a two-inch metal shield behind the pilot and under the pilot. The Japanese were trying to get more speed, so they took the armor plating out. These planes had three 50 caliber machine guns in each wing plus a wing camera on the left wing. We could carry one 500-lb. bomb under the belly of the plane and three 8-inch rockets under each wing. On machine guns they had it so they would crossfire at a distance. Two outboard guns would merge at 300 yards; two middle guns at 200 yards; two inboard ones at 100 yards.

On the windshield of the Corsair there was an electronic gunsight. It had all those crosslines so that when you had the enemy plane there, you pulled the trigger and that was about the end of it.

I got credit for six airplanes. The two planes and the ship that I got the day I was shot down I couldn't claim. And I had another plane that I got that I couldn't claim because it was a Jap Zero that was on my tail. I couldn't shake him. Our intelligence briefing had stressed that Zeroes were not structured for a sharp right bank. The only way I could figure to get rid of that guy was to go right down on the ocean. When I got him down there, I just made a real sharp right turn, pulled up. He went into the water. I knew I got him!

They called that trip up to Bougainville The Slot.

I was a Division leader, four planes in a division: the lead plane and his wing man; another plane and his wing man. Our whole squadron might have four of those divisions. We had to adhere to certain regulations until we got into combat and then it depended upon the situation. My main purpose was to keep the division organized; didn't always work. We were always crisscrossing in our division so that everybody was look-ing in some direction all the time. We'd keep radio silence as long as we could, but once the action started, there was all kinds of stuff on the air.

When I went down I was scared—anyone is. Don't let them tell you any different. But then I got mad, the same as in com-bat when someone started shooting at me.

Telegram to Father

Deeply regret to inform you that your son Captain Sheldon O. Hall U.S. Marine Corps has been reported missing in action in the performance of his duty and in the service of his coun-try. I realize your great anxiety and will furnish you further infor-mation promptly when received. To prevent possible aid to our enemies please do not divulge the name of his ship or station.

Telegram to Mother

Glad to inform you that your son Captain Sheldon O. Hall U.S. Marine Corps Reserve previously reported missing in action in the performance of his duty is now reported a survivor. He will doubtless communicate with you directly informing you of his welfare. The anxiety caused you by the previous message is regretted.

• • •

DID YOU KNOW THAT...

In 1942, because of a shortage of aluminum and other metals, a contract was given to Kaiser-Hughes Aircraft Corp. for three wood-and-plywood cargo planes. The contract was later cancelled because production of aluminum increased while the supply of wood diminished due to shortages of workers.66

VERNON HOYING
FT. LORAMIE, OHIO

Marine Corps, Corporal, 1944-46
Basic Training: San Diego, California
Duty in Pacific

The battle to capture Okinawa from the Japanese began with an amphibious landing on Easter Sunday, April 1, 1945. It would take nearly three months of fighting not only the Japanese, but heat, rain and disease as well, to capture the 554-square-mile island south of Japan. Of all the islands on which American soldiers landed and captured in the Pacific, Okinawa was the closest to Japan and the last to be attacked. A little more than a month later, the United States dropped two atomic bombs on Hiroshima and Nagasaki, speeding the enemy's surrender.

The Marine private was hit in the arm by shrapnel as the Marines were routing out the last pockets of enemy forces on the southern end of the island. After about a week of medical rehabilitation on Okinawa, Hoying returned for duty. He received the Purple Heart.

Hoying happened to be near 10th Army Chief, Lt. Gen. Simon Bolivar Buckner Jr., at the time of the blast. The general, who was commander of all ground forces in Okinawa, had gone to the front lines to see how mopping up operations were going when what Hoying described as an "air burst" occurred some distance off....

A large chunk of metal hit the general. Ten minutes later, despite frantic efforts to save him, Buckner died. Buckner, the son of one of the Confederacy's ablest division commanders during the Civil War, was the only commander of an American army to be killed in action in World War II.

At dawn on Easter Sunday, roughly 1200 ships approached Okinawa. Japanese planes attacked the approaching ships. Carrying his rifle and a 60-pound pack on his back, Hoying climbed down the nets along the side of the ship into awaiting amphibious vessels, which set off for shore.

"Nobody talked," Hoying said of the mood in the vessel as they approached the beach.

Vernon Hoying

The Marines met surprisingly little firepower from the Japanese in the landing. Hoying said successful planning by Allied commanders had fooled the enemy as to the location of the main landing.

During the next three weeks, the troops faced stiffer resistance from the weather than from the Japanese. It rained for nearly the entire period, and the Marines' advance bogged down in the mud. The 100-degree heat was stifling.

In the middle of May, Hoying took part in a week-long battle to capture Sugar Loaf hill. The enemy had heavily fortified the hill and was dug in for the long haul. Tunnels connected Sugar Loaf with other hills called Half Moon and Horseshoe, all three of which were covered with heavy guns.

Hoying was with the Marines who made the first assault on Sugar Loaf. They reached the summit, but with 60 percent casualties. They were driven back in an enemy counterattack. The next day they tried again, only to be turned back in a counterattack. The next day was the same. It was not until six days later that the Marines could claim victory, but not until 2,662 of the...Division were killed or wounded.

Of the 60 fellow Marines with whom he became acquainted during training, only Hoying and four others survived the battle for Okinawa....It was only "prayers from home and a lot of luck" which got him through the fighting.

He also spoke highly of the corpsmen, or medical personnel, who assisted fallen soldiers in the heat of battle. He said on one occasion, he saw two corpsmen killed as one, then the other, tried to help a fallen Marine.

Reprinted with permission from *The Sidney* (Ohio) *Daily News* and Dan Liggett.

• • •

DID YOU KNOW THAT...

The USS Arizona Memorial was designed by a German architect who had been interned in Hawaii in 1941 as an enemy alien.[67]

ROLAND A. MARBAUGH

CONYERS, GEORGIA (FORMERLY WILLSHIRE, OHIO)

U.S. Marines, Private to Major, Infantry, 1938-54
Basic Training: Parris Island, South Carolina
Duty in South Pacific

The Third Marine Division invaded Bougainville in the Northern Solomon Islands on November 1, 1943. The spot where the invasion was made was selected because the enemy would never expect a landing there. The conditions were that bad; it was an unimaginable swamp.

The first night was miserable, as all nights would be on "Boogie." We were exhausted. We had risen at 2:00A.M., landed, fought and sloshed our way several hundred yards inland. The insects were terrible and would literally eat you alive. Dig a four-inch hole and you had 3½ inches of water.

I shared a soggy foxhole with my gunnery sergeant. He had a huge handlebar moustache. On Samoa he waxed it with Lifebuoy soap and one night a rat chewed some of it off, to the amusement of the men. I warned him several times to get rid of it as it would be hard to care for in combat. He would always say, "Lt., I'm taking this off when they send me home!"

We had no time to eat, but I mixed up a canteen cup of lemon powdered drink, laced it with sugar, and Gunny and I shared it in the rain. I took the first watch after dark. You could hear some of the Japs, whom we'd by-passed trying to sneak through our lines. Gunny tried to sleep but he would snort, snuff, and sneeze. I shook him and whispered, "Sarge, you've got to be quiet. The Nips are crawling all around and I want to hear. You're driving me nuts!"

"Lt., if I live until morning, I'm shaving this moustache off!" He said it itched, tickled, and felt like it was going up his nose.

No one slept that night. We had just settled in when we heard planes, Jap bombers. Their motors were unsynchronized so they sounded like old gas-powered washing machines. That was the name we slapped on them on Guadalcanal— "Washing Machine Charlie" and he visited us every night, week in and week out.

They circled and dived one at a time, time after time. We

had plenty of air coverage in the daytime but none at night. All we could do was hope our time had not come. The rain let up a little and then came down in torrents.

A big naval battle rumbled out at sea, miles to the northwest. From the beach they could see the sky light up like lightning from the big guns. The Japs had sent a big convoy of ships from Rabaul to bomb us off the map. Our Navy rushed out, intercepted them, and sent them back to Rabaul minus a lot of ships.

We lived through the night and the blessed dawn came. I inspected Gunny's moustache and it had thousands of tiny red ants in it after the sugar from that lemon drink. Gunny swore it was a diabolical plot of mine to get rid of his moustache. The men had a good laugh and he shaved it off. For a few days his upper lip looked like a horse had kicked him. The men pretended they didn't know him when he ordered them to do something.

In the jungle at the crack of dawn you drag yourself out of your foxhole, spread your poncho, field strip, and clean your weapon, relieve yourself in the bushes while your buddy stands guard, have a smoke and a canteen cup of cold coffee, dry out the best you can, and open a can of cold C-Rations. Then you pack up and, after the patrols return to the lines, move out. The day's objective: To advance the front several hundred yards farther inland.

There was one thing I wish I had a picture of. The jungle was wet and damp, the swamp and mud was bad, and it rained every whipstitch. To protect their rifles from the elements, everyone slipped a condom over the muzzle. I was always amused to see those columns of limp condoms go by.

Note: Bougainville was the bloodiest beach in all the Solomon Island campaigns.

Now about Samoa. The Samoan love song was a beautiful thing. I tried to get the chief's daughter to translate it into English for me. I never did get her to understand what I wanted. Each time she would start out: "A long time ago nothing grew and we were starving. A man took a boat and went to sea. When he returned he had pigs in the boat. We've never been hungry since." Oh, well....

The Samoans were deathly afraid of "iitus," (ghosts) and burned lights all night, either a fire or kerosene lamp. This worried "The Brass." So we tried to explain to the natives that lights made good targets for Jap ships, subs, and airplanes, but to no avail. We finally got orders to extinguish them by force— they were relit as soon as we left. We got orders to threaten to shoot the lawbreakers. They just said, "Me no care. Me do no wrong. Me go to heaven." The lights burned on as long as I was there.

The Samoan beaches are among the most magnificent in the world to look at. As you draw near them, however, you notice a strange odor. All over these beautiful spots the Samoans dig little holes and defecate in them. When we made practice landings, I was careful not to hit the deck until clear of the sand!

General Larson, the island commander, said this had to stop. So we started patrolling the beaches. Daytime was easy, but at night, when a light was shone down the beach, there they were, squatting like chickens going to roost. We even fired warning shots, but that stopped nothing.

It was finally decided to build long wooden walkways out over the water and to put 6-holer outhouses there. We had learned that nothing was ever accomplished without a 3-day feast, which all officers had to attend. We had the feast and my chief took me along. It was a gala affair with singing, dancing, and quantities of food and drink. Finally it was agreed that, if we built them, the chiefs would see that they were used. In all the time I spent on Samoa, I never saw one person except an occasional Marine, use these outhouses.

The next crisis to arise was the fact that most of the women wore a Lava Lava around their waist but nothing above. General Larson was bound to cover those mounds with cloth. The feast was called and it was even better than the outhouse feast: fire dances, sword and axe dances, roast pig, kava-kava, and the whole nine yards. The decision was, after the third day, that, if the Navy issued two green T-shirts to each woman, the chiefs would see that they were worn. The morning after the issue the women all appeared wearing the T-shirts, but they had cut two holes in front and every breast was bare. Later they started wearing the Lava Lava up to their armpits.

The Seabees built a huge reservoir high in the hills. All camps had running water. A pipe was run to each village and out in the village square it was elevated and curved into a shower and laundry. Now the women could beat their clothes clean on a cement floor and bathe without going to the streams.

At about 5:00 p.m. every day the women and girls gathered at the shower to bathe, after their daily chores. The Marines gathered, also. This was fine except there were complaints that the boys were laughing and making snide remarks. A one-day feast was called and afterwards a general order was issued and posted stating that it was permissible to watch the bathing in silence and with a straight face. Our company commander told us, "Okay, you can watch the butt-scrubbing, but I'll bust the first man to crack a smile!"

If by relating some of these incidents I am conveying a wrong impression of the Samoans, let me put it straight. They were one of the most moral and beautiful people I have ever seen. Those who originally thought they were in for easy times soon found out differently. Any Marine who at first thought the scanty dress was a sign of easy times was soon discouraged. It was just a mark of innocence as was the salty language they picked up.

Every night at bedtime each family would gather in a circle in their fale (house) and sing a religious song. Sometimes I'd be walking along and stop outside those fales to listen to that beautiful harmony. It always sent a thrill up my spine.

• • •

DID YOU KNOW THAT...

Navajo Indians, who were forced to ignore their own language and speak English in school, were found to be invaluable in the Pacific. From Guadalcanal to Okinawa, approximately 400 Navajo Marines used a code developed from their language, that the enemy never broke. On Iwo Jima, with these Navajo Marines protected by assigned bodyguards, 800 secret messages were sent. Without these "Code Talkers," battle results could have been different.[68]

EDWARD SEVERT

COLDWATER, OHIO

USMC, 4th Div., HQ Co., 1st Bat., 23rd Reg.
Cpl., Infantry and Half Tracks, 1944-46
Basic Training: San Diego, California
Duty in Pacific

I wanted to go into the Navy, but in Columbus my group was asked for two volunteers for the Marine Corps. When no one volunteered, we were all asked to stand up. The two tallest were "volunteered" into the Marines.

When arriving in San Diego, I soon learned the way of the Corps: the group was asked, "Any truck drivers?" Those with their hands up were assigned to latrine duty. Also, during Basic someone goofed, and no one came forth. The entire group was finally released for bed at 10:00P.M., but at midnight all were turned out with rifles, bayonets, and scrub buckets on their heads for an hour of close order drill. After not having the number of our rifle down pat, we had to write it 2,000 times.

After half-track training at Camp Pendleton, there was more training in Maui, including 21-mile hikes. As we went down both sides of the road when pineapple trucks approached, we got closer and closer to each other so that we could take pineapples off the truck as it went through. One truck lost 280 pineapples going through the company.

In three days after arriving at Saipan, via Eniwetok, we were rehearsing an invasion off Tinian. A couple of days later we were part of the Iwo Jima invasion.

Iwo Jima is an island less than eight square miles, made up of twin cones of volcano that had risen from the sea. Although small, the American military planners wanted the island as an emergency landing field for the bombers going to and from Japan. They thought it was lightly defended and could be easily taken. This turned out to be incorrect; the battle for Iwo Jima was one of the bloodiest of the war.

Around 11:00P.M., February 18, we were awakened for the big meal of steak, etc., knowing that for many, this would be their last meal. Around 1:00 or 2:00 we were transferred from the troopship, down rope ladders, to Higgins boats. Our Lt. got us lost, pulling up aside a battleship and looking right into the barrels of twelve or more guns. It scared the hell out of us; all of this was done with lights out. After some conversation with the captain of the ship, we went in the direction we were supposed to, arriving just in time to see the first wave going in. I think we were in the sixth wave to start, but God only knows which wave we landed with. Some part-waves and some whole-waves were eliminated. Just to the right of our beach was the smokestack of a ship, more than six feet in diameter, which we thought was abandoned; however, it had been made into a communication center for the whole island by the Imperial Japanese Marines and commanded all of this beach. Until this became known, every wave was simply sitting ducks.

Edward Severt

The beaches were on an incline and the coral sand was loose and thick; we could not get a toe-hold and no vehicles could move. Since half-tracks could not operate here, I was transferred to A Company.

After crawling across the beach sand, there was about 400 feet of level ground. In this area we were looking into the barrels of tanks buried in the base of Air Fields #1 amd #2, plus

Charley Dog Ridge, Turkey Knob, the Amphitheatre, and the Quarry.

This was more than we needed, but we also had to contend with underground mortars buried under the hills. The Jap mortar guns were on carts and rolled back and forth underground on tracks. They would roll them forward to an opening, fire them, then pull them back to reload. General Kuribayashi's headquarters were also located 75 feet underground with 500 feet of tunnels.

My foxhole mate was an original A Company man who taught me real quick how to set up for the night. "DO NOT fire your rifle at night; just fix bayonets and get plenty of hand grenades. When you fire at night, you give your position away. Keep quiet and listen at night. The English-speaking Japs will call a common name, or ask for a Corpsman. They will try to test our nerves."

When we were getting ready for this invasion, we were told the island could be taken in about three days; that was February 19. About the 9th or 10th of March, just before sundown, we got the word to spread out as we were losing too many men. We had to cover another 3-400 yards to our left. We did this and, as we moved the mortars, we got word to cover the same area. Until we got the mortars stopped, a rock the size of a gallon bucket was the only cover we had.

On March 12 a mortar shell landed about 10 feet from my feet. I was knocked out for some time. The next thing I knew I was in a Jeep ambulance going to the island hospital. By this time they had half my clothes off to stop the bleeding. After some surgery and stitches and blood, I was transferred on a wire stretcher, by a small boat, to a hospital ship. I was raised up to the deck with a rope and pulleys along a boom. When on ship they put me down, cut off the rest of my clothes, burned them, and sprayed me down with disinfectant. Then they washed me up and put me to bed naked as a Jaybird. Later I had more surgery, more cutting, and more sewing. The hospital ship went to Guam, where I had more work. Gangrene had set in.

After three weeks I was transferred to Eniwetok by flying boxcar, a plane full of stretcher patients, all strapped to the outside walls. There we were unstrapped, carried into a mess hall for a meal, and then flown to Johnston Island on the refueled plane.

After eating and refueling there, we flew to Pearl Harbor, where I was in Base 8 Hospital. I was confined there for about three months, mostly bedfast, getting more surgery, more stitches, and a barrel of penicillin. When I was able, I was allowed to leave the hospital from 9:00A.M. to 4:00P.M. I visited Paul Bettinger, which was not easy. They said Paul was spending too much time visiting everyone from Mercer County that came through Pearl Harbor.

Hospital ship Ed was on

From the hospital I was transferred to the Marine Transit Center to wait for transportation to Maui to rejoin A Company, where I visited with Pete Liette from Burkettsville.

At Maui the 4th Marine Division was getting ready for the invasion of Japan. I found that of 280 men who landed on Iwo Jima, only 52 walked off the island. The others were killed or wounded.

In August, 1945, I received the birthday cake that my mother had sent me in 1944.

The war ended and I was transferred to Saipan for guard duty. Around forty Marines were guarding 1200 Japanese prisoners. Each day thirty to forty Japanese went on work details with one Marine guard. Some prisoners, whom the guards thought they could trust, were barbers or did laundry. There were no problems and the Marines found time to complete some "projects," such as a 12 x 12 sundeck in the ocean, secured to a rock; a motorboat made of sheets of plywood and a Jeep motor; a motorized bike made from Japanese bike parts and a small gasoline engine.

On Iwo the Americans found the Japanese Field Hospital 100 feet below ground.

DID YOU KNOW THAT...

There were two flag raisings on Iwo Jima. T/Sgt. Louis Lowery, of *Leatherneck* magazine, took the picture of raising the flag as soon as the patrol had reached the top of Mt. Suribachi. There was great jubilation over seeing the flag flying, troops cheering, ships blowing their whistles; however, the commanding general of the Fifth Marine Division felt the flag was not large enough to be seen from all points on the island, and so planned to raise a larger one.

Media photographers were told there was to be a second flag raising, but the only one to go up was Joe Rosenthal from AP. With Rosenthal's picture being sent by wire and reaching the U.S. first, it was the one that received the publicity, became one of the most familiar and most recognized of all combat photographs. Lowery's picture, as a result, did not receive the attention it deserved.[69]

WILLIAM GLENN TEETS
WINSTON-SALEM, NORTH CAROLINA (DECEASED)

U.S. Marines, Corporal, 1943-45

ON TARAWA

With the wind around us raging, And the rain in torrents fell,
We drifted out with the ocean tide, away from an earthly hell.

On this atoll I had pleasures, and joys that come with war;
But, too, I saw grief and sadness, that I care to see no more.

This tiny spot of tropical land, so peaceful and quiet now,
Takes on an air of graciousness, although I know not how.

Her shores are one of many more, whose sand is really red,
And only through the will of God, her enemy has fled.

He fled from this scene of peril; This and many more;
But not before he vainly shed, his blood upon the shore.

My comrades fell on my either sides, as the enemy did before,
But the latter fell so thick and fast, I counted them by scores.

The earth around erupt' and quaked, and claimed her share of
    dead;
The sky spit forth a rain of hell, like thunder overhead.

How man could live through such a thing, is not for me to say,
For e'en the trees and lowest shrubs, were never there to stay.

My buddies fought; the enemy fell; they didn't know our men.
They thought us the army but later cried, "Run! The Marines
    again!"

They ran and fell and ran again, and screamed a mournful
    sound.
They howled and ran bewilderedly, and scattered on the
    ground.

They scatter but they leave behind, an arm, a leg, a head.

They spill their blood upon our hands; These men are surely dead.

But no! They crawl away thru' life's own blood, to kill and be killed once o'er.

They die a thousand deaths this day, and succumb upon the shore.

Three days and nights this hell raged high; it seemed to never cease.

But when our guns were all that spoke, 'twas then we had our peace.

Now trees grow not on this barren land; birds-there are none to sing;

The wind blows not; the sun is hot; this peace-a mournful thing.

It's now a spot in the distant haze, it's shore is all aglow;

It's moving fast from in my sight, And I'm glad to see it go.

God bless the men that died this day; God pray it be no more;

God wash my mind of memories; Lord, wash this sandy shore!

Written on leaving Tarawa April, 1944, by Pfc. William G. Teets, U.S. Marine Corps. Printed with permission of his widow, Marjorie Teets Smith.

William Glenn Teets

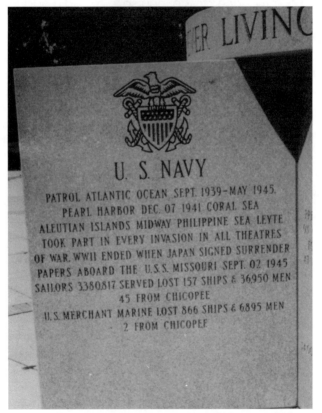

ER LIVING

U. S. NAVY

PATROL ATLANTIC OCEAN SEPT. 1939-MAY 1945.
PEARL HARBOR DEC. 07 1941 CORAL SEA
ALEUTIAN ISLANDS MIDWAY PHILIPPINE SEA LEYTE
TOOK PART IN EVERY INVASION IN ALL THEATRES
OF WAR. WWII ENDED WHEN JAPAN SIGNED SURRENDER
PAPERS ABOARD THE U.S.S. MISSOURI SEPT. 02 1945
SAILORS 3,380,817 SERVED LOST 157 SHIPS & 36,950 MEN
45 FROM CHICOPEE
U.S. MERCHANT MARINE LOST 866 SHIPS & 6,895 MEN
2 FROM CHICOPEE

One of ten panels on monument, Chicopee, MA.
Courtesy Delfo Barabani

JOHN BARRA
COLUMBUS, OHIO

USNR, Discharge Personnel Man 2nd Class, 1945-49
Basic Training: Great Lakes, Illinois
Duty in South Pacific

I was sworn into service in April, 1945; Germany surrendered in May (I always claim they knew I was coming). While on a troop train to San Francisco to catch a ship for the Pacific, Japan surrendered (again, they heard I was coming), so I take personal credit for ending the war. Some people, however, consider it a coincidence, and, of course, the media had their own agenda. They gave credit to the atomic bomb because it had more scare value.

At Treasure Island several hundred of us were placed on an *army* ship manned by *Merchant Marine*, and *we sailors* were hauled as passengers to Buckner Bay, Okinawa. The sailors were put on shore and trained the whole ten days we were there. We lived two to a tent on the side of a hill with running water most of the time because of the heavy rains. The first four or five days we had K-rations. Finally a chow line was set up, but I think that only provided warmed-up C-rations. However, on two occasions Japanese soldiers, who had come down out of the hills, were captured when they got in line for food. They had been left there when the Japanese army evacuated.

Ten of us sailors were finally assigned to a Coast Guard ship in Buckner Bay, refueling ships at sea. When ordered back to the U.S., one day out of Hawaii we lost a main bearing out of our engine and were towed into Pearl Harbor. The ten sailors were put ashore and later assigned to a troop transport bound for the U.S.

. . .

DID YOU KNOW THAT...

Blimps, which were used mostly for public relations purposes before WW II, suddenly acquired the role of ships' guardian angels. Crisscrossing over and around the ships, they were on the lookout for German submarines. While hovering over the spotted subs, fixed-wing or surface craft would be notified by radio. Admiral Donitz, the German naval commander, later admitted that the blimps deterred their operations by causing them to stay submerged.

NAS Museum, Pensacola, FL

Airships patrolled three million square miles, escorting 70,000 vessels in the Atlantic, 11,000 in the Pacific.

Besides escorting convoys, searching for, detecting, and tracking enemy submarines, blimps were also designed to destroy the subs. "Internal and external ordnance racks carried depth charges, bombs, and homing torpedoes. Crew positions included three pilots, a navigator, equipment operators, and riggers. Normal cruising altitude was 500 feet over water, and 6500 to 9500 feet over land." Usual cruising speed was 47 miles per hour, with a maximum of 75, covering a range of 2,000 miles.

The crews at Moffett Field, California, were also trained to help commercial fishermen by reporting to them when they spotted schools of fish. This preserved the fuel of the fishermen and added to the food supply of the nation.

One year after Pearl Harbor there were six LTA (lighter-than-air) craft, commonly known as "blimps" being used by the Navy. Between 1931 and 1952 about one hundred twenty were produced, with thirty being modified for operation aboard aircraft carriers.

Not much of the $8,500,000 once important naval air station, "the blimp base," at Hitchcock, Texas, remains, as the focus has gone to the nuclear and space age. It was noted that the 17-story-high hangar, one of the largest wooden structures in the world, one large enough to hold six blimps or a DC-3 plane, could easily have held the entire rice harvest of Texas.

Other blimp stations were in California, Oregon, Georgia, Massachusetts, North Carolina, Louisiana, New Jersey, and Florida.

A 45-year saga was ended in August, 1962, with the last flight of a Navy airship.[70]

PRESTON CRAFT

ROANOKE, VIRGINIA

Navy, SKD2C, Storekeeping Disbursement, 1943-46
Basic Training: Bainbridge
Duty in Pacific

A movie was to be shown twice. One guy dcided to go to the first movie, and another to the second. A suicide plane hit the ship while the movie was being rewound for the second showing. The fellow was still sitting on the hangar deck when the plane hit and was killed, burned up.

A sonar man was on duty and spotted three torpedoes that had been fired at the Randolph. The Captain was on the bridge and slowed the ship, missing the first torpedo; it went past us. And he went in between the next two. This was the story told to me; I cannot verify it.

We pulled in to the island of Ulithe, a horseshoe-shaped island, and anchored. While there, I had a hernia operation. They kept me in sick bay 26 days, lying in bed eight days. On that eighth day the ship was bouncing like a cork; a big pipeline broke in sick bay and the room was filling with water. All the corpsmen left, left me by myself. After a few minutes the hatch opened up and they started carrying men down. One of the doctors asked what was wrong with me. When I told him, he said I could stay. They filled up sick bay with patients and turned the hangar deck into a hospital. Doctors and corpsmen came from other ships. We had been hit, through the flight deck, the galley deck, into the hangar deck. They laid a boy down beside me that had half his leg blown off, started giving him plasma. There was a lot of confusion, people in and out. A corpsman looked at the boy and asked how much plasma he had received. I said, "Four bottles." "How do you know?" "I've been lying here the whole time watching." He thanked me and went on. About ten years later my sister had a party and invited a friend that she worked with. This lady's husband came to pick her up later and, as we started talking about the service, I said I was in the Navy, on the Randolph. Coincidentally, he was the fellow that had asked about the plasma.

We were in Task Force 58, which became 38 when Admiral Bull Halsey took over. Our carrier's planes made the first raids on Japan. Doolittle flew off a carrier earlier but landed in China; his group was not based on a carrier.

I joined the fleet at Ulithi. There were other fleets out there, but this was the major fleet of the Pacific war. I don't know how many big carriers we had, but at that time they were the Essex Class, straight deck. They were 80 or 90 ft. wide and 900 or more ft. long. When the planes landed, the arresting cables came up and the tailhook caught. If you missed all those tail-hooks, you went into a cable barrier, protecting the planes that were already there. The new carriers today go at an angle. If they miss, they take off and come around again. They land into the wind.

There were baby or jeep carriers. CV is what we were. C for Carrier, V for heavier than air. CVA came later meaning an attack carrier. Still later CVS meant anti-submarine duty.

The Randolph picked up John Glenn when he made his original space flight. They picked him up in a destroyer but brought him to the Randolph.

We didn't have helicopters, so to transfer guys that were sick to hospital ships, they were put in a little chair and pulled across on a "High Line." A line was shot-fired across to the other ship. A bigger line then ran through two pulleys. A number of men were on each end to keep the line tight; if it got too loose, a man went into the water.

There were 103 planes on the ship, a full load. The present-day ships carry fewer because the planes are bigger. We had fighters, torpedo planes, and bombers.

The movie, "Midway," tells the story of 12 PBY Catalinas, floating planes, being sent out in different directions to look for the Japanese fleet. One plane found the fleet, so all of the car-rier planes took off in that direction. The torpedo group was supposed to have a fighter group going along to protect it, but when the planes got to the fleet, the fighter group wasn't there; it had gotten lost. The torpedo group went in, and out of 20 men in that group, all were killed but one. He was hit but not killed. He went down in the water and grabbed up a flotation pillow and watched the whole battle going on. That surviving Ensign (the real one) visited the families of all the members of the squadron. These planes were from another ship but the same type as ours.

Our ship started launching about 4:30A.M. We had 400 pilots, so the planes would go on their mission, come back, refuel, rearm, and another pilot would get in. Each plane would be flown three to five times a day.

When the Japanese said they were giving up, the 80 Marines on our ship were put in amphibious boats to land like an invasion. Photographers also went, getting there before the Marines, and the Japanese had their hands up. When the Marines came charging up, the photographers and Japanese were sitting there waiting for them.

The Randolph was exactly like the Yorktown, which is berthed at Patriots Point, Charleston, South Carolina. Three types of guns are on a carrier: 20 mm, which the guy straps himself in and shoots; every fifth bullet is a tracer, so he can tell what he's hitting. The Quad 40s have a 40 mm shell; one side goes up and fires two, then the other side fires two. It takes 16 men to load it.

When the suicide planes came, they were in groups with a leader bringing them out. The leader had a good plane and a parachute. One leader got too close to us and we shot him out of the air. Our shells blew his plane into three pieces, and he parachuted down.

We had a company of Marines on our ship, about 80. The battleships and carriers had one Marine that went around with the Captain. When going into port, one stands at the gangplank and guards against anyone coming aboard. During combat they man many of the big guns. They do not fire the five-inch guns; they are specialty men. One group loads and the other fires it.

We had blacks on our ship, but at that time they were only allowed to be cooks for officers, stewards. They had their own division, with no rate or rank other than steward. They had their own compartment, all slept in one area.

There was "Officers' Country" on ship and, even in battle, there were certain hatches and places where we weren't allowed to walk. There was a hatch near the pay office, but three feet of that was "Officers' Country" so we had to go down another one. The little dog, the mascot, could go down but we couldn't.

When I was in sick bay there was a boy brought in. I asked what was wrong and was told, "He's got stomach trouble; he's been on bread and water for 20 days." That was an acceptable punishment then.

· · ·

DID YOU KNOW THAT...

Bobbie and Paul Cope, twins from Kentucky, met their death on the Hornet when a Japanese bomber crashed into it October 26, 1942. Most of those on the Signal Bridge were sprayed with burning gasoline, dying almost instantly. While one twin stood screaming as he burned to death, the other twin, who had not been touched by the fire, ran in, put his arms around his brother, and they died together.

The Hornet was a well-publicized carrier because of Jimmy Doolittle's Raiders taking off from it to bomb Tokyo, April 18, 1942. 71

The Hornet — NAS Museum, Pensacola, FL

GAIL DIAMOND

TWIN FALLS, IDAHO

U.S. Navy, CTM, Submarine, Chief Torpedo man, Chief of Boat
Duty in Pacific

Story told by Marion L. Shinn, Lewiston, Idaho

In the first two weeks in the war zone the officers and men on the Scorpion had a taste of most of the hazards of submarine life. They laid mines, engaged in four gun battles, sunk enemy vessels with torpedoes, felt the impact of depth charges, had one of her officers killed in action by enemy gunfire, and five crew members injured by bullets.

On April 5, 1943, the boat left Pearl for the war zone. There were 9 officers and 60 enlisted men aboard. In the forward torpedo room we were carrying 11 torpedoes and 12 mines; the after room had three torpedoes and 10 mines. I was a First Class Torpedo man and was in charge of the after room. Our first priority was to lay the 22 mines in the traffic lanes outside Yokohama harbor, which was on the main Japanese island of Honshu. After laying the mines we were free to use our guns or torpedoes to attack the Japanese.

The International Date Line was crossed on April 10 and that day was lost, according to the calendar. We were making about 15 knots on the surface. About 0200 the morning of April 19 we approached the Japanese coast; the lookouts started sighting small Japanese boats. At one time eight small vessels were in view; some were patrol boats and others were fishermen. It was hard to tell them apart. Most of the little boats were from 30 to 60 feet long; no guns were visible on any of them. Mr. Raymond, our Executive Officer, made the remark that "We could hold a field day on them (the little boats) before we left to go back to Pearl Harbor."

Our first concern, of course, was to dispose of our mines. At about 2100 hours a terrible banging sound on the outside of the boat startled the whole crew. Most of us were very scared; not even the Captain knew what was happening. Later we determined that the boat was hung up in a Japanese fishing net. The crashing sounds were the glass balls on the net being banged against the hull. Much of the net clung to the boat until we surfaced, but the balls were broken and the banging ceased.

There was enough confusion and noise around us that patrol boats were alerted. Two of them tried to locate us with grappling hooks. The clanging of the chains on deck rattled throughout the boat. In an attempt to escape the patrol boats, we went to 430 feet. The boat had been tested for only 300 feet; probably we could have gone deeper, but none of us wanted to try it. When the sound above stopped and everything appeared to be clear, we worked our way close to the beach and prepared to lay our mines. The mines were slightly less than 21 inches in diameter. Two mines were stored on one torpedo skid and they fit snugly into the torpedo tubes when they were ready to fire.

One at a time the mines were shot out of the torpedo tubes with compressed air—the same as torpedoes. Sea water rushed into the open torpedo tube after the firing; the air used to push out the mine wads bled back into the submarine to prevent a bubble rising to the surface. The extra air increased the pressure in the boat, but we could not run our air compressors because of the noise.

The crew in the forward room started laying mines about 1700 hours. The twelve mines were out and the job completed in about an hour and a quarter. At 1830 hours the after room started putting our 10 mines out. The mines we had shot out were resting on the bottom at a depth of about 200 feet. Our escape route was back over them. The time clocks on the mines were set to start releasing a cable with the explosive head in about three hours. A cable arrangement allowed the buoyant explosive head to slowly rise in the water to the assigned depth.

At 2015 we surfaced after being submerged 16 hours and 15 minutes. Everyone was complaining of headaches; the increase of pressure inside the boat made us very uncomfortable.

About 1130 hours on Tuesday, September 20 the alarm sounded for Battle Stations—Torpedoes. The Executive Officer passed the word over the loudspeaker that a freighter was in view about 7000 yards away and she looked like a sure thing. The order was given to make three torpedoes ready forward;

about four minutes later the after room was given the same instructions. Almost immediately the order was given, "Fire 8, Fire 9, Fire 7." A minute and 20 seconds after the ship was hit with one torpedo, she sank stern first. The man on the periscope could see 8 survivors clinging to 3 different pieces of wreckage and not making out so hot. The ship was small; about 3000 tons....I had painted "Norma," my wife's name, on the torpedo that hit the ship. The after room torpedo men were excited; the Scorpion wasn't a virgin any more.

Minutes after midnight on April 21 we dove and prepared for battle stations — deck guns. As the gun crew waited in the conning tower, the Captain told us that we had a boat lined up to sink. It was about 160 feet long with a 10 foot beam; there was no way to determine whether she was armed, but we would try our luck with our deck guns.

The three-inch gun crew included the trainer, pointer, sight setter, first loader, hot shell man, second loader, and several ammunition passers. My battle station was trainer and my responsibility was to train the gun horizontally. Mack was the pointer; he moved the gun vertically and fired the gun with a foot lever when given the word by the sight setter. I was a little scared. The gun crew had fired the three-inch gun many times in practice, but this was the first time at a live target. We had never been in a position where someone might shoot back at us.

We surfaced at 0050 and manned all guns. In addition to the three-inch we had the 20 mm, the 30 calibers, and two tommy guns. The first shell in the 3-inch was a misfire; what an awful time for that to happen. The target was about 1000 yards away and we were heading straight for it.

While we moved toward the target the 20 mm gunner was firing at will. When our gun was clear and reloaded, Mack and I trained on the target and the sight setter gave the word to fire. The first shell went through the wheelhouse; the second hit below the deck and ripped a big hole. The 20s were raking the vessel from bow to stern. The next 3-inch shell hit the engine and exploded as fire broke out midships. Our sound man picked up the noise of a set of screws; we left the area in a hurry.

At 2330 the lookouts sighted another patrol boat, and 20 mm and 30 caliber gun crews were called to action. The 3-inch crew waited impatiently and hoped we would be called on. Our boat made the approach and at 600 yards our crew opened fire. In one minute and 35 seconds the boat, about the same size as the one the day before, was sinking stern first.

Our action was not unnoticed by the enemy. Four hours after the attack (about 0400) a plane was picked up on the SD radar coming in fast. About the same time a tin can suddenly appeared coming toward us at about 35 knots. We crash dived to 380 feet. A couple depth charges were heard in the distance, but they did not even shake us. A second destroyer came and the two searched for us until about noon.

Friday, April 23 started off with a bang! At 0010 another patrol boat was sighted. Again the 20 mm and 30 caliber gun crews were called. They opened up on the target at about 650 yards. There were lights on the boat, but after the first blast they were gone. In a minute and forty five seconds the boat was gone. She weighed about 50 tons. While the gun crew was still on deck another patrol boat was sighted so we went after it. In about two minutes that boat was no more. There were no survivors on any of the three little boats.

I had just been called for the 0400 watch when the word was passed that we had a target of about 15,000 tons; it was escorted by two destroyers. A few minutes later another ship was sighted. About 0415 the forward room was instructed to make tubes ready. We fired four fish, three at the big ship and one at the smaller vessel. About two minutes later we heard a loud explosion followed by others. Quickly we dove to 380 feet and underwent a depth charge attack. Fourteen depth charges were dropped, but they were not close. We went deeper, to 430 feet. That was the deepest our boat had ever been and most of us did not want to go deeper. When the depth charges stopped, we rose to periscope depth. One of the ships was in flames and her speed was slakened to about 5 knots.

The morning of April 27 we dove at 0330 as daylight approached. An hour later the word was passed that a convoy was approaching. Four merchant ships were escorted by one destroyer. We started the approach when the convoy was about 2500 yards. Six tubes in the forward room were prepared to fire. When the convoy was at 2200 yards four torpedoes were fired at the largest ship; it weighed about 9,000 tons. The first explosion came in a minute and a half, a second explosion was heard about ten seconds later. Two more torpedoes were fired at the second ship. By the time the second batch of torpedoes left the tubes the destroyer escort was coming toward us at full speed. There was not time to see if the first ship was sinking!

We dove to 250 feet! In my opinion that was not near deep enough! Suddenly, all hell broke loose. Eight depth charges of the 600-pound class were dropped on us. Fortunately, we had no damage. After the charges stopped, we came back to the surface for a look. There was a freighter with the bow sticking straight up. The Captain got some pictures before the ship made its final plunge to the bottom. The enemy was still patrolling the area! A Jap plane spotted us and we dove to 200 feet. One aerial bomb dropped but there was no damage. Through the hull we could hear the sounds of the target ship breaking up as the sea engulfed it.

At 0600 on the morning of April 28 we were cruising on the surface with the periscope watch on duty. He spotted a patrol boat so the Captain ordered 20 mm and 30 caliber gun crews topside. When we got about 1800 yards from it our gun crews opened up, but they could not sink the little boat. The Captain called up the 3-inch gun crew. We fired 20 rounds and got 18 hits. Of course, we were only 1000 yards, but the boat was pitching a lot. The wheel house was blown off and there were three Japs hanging on the stern. The boat was burning furiously.

The gunnery officer wanted Mack and me to get more practice so he got permission for us to keep firing. We fired 19 more times and there was nothing left of the boat.

Friday, April 30, was the saddest day I had known in my 28 years. It is one I will remember the rest of my life! The patrol boat we attacked was different from the others we had experienced. The craft was spotted at 0745 and the Captain called for all gun crews. The three-inch gun stayed in control room until the range was about 1800 yards; then we went on deck, made our gun ready, and started firing. Estimated ranges were usually relayed from the periscope watch via the bridge. In all the excitement we got no ranges to help set our gun. Mack and I could not get the range or deflection of the target. After firing 30 rounds with no hits, the Captain changed our course and veered away from the target. We needed time to load the ammo drums for the 20 mm and 30 caliber and get the deck lockers filled with 3-inch ammo.

We returned to the battle at a range of about 1500 yards. The first 3-inch shot was a miss. The second one hit the bridge and caused a fire. In very few minutes forty rounds were laid in along her water line. After we moved in it was discovered this was a different kind of target. The patrol boat had a three-inch gun forward and another one aft. They were also firing at us with a machine gun, and a couple of high powered rifles. Their men on the small arms had the range and the shells were hitting the conning tower with a thud. Every hit made a hole in the superstructure. Their gunners had not found the range with the three-inch guns, but we could hear the projectiles skipping when they hit the water.

I trained on the target's forward three-inch gun and got three direct hits. Then we shifted to the after gun and knocked it out with four shots. Suddenly the Captain shouted, "They've killed Mr. Raymond!" For a few moments we opened up on the vessel furiously with all guns. Then the Captain said to secure the three-inch gun. He then told the Forward room to get the remaining torpedo ready to fire. When it was ready he said, "This is for Mr. Raymond!" Our last fish hit the vessel squarely; I had never witnessed such an explosion in my life. One section of the ship, about 15 feet square, must have blown about 1000 feet straight up. What was left of the ship sank in about 30 seconds.

The excitement level was high on deck!

The 3-inch gun crew was told to go below; suddenly radar picked up a plane bearing down on us at a two-mile distance. We made a crash dive; there was no chance to get Mr. Raymond below. He was lost in the foaming sea. The plane dropped one bomb, but no damage was done.

After we were safely under the water there was time to assess damage to the gun crews. Five men had been hit by small arms fire! The gun boss was hit in the zipper of his sub jacket. The metal zipper deflected the bullet and he received only a break in the skin. I received a bullet wound in the leg. It was not a direct hit; the bullet had ricocheted off the gun mount. Three others on the gun crew, including the first loader, had been hit.

....The Commanding Officer of the Pacific Fleet sent us a radio message with a letter of Commendation on the success of our trip. It said that all the ships in the U.S. Forces should look up to us because of our valiant work. Medals were awarded for bravery during the action....

It was a highly successful patrol. However, the crew was still very sad. In a crew where we try to work as one, it is hard to realize that a single bullet took one of our finest officers....

Reprinted with permission from Marion L. Shinn, Gail Diamond, and the Editor of *POLARIS,* Official Publication of U.S. Submarine Veterans, World War II, June, 1996.72

• • •

DID YOU KNOW THAT...

When asked why soldiers were called dog-faces: "We wear dogtags, sleep in pup tents, are chow hounds if heavy eaters, and come on the run when whistled at."73

PAUL R. GROSS

SIDNEY, OHIO

Navy, HA 1/C, Medic, 1942-45
Basic Training: Great Lakes
Duty in Pacific

During six weeks in Basic, we had light nurses' training, supervised by Navy nurses. We learned to give injections and medicine, but also had to clean floors.

When stationed in Washington, servicemen were everywhere! Had a one-room apartment, $6 or $8 a week. Had a closet that had been made into a kitchen with little sink and stove. Cockroaches were in full force.

Rum and coke was the popular drink; the song came out then. My wife got ration stamps but, because I was supposed to be eating at the base, I didn't have stamps. The grocer, however, was nice and told her to wait until others were gone. Then he gave her what she wanted. Everyone helped everyone else.

In New York a big plate of Hungarian Goulash cost 25 cents.

Paul R. Gross

At Ft. Pierce, Florida, I became attached to the Beach Party, separate from the ship's crew. The Beach Party trained for invasions; had about eight medics and one doctor. They were in addition to the ship's ten or so medics.

Left Norfolk with full load of troops and equipment, 2,000 soldiers. With land swells, everyone got sick. Next day took fire hose and washed ship off. Sailed down past Cuba and through the Panama Canal.

On to Hawaii and then Eniwetok, leaving in convoy with ships as far as you could see. Arrived at Saipan during night. At 4:00A.M. got on landing craft and stood by. Started sending troops in in waves—beach was being shelled. We (medics) went in on fifth wave. Our job was to secure the beach and then after the other medics got up their tents, etc., they could handle it. We gave the wounded First Aid and sent them back to ships. The dead were piled up like cordwood. Buried them in National Cemetery in Saipan.

There was a sugar mill up the way and in the smokestack was a Japanese spotter directing the shelling on the beach, which was hot and heavy. When our guys learned that, they took off the smokestack and things got quieter.

The reef went out almost a mile. LSTs and small landing craft came right up to that reef and let their vehicles off. Ours took on casualties. Seriously wounded went to hospital ships and those with minor injuries went to other ships. We had a doctor and two lieutenants that made the decisions.

There was no shortage of medical supplies. We ran out of food once—had to eat Australian bologna and K-rations. Good food aboard ship except when troops came on board; couldn't prepare food then for so many. A kid gave chickens to some of us medics, and we put them in the sterilizer and got them steamed just right.

Went to Leyte, the first blow at the Philippines. Leyte Beach was quiet. Stood by ship til 9:00A.M. Scary with war planes overhead. Troops from our ship planted the first flag on Philippine soil for the liberation of the islands.

An enemy plane, a Zeke, was shot down by P-38s directly overhead. He flamed, made a beautiful banking turn, and headed for our ship. Fortunately, his starboard wing exploded and he just hit the side of the ship and glanced off into the water. There was fire on the water, but it was soon extinguished.

Also in the Philippines our ship was hit by a suicide plane. The wing hit the upper deck; the body of the plane hit level with the water and knocked a hole in the side of the ship. Big explosion! Water was running in. We didn't see the plane in time to shoot at it. Welders welded the hole up.

Saw Australian cruiser with three stacks. A Jap plane went right in center of those three and took that center one out as slick as a whistle.

Followed coast of Philippines. Air raid every night. Planes couldn't see anything because of smoke screen.

At Iwo Jima we were fortunate enough to receive mail, five days from the States, even while the battle was going on.

When underway to Marianas, 300 Japanese planes came over and the fleet shot them down.

Guadalcanal was the most desolate place we had ever been. At Hollandia, New Guinea, took on troops and that was the first time men saw bread for a long time. They took huge stacks; soon it had to be rationed.

Joined convoy from Hollandia for scheduled invasion of Okinawa—transports, warships, LSTs, LCIs, and other small ships; could only travel eight knots. Troops had dysentery. Dropped them off at Leyte and missed invasion of Okinawa.

While on ship I was tending sick wards. When getting instructions one morning from the doctor, I was told to be sure to get that fellow up who had the appendicitis operation the day before. I could hardly believe that, thought the stitches would be pulled out and the guy would really be in a bad state. My wife and I had just received appendicitis operations not long before that and we had to stay in bed between two and three weeks—that was standard policy then.

After 23 months we were on our way back to the States. Steaming slowly up under the bridges of San Francisco was a thrill. The war was over. I had enough points but the skipper didn't release us. We had nine days in the U.S. with no leave except for emergencies. We were to get liberty in watches, half and half. However, Lady Luck favored us to a limited extent and, because of repairs, alterations, and changing our type of guns, we prolonged our stay. They took our 20 mm and 3-inch guns off and replaced them with 40 mm and 5-inch guns. Reloaded troops, supplies, and headed for Japan. Scheduled for

Nagoya, but mines weren't cleared out. Stayed at a little fishing village, Wakayama, for 27 days with troops aboard. When Nagoya was cleared, we went up there. When we came into the harbor, they sent out a pilot. Our skipper said, "No damn Jap pilot is going to run this ship!" So he took it in and ran on to a sandbar.

During the war I felt particuarly sorry for boys on subs. They would come up shaking like a leech. They would be sent to a hotel to recuperate.

War is hell. We were fighting for our own freedom. If the other side had won, we wouldn't have had any freedom.

I AM THE JAMES O'HARA

I am the James O'Hara, serving under articles of commission in the Navy of the United States of America, as a transport for attack.

In the Spring of 1943 my crew flung the long, thin, pennant to the breeze; tested my engines; fired my guns; tested my rigging; and found me worthy.

After that time I came to know the emerald waters of the Caribbean; the gray spume of the Atlantic; the sky-blue of the Mediterranean. I felt the pounding of the feet of thousands of fighting men; the scraping of their battle gear on my decks; the shuddering jar of depth charges searching out the unseen enemies below the surface of the ocean. I absorbed within me the panting breaths of fearful men. I jerked with the clapping thunder of my heavy batteries; the staccato rattle of my twenty millimeters. I felt the burdened clanking of the debarkation ladders as men went down my sides to the boats which took them to hostile shores. I listened to the harsh breathing and wild babble of men carried aboard, wounded, bleeding, dying. I have drunk their blood into my steel veins and so gained rage, and courage, to carry me on. I have known heroism and cowardice. I knew in turn the mixed scenery and smells of Africa; the fresh green of Ireland and Scotland; the raging crash of the North Atlantic; the nostalgic waters of America.

USS James O'Hara

Initiation when crossing equator on USS James O'Hara

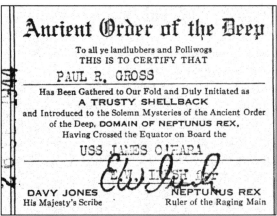

Ancient Order of the Deep

To all ye landlubbers and Polliwogs
THIS IS TO CERTIFY THAT

PAUL R. GROSS

Has Been Gathered to Our Fold and Duly Initiated as
A TRUSTY SHELLBACK
and Introduced to the Solemn Mysteries of the Ancient Order
of the Deep, **DOMAIN OF NEPTUNUS REX,**
Having Crossed the Equator on Board the

USS JAMES O'HARA

DAVY JONES   **NEPTUNUS REX**
His Majesty's Scribe   Ruler of the Raging Main

And so passed the year 1943. I left some of my crew there, on foreign shores and in the deeps of foreign waters, forever. Others went to new ships to pass on the knowledge and experience they gained while with me.

Then, with the new year, came a new world for me and my crew. We steamed slowly through the wild, untamed, beauty of the Panama Canal; the blue-green of the Pacific. We came to know the unparalleled, changing spectrum of Hawaiian waters; the miracles of Diamond Head and Waikiki; the shattered palms and burning sands of Eniwetok; the stink of Guadalcanal; the watery grave of the five Sullivan boys; the mountains of New Guinea; the death-trap of Saipan; the swollen floating bodies at Angaur; the false security of Leyte Gulf; the loss and gain of days over the Date Line; the breathless head of the Equator; the hellish humidity and deadly monotony of all Pacific Islands; the glassy seas and sickening vacuum of the doldrums; the stink of rotting jungle; the endless distances, and the time and memory-destroying stretches of tropic seas; the hush of the passage through Jap infested waters of the Surigao Straits in the dead of night; the awful, slow spiral of burning planes falling into the sea; the horrible futility of a Jap suicide plane crashing my steel skin; the return of MacArthur to Luzon, to Bataan, to Corregidor; the sickening screech and burst of flame and oily smoke as more suicide planes crushed men and ships; the disgust, rage, and tragedy of half-masted colors when dead men slipped off the stern of ships in canvas shrouds; the sickening sweet smell of human blood as it dripped and gushed; the nauseous stink of putre-faction; the slight splash as limbs of the maimed were dropped over the side; the faltering step of men blinded; the palsied, convulsive shiver of nerve-shattered bodies; the click of type-writers listing the dead and wounded, and writing the poor message of condolence.

I know the exhausted looks of the crew after grueling months at sea in combat and monotony of routine. I have watched smiles change to carved lines around eyes and mouths; laughs drop to muttered curses; friendly horseplay to listless steps and dull dejection. I got to know the letters that men write home — letters of hope, pride, fun, love. I saw them change to letters of loneliness, fear, sickness, discouragement, and bitterness. But finally came the joyful letters of men return-ing to their homeland. The glorious sight of America's shores; the wild reunion of man with wife; the proud meeting of mother and son; the shy happiness of boy and girl.

There came the newspaper echo of the atomic bomb—and the enemy quit. And we heard the hoarse, triumphant bel-low of hundreds of sirens and whistles; the rattling clang of bells; the drunken frenzy and needless waste by human beings temporarily mad with victory.

And so, now, I know peace. The peace of waters no longer deadly with submarines; the peace of skies free from shrapnel and bombs; the peace of lands no longer whispering in fear. Now I know the light-hearted tread of men who are confident of returning to their homes; the ecstasy of running at night with lights and open ports.

I have known war...and death...and fear...all these things.

276

But now we are in the home waters of a conquered enemy. I, and my crew, and thousands like us, have dispelled the clouds of tyranny and oppression and hate...We have fought almost around the world. It has been such a long road. But now...now, my work is almost done...and I am content.

PC Kirkpatrick CY

Included in special edition of ship newspaper, *The Invader,* when the war ended and the GIs were returning home. Submitted by Paul R. Gross, U.S. Navy

PAUL H. HEITKAMP

NEW BREMEN, OHIO

Navy, Diesel Mechanics, 1944-46
Basic Training: Great Lakes
Duty in South Pacific

Our ship never got hit, but there were some close ones. The biggest convoy we were in was in Leyte, Philippines—200 ships. We were only a couple thousand feet away from MacArthur when he landed at Leyte.

Paul H. Heitkamp

We had 28 people aboard our LCI (Landing Craft Infantry), 24 enlisted men and four officers. It was designed as a troop carrier with the capability of landing 200 troops directly on the beach. Its fresh water tanks held 37 tons of water; it carried approximately 35 tons of supplies, spare parts and ammunition. It was powered by eight GM diesels with 1800 total horsepower. Two GM diesel generators provided electrical power. We had smoke generators to blanket the ship during air attacks or to fog the bay during an invasion.

There were 912 LCIs built in the U.S. between 1942 and 1944, 220 of which were on loan to the United Kingdom; 30 were lent to Russia; 662 were manned by U.S. Navy and Coast Guard personnel.

The crew on our ship was like a happy family. We had a small PX where we could buy candy, nuts, cigarettes, etc. We had to do our own laundry.

We didn't get mail for three months because our sister ship was sunk by a kamikaze plane and the numbers on the two ships got mixed up.

We went to China and took Chinese troops to Formosa. In Shanghai they were using charcoal burners on the cars and trucks; used a lot of bicycles.

LCI (L) 1064

. . .

DID YOU KNOW THAT...

Copeland Refrigeration Corporation, Sidney, Ohio, was supplying refrigeration on Navy vessels before WW II. In 1937 a complete Copeland ship program was started with refrigeration equipment designed to meet the extremely rigid requirements.

Civilian production lines were eliminated during the war and the program for the Navy, Army, and other governmental agencies increased. Copeland also manufactured parts for bomber carburetors, tanks, and anti-aircraft guns.[74]

DICK HURST
BELLEFONTAINE, OHIO

Navy, Petty Officer 2nd Class, 1943-46
Basic Training: Great Lakes
Duty in Atlantic and Pacific

I was on the USS Weber, a new destroyer, with a crew of 400 plus, out of Pier 92 in Brooklyn. It had 6-inch guns and pom-poms, 40 and 20 mm. I was a signalman on the bridge.

Being a signalman we used the flashing lights during the day and nothing at night. By that time they had a Nan Gear, an electronic device to put on a searchlight. With it we could see through the sights and send messages back and forth; it was a reddish beam and we'd read that beam; you couldn't see it with the naked eye. It was Top Secret stuff at that time. It wouldn't mean anything today, but when the war was over, they really confiscated that model. I think we picked it up at San Diego but never used it until we hit Okinawa.

We took a shakedown cruise up to Casco Bay, Maine. Made our first trip escorting convoys to England, went in at Londonderry. That's where we would stay and get repairs. Then we'd come back, get another convoy. We crossed four different times, and the last time we went into the Mediterranean and got our bow smacked. A Portuguese fishing boat came across the convoy. The commander told us to take them; how, he didn't care. We fired a shot across and they still kept coming in, so we rammed them, tore a big hole in our bow. The fishing boat sank when we rammed them. We took the people on to our boat and then dropped them off at the Rock of Gibraltar.

At the mouth of the Mediterranean the submarines would watch for us. We got into it with one. We'd go in General Quarters and there'd be a sonar with a ping in it, which would be a submarine alert. We'd drop depth charges, or what we called hedgehogs, off the front; roll them off the back; shoot them off to the side, and lay down the whole pattern. There would be other destroyers following with their depth charge pattern. In this case, the destroyer was the Otter. Together, we got the sub. The ships we were escorting were carrying high octane gas for aviation. We knew the submarine was going to try to knock out the whole convoy. Of course, they'd knock off the tin cans (destroyers) cause then they could get in to the other ships easier. We had to zigzag all the way.

We went up through the Mediterranean, in to Palermo, Sicily, dry dock. While there, an officer told me that the person I was looking at through the binoculars was General Patton; I'm not sure.

We were there for quite some time, and then went in to Normandy, France, D-Day plus 2. Immediately we got into a minefield. Another ship alerted us, so we had to back off. We helped to cover the troops that were still coming in.

Back in the Philadephia Navy Yard they converted us, taking our torpedo tubes off and putting on Higgins boats, which were landing craft.

In San Diego we loaded up with ammo, etc., and went out to Pearl, Eniwetok, Saipan, and Okinawa. At Okinawa nothing happened for a day or two and then, here they came! We were on picket duty for the task force, meaning that we were so many square miles out from an island, trying to protect our incoming troop ships, flattops, battlewagons, and cruisers from the kamikaze planes. We used the 6-incher some. This was off Naha, the airstrip, in Buckner Bay. They had a cove there called Wiseman's Cove, and suicide boats came and tried to knock us out at night. They were about the size of a PT boat.

We operated with a ship called the USS Laffey, which was a destroyer in the Atlantic and the Pacific. It took a bad hit. The aircraft carrier Franklin had a bad hit, too, but it got back on its own. The Laffey lost 80 plus men, I think, in 20 seconds, but it also got back.

A few years ago we went to Charleston and the Laffey is there. It had a plaque with the names of the ships they operated with in gold and my ship's name was on it. My destroyer was the same class as the Laffey.

They had a hard time getting mail to us at Okinawa because we hit a typhoon and our ship was listed as lost. Christmas presents and everything were returned. Our water tanks went bad once, and we could only wet our lips and fingertips for ten days or longer. Couldn't even shave.

It was at Okinawa that I saw George Young and Dick Buckenroth from Bellefontaine; also Bob Lewis who was on the cruiser Biloxi.

USS Laffey

I was in China, up where The Great Wall starts. We escorted the troop ships which were carrying the Nationalists to fight the Communists.

We left Okinawa and went to Leyte in the Philippines. They dropped the bomb at Hiroshima and Nagasaki; two weeks after that we went in at Nagasaki. In the harbor there was a minesweeper and the hospital ship, New Haven, us, and a cruiser. We went on shore and liberated prisoners of war, Dutch, English, and American, all skin over bones. Terrible sight! Took them out to the hospital ship. The POWs had been working in the mines, which they said saved them from the bomb.

The people were burned, were eating roots, living in tunnels dug back in the hillside. We didn't do anything about them, but after about a week the Army and big transports came in for the occupation, and they probably started helping them. As far as feeling sorry for them, I didn't. Under the circumstances, we just couldn't. They killed my uncle; he was one of the first ones from Logan County to be killed. In the Coral Sea battle he was on the destroyer Sims.

A lot of guys came home and thought the world owed them a living, but I didn't feel that way. It was only a short time, considering our whole lifetime.

• • •

DID YOU KNOW THAT...

When German submarines first approached Galveston Island, Texas, at the beginning of the war, it was tourist season and lights were burning brightly. Eight ships were blown up that night.

During the first half of 1942, German subs were busy off the northern half of the eastern shoreline. After American defenses were put in place there, the subs moved to the southern part of the coast. They were so close to shore that sometimes people on the beach could hear or see them. Thirty-seven American ships were sunk or damaged between April and July, 1942, in the coastal waters off Florida.

Twenty-four German submarines sank fifty-six merchant ships and damaged fourteen more in the Gulf of Mexico between 1942 and 1943.

But the highest toll in the Western Hemisphere was taken off the shores of North Carolina, causing it to be called the "Graveyard of the Atlantic."

Residents of all these states were told not to discuss with others what they heard or saw in the coastal waters so as not to alarm citizens.75

6-inch Shield Gun, Ft. Pickens, FL

KENNETH D. KELLY

SPRING LAKE, MICHIGAN

Navy Seabees, Carpenters Mate 3rd Class, 127th Battalion, 1943-46
Basic Training: Camp Peary, Virginia
Duty in Pacific

The Navy Seabees, or Construction Battalions, were formed in 1941, to provide a force that would be equivalent to the Army Engineers. Since the war was on and the Navy needed to get these units into operation quickly, they adopted a policy of recruiting experienced construction men so they could proceed with advanced base construction projects without extensive training. They gave them ratings commensurate with their experience and education.

The typical construction battalion consisted of 1100 men in four letter companies (A,B,C,D) and a headquarters company. The units were officered by trained Civil Engineers who were members of the Navy Civil Engineer Corp. There were about 350,000 Seabees in WW II, forming 146 construction battalions and 20 or 30 smaller units called CBMUs (Construction Battalion Maintenance Units).

Some Seabees went in on invasions ahead of the Marines and Army Infantry, but they were very few and had special training in demolition and heavy-equipment operation. Their responsibilities included clearing the way for the invasions and using their heavy earth-moving equipment to clear roads and pathways for the invading infantrymen.

The Seabees' main function was exercised after an invasion took place. They would move in with all of their equipment and build bases the Navy, Marines, Army and Army Air Force needed in their advance against the enemy.

At Camp Peary we learned to wash our clothes by wetting them down, laying them on a flat board and scrubbing them with a stiff-bristled scrub brush, using plenty of soap and elbow grease. After rinsing, we would hang them on a clothesline using what the Navy called "clothes stops." These were short pieces of braided cord about 1/8" in diameter and 12 to 18" long with metal clips on each end to keep them from unraveling. When the clothes were dry, we took them down and rolled them individually into neat, tight bundles and tied them with the clothes stops. The Navy said if we did this properly, the clothes would not need pressing. After many times we did achieve a reasonable degree of skill in rolling them that resulted in our making a presentable appearance in morning inspection.

We were also told that there were three ways to accomplish something. They were: the right way, the wrong way, and the Navy way, and, by God, we were going to learn the Navy way.

After boot training came Marine combat training. Marine Corps drill instructors taught us large unit tactics, combat techniques, how to take care of and shoot our pieces. Our rifles were our "piece." If anyone was heard calling it a rifle or gun, he was made to run around the drill field in double time, holding his piece at high port (position in front of and parallel to the body, holding the piece with both hands with barrel pointing up to your left at angle of 45 degrees), shouting "This is my piece, this is my piece."

On our trip to the South Pacific, toilet facilities were deep troughs with a rapid stream of sea water flowing through, emptying over the side of the ship. The tops of the trough on both sides were covered with a 2x6, which you sat on with your business end hanging out over the running water.

After several stops, we arrived at Los Negros in the Admiralty Group, north of New Guinea, 25 to 30 days after the invasion. The campsite was situated in a beautiful grove of palm trees alongside the former Japanese Momote Airstrip; on the other side was a sandy beach. When trying to drive the wooden tent stakes into the ground, we learned there was only a two- or three-inch layer of soil on top of very hard impenetrable coral. Then we followed the lead of our predecessors and anchored the tent guy ropes with steel-reinforcing bar stakes.

My first assignment was filling in bomb and shell craters, fox holes, trenches, burning trashed trees, logs and other debris. We also disposed of wrecked equipment and buried dead Japanese soldiers we found.

My next job was laying steel pipe from the dock area to fuel storage tanks. The 17th regiment was expanding the Momote airstrip into an airport for B-24 Liberator 4-engine bombers and single-engine fighters. We extended and widened the airstrip, built hard stands (parking areas for planes), constructed barracks (mostly Quonset huts), mess halls, hospitals, toilets, parachute lofts, bomb storage areas, repair and maintenance building, cemeteries.

Most of the time in the Pacific we worked in shifts, with the work going on 24 hours a day, seven days a week. We had constructed portable light towers with gasoline generators to light our work areas at night. We always said that tough projects we could do immediately and the impossible ones took a little longer.

The Seabees use a colorful shoulder patch of the little fighting, flying bee with a tommy gun, monkey wrench, hammer, Navy white hat, and Navy rating badges on his arm.

Seabee patch

On the island of Manus we constructed a Communications Center (radio transmitting and receiving station). I worked with a man assigned the job of dynamiting holes in the coral rock so we could pour concrete foundations for the radio antenna towers. He had learned his dynamiting skills in the coal mines of West Virginia. We drilled holes in the coral and inserted dynamite sticks in them, into which we had previously inserted blasting caps; strung wire from the caps to our charge box which we located nearby behind a tree or a convenient pile of dirt. If the area was clear of people, we'd shout, "fire in the hole" and press the lever down that exploded the dynamite. Usually with one stick of dynamite we could blast a 4-5 ft. diameter hole 3-4 ft. deep.

My next job was working with a pile driver. The Section Base required a "T" shaped dock where the minesweepers could tie up for their required maintenance and servicing. I was to fasten the lifting lines from the pile-driving crane to the piling when it was on the ground or floating in the water. After the crane had lifted the piling to the vertical position, I had to climb up on the leads and work the suspended piling into the opening so the hammer could be dropped on their tops and drive them into the bottom of the harbor. I thought it was a fun job because many of the older men wouldn't do it.

We also had to drive some piling clusters in the harbor about 50 feet out from the dock we built. These were for tying up larger supply ships which came in from time to time when the dock space was occupied by minesweepers being serviced.

We had completed our first piling cluster of about ten pilings when we heard that a supply ship was coming in. We pulled our pile-driving crane barge back to the docks and stood back to watch the supply ship come in. It was a good-size ship and, as it came in, it didn't slow down appreciably but steered alongside our piling cluster and dropped the loop of a mooring line on the center piling, which we had left extended above the others about four feet. Then they snubbed off the other end of the line on a bollard on the ship, expecting to stop moving when the line became taut. Well, they didn't stop. Our piling cluster wasn't set in the harbor bottom strong enough to hold the ship; it pulled them all loose.

We thought our handiwork was strong enough to hold any ship. The next day, after the ship pulled out, we went back to work, using longer piling and driving them deeper and more firmly into the harbor bottom. The next time a ship came in we were pleased to see our cluster project hold up very well.

We were working with a crane and I was turned away from the harbor. Suddenly one of the fellows yelled at me to look! Where one of the ships had been anchored there was a huge mass of smoke and flame climbing skyward. One of the quicker-thinking fellows in our crew said, "Get under the crane, there may be a concussion coming, as well as falling debris!" So we crawled under the crane and in a short time we could hear debris falling around us but felt no appreciable concussion.

We later learned that a Navy ammunition ship had its load of ammunition explode. The crew of over 300 were killed and never found. Seventy or eighty in nearby ships were also killed, plus many injured. One of our corpsmen was assigned to help identify the wounded and killed and to strip the dead of their rings, watches, wallets and other valuables.

Going from New Caledonia to Okinawa, we stopped at Eniwetok, where I had the opportunity of visiting my cousin. Then on to Ulithi in the Caroline Islands, which served as one of the major advanced bases for the recapture of the Philippines and the invasions of Iwo Jima, Okinawa, and ultimately, Japan. There were eight aircraft carriers all anchored in a row. There was also a destroyer with no superstructure. It had just arrived from Okinawa where it had been hit by a Kamikaze suicide plane. It had come in under the command of a Chief Petty officer because all of the officers had been killed by the suicide plane.

The part that I particularly remember about Okinawa was meeting my brother Dale. What a happy reunion we had on this war-torn Pacific Island!

Three days after we arrived on Okinawa, Lt. Gen. Buckner, the Commanding General of the 10th Army, was killed by an enemy artillery shell that struck a rock near where he was standing.* The fragments from the rock and shell hit him in the chest. His grandfather was the Confederate Gen. Buckner in the Civil War who surrendered Fort Donaldson to Union Gen. Grant.

One night at 2:00 A.M. while we were working, we saw anti-aircraft shell bursts and machine gun tracer bullets going skyward. We went through our lights-out, crawl under tractor drill, to wait for the raid to end. As we lay there in the quiet with our tractors shut down, we could hear trucks out on the airstrip and also the cheers of men nearby. Someone got out from under his tractor and went to the airstrip to find out what was happening. We learned of the Japanese acceptance of our surrender terms and that the war was over. So after we had shouted and cheered a short time, we got on our transport trucks and headed back to camp, two or three miles away. When we got there we were chastised by our superiors for leaving work before quitting time. However, we only worked on the airfield about another week and then quit for good.

Three or four weeks after the end of the war we were assigned work on an area to be used for an ammunition dump. We noticed some round holes about twelve inches in diameter. When we got down four or five feet we struck metal. Upon closer inspection we discovered that the metal objects were tailfins of live bombs; apparently a plane had jettisoned its bombs. The bomb disposal people very carefully disarmed them. First, though, we had to uncover them completely, which was done by our most skillful bulldozer operator, along with some men with shovels. The bomb disposal people said they were American bombs that had not dropped far enough to activate the fuses that caused them to explode on impact. The vibrations from our heavy nine- and ten-ton tractors traveling on the ground above them could have very easily set them off. We were very lucky!

When I returned to Okinawa with a reunion group 50 years later, June, 1995, there were some Japanese veterans there, also. A Lieutenant in the 65th Imperial Japanese brigade asked if there were any Marines present who had been on the Shuri battle line on May 6, 1945. Eight or ten raised their hands. He went on to say, "You killed all of my men." Apparently, on that specific day his brigade was ordered to counterattack our forces on that battle line. He commanded 23 men and they were all killed in the attack. He had 13 battle wounds, one of which almost severed his arm. That wounded arm interfered with his crawling back to the Japanese lines for treatment, so he cut it off with his battle sword. Then he made his way back to an aid station where he received treatment. He returned to duty during the battle and surrendered with ten men in his command at the end of the war.

*This is the same Colonel Simon Bolivar Buckner, Jr., who commanded the troops in the Aleutian Islands.

• • •

DID YOU KNOW THAT...

The Queen Elizabeth and Queen Mary could each carry 15,000 troops, having them sleep in three shifts, known as triple bunking.76

CHARLES MANNING
SIDNEY, OHIO

Navy, GMMC 3/C, Gunner's Mate, 1943-46
Basic Training: Great Lakes
Duty in Pacific

Went in Air Force in 1943, 16 years old. They gave me a certificate, said I was out. Went across street and joined the Navy.

I was assigned to a destroyer, within a convoy, from Pearl Harbor to Okinawa for the invasion. Stole a dog in Pearl Harbor, had him four or five months, then gave him to another ship and he jumped off.

Amber

We were at sea maybe four days; looked around and no convoy, just five destroyers. We kept going and going and got fired at. That ship could take on a light cruiser and sink it. We were loaded for bear on that little dude, but we ran like scared rabbits. The Captain came on the horn and said that we were on a different mission and should not in any way engage the enemy.

Another day goes by and sonar picks up a submarine. That thing set off our stern for about three days, about a mile or so behind us. They all knew that. Kept giving codes, Who are you? What are you doing? On the third morning I got this beep, beep. My chore was setting the depth charges, not the hedgehogs, but the cans you roll over; set them for time and depth. We blew the heck out of that sub! Still don't know whether it was ours, Japanese, German, English, but we got it.

Charles Manning

We kept on going through a typhoon to Okinawa; it took planes right off the aircraft carrier. All big ships tried to make anchor, it didn't matter where. And we were on this little dude right in the middle of the South Pacific! For two days we were riding 135 ft. waves. The third day it calmed down a little to 80 and 90 ft. waves. We thought we were home! Went down in the galley; there was only a little soup in those big soup kettles, but it went right out over the top. Bologna sandwiches are all we had for three days.

After the storm we passed Wake Island. Refueled at Guam. Between Guam and China the war ended. We went in and delivered the gold bullion to Formosa on somebody's ship—no one knew which ship it was on. That was 5 billion dollars! It was to reinforce Nationalist China for Chiang Kai-shek.

We went into Hong Kong just as the war ended, the first American ships in. We ran patrol, picket duty between Hong Kong and Shanghai. We'd go up the little rivers as far as we could go and we'd catch these pigboats or Japanese gunboats. Guys were still coming out of Burma, so we protected the Chinese people the best we could; fed them out of our garbage.

I was a diver, no special training. They had a hand pump. When we'd go ashore we'd drop an anchor about 50-100 yards out, depending on the depth of the water. When we'd leave we'd put this big wench in reverse and it would pull us off the shore. The propeller would get tangled in the cable and we couldn't go any place. So I went down and cut the cable.

Charles Manning

I got off the destroyer at Hong Kong. Transferred to a destroyer escort. We were the peace-makers, ambassadors; went in taking money to all these ports and spreading PR. We stopped at Singapore, India, Suez Canal, Pt. Saib, Madeira Islands, Spain, Rock of Gibraltar, two days in each port. Half of the crew at liberty at a time. Anything we had that they wanted, they got. But they told us to clean up the shipping lanes, blow up the floating mines. So our ambassador ships, four destroyer escorts, would spread out and if we'd see a floating mine, we'd signal and everybody would back off and we would shoot it.

Royal Band, Singapore, 1945

Marseilles, France 1934

Ceylon—saw hands hanging on tree; person had been caught stealing.

Came in at Charleston and saw these signs: "Sailors and dogs keep off the grass." That didn't go down well with us!

Went in inactive reserves. Started flying right away in 1946. Became stunt pilot. Then I joined the Confederate Air Force, based at Harlingen, Texas. There's now a wing in Indiana and northern Ohio. They get WW II aircraft, fix them up, and fly them in air shows.

Met Captain Edward V. Rickenbacher at an air show. We wrote back and forth but weren't real friends. He sent me auto-graphed copies of his *Fighting the Flying Circus; Rickenbacher, an Autobiography;* and *Rickenbacher's Full Story: Seven Came Through.* We used to sit down at the Officers Club in Harlingen, Texas, and drink a lot of beer with Pappy Boyington. He signed and sent me *Baa Baa Black Sheep,* October 8, 1978. Met General Doolittle at an air show in California; we wrote back and forth a few times.

One time while I was up in one of the old planes, a DC-3, I lost a rudder. I set it down in the sand; no one got hurt. And I learned parachute jumping while in the Confederate Air Force.

Pappy Boyington

I used to fly an Aeronca for the Civil Air Patrol. They were used as Scouters for artillery in Europe and the African Desert. A few were used in the Pacific but they didn't work too well because of the humidity, and they were canvas.

Well, going back to WW II, WE HAD SOMETHING TO FIGHT FOR—OUR COUNTRY AND HER FREEDOM!

. . .

DID YOU KNOW THAT...

Sidney, Ohio, was cited as an example of patriotism in *The Saturday Evening Post*, March 27, 1943. The article, "Sidney's Answer to the Manpower Problem," told how employees were working double time, doing two jobs rather than one, putting in sixteen or more hours a day.

With a scarcity of automobiles, parts, and gasoline, transportation had to be provided for those coming in from the country. Sidney took over ten school busses. One worker drove the bus to work, picking up others; a group coming off their shift took it on the route home. A third group took it back to the factory, and the original group took it on the route home. Similar arrangements were made by groups with station wagons.

All the Sidney citizens seemed to agree that working eight hours a day, seven days a week, in a factory, and then going to another job was worth it, because it could "...mean the difference between victory and defeat."

"Sidney is just an American town... Its citizens are human. ...But Sidney has handled uniquely and with surprising success the toughest problem war has left on the doorstep of the home front, and, in doing it, has blazed a trail which may well be followed in many communities throughout the country." [77]

HERBERT RISMILLER

VERSAILLES, OHIO

Navy, Armed Guard on Merchant Marine ship, 1943-45
Basic Training: Great Lakes
Duty in Atlantic

I was on a cargo ship, a Liberty ship. About 2700 of them were built; roughly 400 ft. long and 52 ft. wide; flat bottom. One-fourth of them got sunk. Germans were really after them because they were carrying freight, army supplies, ammunition, food, and all kinds of equipment that was needed. I made five trips to Europe and one to the Far East. We had combat attacks in the Mediterranean; shot down two German planes; they missed all five of our ships.

Going to Murmansk, Russia, eight out of ten ships were sunk. Loads that went to Iran went from there to Russia by land. We were in Iran in the spring and it was 140 degrees. The American soldiers stationed there were only supposed to be there ten months, but if no relief came, they could be there as long as two years.

In 1942-43 we went across with no guns. There were telephone poles to look like guns. That's how ill-prepared we were. It cost many, many lives. There was generally a 538 on the bow and maybe a 350; on the stern you'd have a 538 or a 551 plus eight 20 mm.

The Merchant Marine is a sea-going civilian; has no benefits of the Navy; gets hazardous duty pay. I never felt this was right. Merchant Marines were out before the war; they manned the ships. As long as they were in the Merchant Marines, they weren't drafted, but if they didn't re-sign and go back out to duty, they were subject to the draft. We had guys 18-20 years old; some were black. My boss was a Navy Lieutenant, but the Captain of the ship was over the whole works.

There was good food on the ship. We went *to* the diningroom and the *food was served to us*. At the evening meal we had a choice of meats. It wasn't geared up for a chow line.

In early 1945, it was considered to be relatively safe. Earlier when we crossed the Atlantic there was a convoy with as many as 100 ships at a time, ten deep and ten wide. There'd be two or 3 destroyers scout around ahead and behind. They didn't go in between the ships, scouted around the outside for German subs.

As we came back from Iran, empty, a German sub laid out there all day. Could have shot at us any time. I guess because we were empty they thought we weren't worth blowing up. Our captain said, "Don't fire. Be at your station. We can't ask for trouble." Around 4 or 5:00 in the afternoon the sub disappeared. We came back through the Gulf of Eden through the Red Sea and Suez Canal.

No ships got hit in any of the convoys I was in. I was out at sea about 21 months. I asked for the Navy and they put me here. After boot camp at Great Lakes, went to Norfolk for gunnery training. I got 20 percent extra for sea duty. Seaman 1st Class, $66 a month. In late 1941-42, it was $21 a month for a private, plain old Seaman. Could ride subway free in New York; the ferry for nothing to Staten Island.

We'd make a trip to England, unload and come right back. While they were loading the ship I could come home, usually on a four-day leave. It cost $19 from New York. I'd get on the Pennsylvania Railroad and come straight through to Xenia. My sisters in Dayton would bring me home.

We stockpiled men and materials in England before the Normandy invasion. Our government rented houses, just one or two rooms, to take care of soldiers. It's a wonder we didn't sink England with as much stuff as we stacked in there. We'd unload and come back to get more supplies. After the invasion we'd go into Swansea, England. The ship would be roughly 30-35 feet in the water, fully loaded and, as they took off about half, the ship would come up in the water. Then we'd go over to the beachhead and they'd take off the rest. A "duck" would come out and get it.

I was in Liverpool, England, went in just behind a submarine net; had to wait a few days to unload. We left there and went to Belfast, Ireland, and that's the night they went from a blackout to a dim-out. England and all those countries used a 50- or even 25-watt bulb; double curtains over all their windows and doors, no light anywhere. They let them put 50-watt bulbs in their street lights that night, and were they ever celebrating! Apparently, the Captain of the ship knew this and he took us all in to help them celebrate. They had been like that since 1939, almost six years.

To get to England it took 17-21 days, depending on the weather. We weren't supposed to take any notes because they might get into enemy hands. The first time out we got in a bad storm. There were about ten of us who were on our first trip, and we were really sick; you hope you will die and are afraid you won't. Our ship had to leave the convoy because the ship was going too far sideways, could capsize.

It took around a month to load the ship; ammunition isn't just thrown in the bottom of a ship. Everything had to be secure, so when we started rocking, everything would stay in place. Unloading didn't take quite as long, maybe two or three weeks. It was amazing how all those things got over there and were organized.

On my last trip we headed for Antwerp, Belgium, but got to the White Cliffs of Dover on V-E night; anchored there and didn't get to go ashore. From there went to Antwerp, where they unloaded us. Then to Hull, England, loaded some things, medical supplies, I think, and went to Oslo, Norway. How they would have had anything to spare we don't know. The German forces had Norway occupied with air and submarine bases. We weren't allowed to go into the city of Oslo because there were mines that hadn't been cleaned up, could see them floating.

The ship went about 11 knots and a knot is 1-1/8 miles, roughly 12-13 miles per hour. Some of the older ships wouldn't go quite that fast, and, of course, in convoy they had to stay with the slowest. Those liberty ships rolled because of the flat bottom. They are like a washtub. When I got assigned to this unit, a guy told me that crossing an ocean in one of those ships was like going out in a washtub with a popgun.

• • •

DID YOU KNOW THAT...

"Some 250,000 seamen of the U.S. Merchant Marine [who] served aboard overseas-bound vessels during WW II" were not declared "veterans" until 1988.[78]

MARION L. SHINN

LEWISTON, IDAHO

Navy, RT 2/C, USS Guavina (submarine)
Basic Training: Bremerton, Washington
Duty in Pacific

Ordinary activities taken for granted on the beach become problems on a submarine at sea. Tanks inside the hull are filled with fresh water before leaving port. The water was excellent for a few days, but it tasted like something was growing in it before the run was over. The water evaporator was in the forward part of the Engine Room. The engine crew pumped salty sea water through an evaporator, and a low grade of potable water resulted. ...A saline taste remained. It did not take long to decide not to drink water straight. The coffeepot was always hot. Cooks made about a gallon per person each day in the mess hall....

Marion L. Shinn

The washroom was a small compartment at the after end of crews quarters; it consisted of a wash basin and a cramped shower stall. Since the supply of fresh water was limited, the use for personal cleanliness was restricted....instructions were to "wet down, soap, rinse." Washing clothes was a chore, and we did not put on clean clothes every day....Most of the guys wore navy-issue strap toed leather sandals without socks to keep the jungle rot from attacking the ever-moist, soft skin between the toes.

Using the head (toilet) on a submarine was a new experience. Two individual stalls were near crew quarters across from the washroom; one stall in the forward room was officially reserved for the officers. The toilet stool looked much like those used on land, except for a long handle on the side. That lever raised and lowered the ladle that created a seal at the bottom of the bowl. Two nearby valves, not clearly labeled, gave the operator the choice of air or water to move the fecal material to the sanitary tank. Since water was a scarce item, it was desirable to use air whenever possible, and a turn of the knob did the job. Newcomers soon learned the ladle must be held securely in the closed position when flushing....Men making a mistake while flushing the toilet seldom made it a second time. A blast of misdirected air would blow the feces in the ladle back on the bulkheads and the unfortuate sailor....

Officers' head

I was the only person assigned to my bunk....the middle bunk in a three tier set; I thought it was the best of the lot. The lower bunk was only three or four inches from the floor. The dust and dirt from shuffling feet sifted onto the mattress. The top bunk was hard to enter and harder to ride in rough weather. Being next to the passageway, leading between the mess hall and the head (toilet), was not an advantage. There was a constant parade of men walking through the darkened compartment; the edge of my bed was an effective hand rail for passer-bys. The Pharmacist Mate's bunk was next to mine. All medical emergencies and sick calls were treated a couple of feet from my sleeping quarters....A half dozen of the new men "hot bunked." They shared bunks with someone on the opposite shift.

The deck crew carried enough food aboard to feed eighty men for two months. The selection of food looked good; the cost of food per man per day for submariners was about $1.25, compared to 63 cents for the navy as a whole. Below the mess hall and galley was a large cooler for fresh meats and eggs. Most of our food was stored in the large storeroom below the galley, but early in the run every nook and cranny on the boat was filled with the overflow boxes....

Tender and subs

In addition to the base amount for our specific rate (of pay), we were allowed 50% additional for submarine pay and 20% more for being overseas. My monthly income was nearly $200 per month in addition to board, room and clothes. That was more than double what I earned as an elementary school teacher in Idaho....

A small puppy, Tessie, was discovered several hours after we put to sea. She was smuggled aboard by a couple of Motor

Macs. The little dog took the dives and rolls very well after the first day or two. The watertight doors between the compartments were a couple of feet off the deck; Tessie could not jump high enough to get through. Whenever she wanted to change compartments a passing man would reach down and lift her through the opening....

The over supervision by the Captain was hard to put aside in my mind....a little event made me feel justice prevails, at least sometimes. It was a sunny day with little aircraft activity. The boat was cruising slowly on the surface on the dinky engine. We were just waiting for something to break the monotony. The Captain came out of his stateroom after breakfast dressed in a light tan short sleeve shirt with beige shorts. Obviously, he had taken time to shower and give unusual care with his morning grooming including the thinning crop of light colored hair. A few minutes after he went to the bridge, the unexpected happened; a glob of grease from the top bearing of the rotating SJ radar mast broke loose and dropped. It barely missed his balding spot, slithered down his right ear, and onto the shoulder of his immaculate shirt. The Captain immediately left the bridge; he did not look to right or left as he passed through the control room. Nothing was said as he turned left, stepped through the watertight door and headed toward his wardroom. I expected the oil to work out of the bearing; it was inwardly pleasing that it dropped at that particular moment. My resolve to take a rag up and wipe the bearing was not necessary. The next day my shift was changed back to days. I was no longer on the greasing detail....

Captain...was an exacting man; he gave specific orders. There would be no coffee topside....The men topside followed his orders explicitly during the day, but at night it was different. When the temperature cooled, word passed quietly for coffee to be sent to the bridge....Cups of the steaming brew were relayed from the galley to the bridge. Sometimes the Captain would wake in the middle of the night and decide to go to the bridge; he would appear topside unannounced. The reaction from rule violators was instantaneous; the coffee and the cups went over the side and disappeared in the ocean. By the end of the run, coffee cups were in short supply. The Commissary Officer would order a whole set of new ones for the next run....

Our operating station was directly on the equator. The navigator determined the exact location and set the course to follow that imaginary line. During the afternoon, we zig-zagged across the equator hundreds of times....The rays of the sun beat directly down on the water; the temperature at the surface went up to 87 degrees Fahrenheit. Twisting columns of air created waterspouts; they siphoned the hot surface water into little scattered spots of gray clouds. Those dense spots in the sky caused hundreds of small false pips on the radar. The operators reported many of them as possible airplane contacts; this created unneeded concerns on the bridge....

...the message came to return to Brisbane for repair.... Everyone was glad to be on our way back to Australia. ....The fast transit system in Sydney was the most efficient I had ever seen. Street traffic was light; most of the battered, old cars were taxis or government vehicles. Australia had no oil reserves; petrol was in short supply, and ordinary people did not own cars. The few cars that operated used propane or butane gas stored in a large rubber fuel bag on top of the vehicle. When the bag was full it stood half as tall as the car itself. When the fuel supply was low, the bag collapsed flat against the car-top....

(In Perth) A charcoal burner replaced the usual gasoline tank as a fuel source; modifying the carburetor allowed the engine to burn carbon monoxide instead of gasoline. Some operators removed the trunk lid to install the charcoal burner; others hauled their charcoal burner in a small trailer....One night (our) taxi was an old Nash sedan with the burner in the trunk. The driver got out of his car, went to the charcoal burner, and stoked the fire. He added charcoal and closed the tight burner door. When enough carbon monoxide was generated, he started the engine, and we were underway. The car had no pick-up; we crept along, hugging the outer edge of the road. At least twice, he stopped, stirred the fire, and waited for gas to be generated....

Most of us had never seen a kangaroo, but hunting them sounded like great fun. The "roos" were ravaging the range; the locals wanted to decrease their number. Brother Hadley and three or four of his boys went with us on the hunt. The bus rumbled out on a dirt road for some distance. When it stopped, all of us climbed out and started wandering around. The Brother told us to walk in a straight line, about 8 feet apart, through the bush. By staying in a straight line, we would sweep the kangaroos ahead of us. It also would reduce the danger of shooting each other....Low bushes and short gum trees covered the rolling hills. Large protruding rocky ledges dotted the countryside.

The kangaroos remained hidden behind the trees or rocks until we almost reached them. The big red kangaroos were more than six feet tall. As we approached, the large animals would jump straight in the air like a jack-in-the-box. While we were frantically swinging guns in that direction, they would gracefully bounce away. Their huge tail was used for balance; they glided easily across the rough terrain. A volley of shots followed each fleeing animal, but none of the shots came close to their mark.

After walking a long time and firing our guns, Bill, our gunners mate, shot a little wallaby. It was about 3 feet tall. As soon as the animal hit the ground, a couple of the barefoot boys raced up and cut its throat. One of the boys thrust his hand into the pouch in the front of the wallaby and pulled out a tiny pink object about the size of a thumb. The wallaby had a little Joey hanging on to the teat inside the pouch. The size of the tiny immature baby was surprising; the pink mass was more like an embryo than a baby animal. Immediately, the boys took over; they started gutting out the animal and skinning it....The skin was removed carefully; it was handed to the mighty hunter, Bill McKay. He rolled the skin flesh side in, and tucked it under his arm....(He) proudly carried his wallaby skin back to the hotel and stored it under the bed. Before the week was over, the smell of rotting flesh was too strong for the room; the trophy was thrown away....

...one of those low flying planes almost got us. Our radar operator spotted it at 14 miles, low, about 3 degrees above the water, coming in fast....By the time the Captain arrived on deck, the plane was almost too close. The Captain shouted "Crash Dive"; the men topside cleared the bridge in seconds. Just as the bow started down the boat rocked from a violent explosion, an aerial bomb. The noise of the explosion was deafening, and the impact came from the forward part of the boat. The bow of the boat changed directions; it suddenly popped back toward the surface, and the stern dropped like a rock. The two seamen on the bow and stern planes pushed and pulled

304

on their controls; the boat continued to sink deeper and deeper stern first. When the boat came to a stop, the stern was about 300 feet under water; the bow was sticking up at a twenty or thirty degree angle. This was an ususual position; all the books, charts, coffee cups, and everything else loose tumbled backward onto the decks. All of us froze in position, bracing to keep from falling.

Mr. MacKay climbed the inclined deck to the pumps on the water manifold....the Bosun...sat with one hand on the hydraulic manifold handles. His eyes never left the lights on the Christmas Tree....the auxiliary man on duty, was standing by the air panel. He was rigid and ready, but one hand reached around and thumbed the Bible; he always kept it in his back pocket. The crash dive happened so quickly there was no time to "flood negative" to get weight in the belly of the boat. Venting negative allowed water from the sea to fill the tank and add weight amidships. The increased air venting into our closed container caused the air pressure in the boat to rise rapidly. Suddenly, with the increased pressure, the atmosphere became oppressive; everyone broke out in a cold sweat. It was just like we were sitting in a pressure cooker. Sweat droplets popped out all over our bodies; it left us with a clammy cold feeling. A feeling of sheer terror came over me. I tried to stand on that precariously tipped deck and keep loose objects from falling off of every shelf and piece of equipment. Officially I was a qualified submariner. However, I had no idea what was happening or what to do about it.

...slowly the boat eased down into a horizontal position. When it was over the guys in the mess hall joked a little about the experience. Most of us were trying to cover up our fright with a little bravado....

The next morning...our location was west of Mindoro Island, and about 60 miles southwest of Manila Harbor. Many small water channels divided the towering rocky cliffs; none were deep enough for a submerged submarine to enter....As soon as it was dusk, we surfaced and put the SJ radar in operation. About 2200 hours, the radar operator picked up a pip at 15,000 yards. It did not look like the land images around it. Only a tiny, fuzzy difference distinguished the image of land from a ship, but our operator picked it up. The Captain eased closer into the shallow channel; finally he sighted a ship. It looked like a middle sized merchantman of the Maru class; it was resting at anchor. The shallow water and the rocky cliffs protected the tanker from most potential enemies. There was a fire burning on the after deck; she had been in trouble before.

We approached as close as the channel would allow; the Captain fired from the forward room. The first torpedo was on target. As that 600-pound chunk of torpex hit the ship and exploded, the whole mountainside reverberated. Shock waves bounced us gently, even in the deeper water at the mouth of the channel. Apparently the cargo was aviation fuel. Flames covered the surface of the water around the ship; the highly flammable liquid burned as it flowed from the damaged vessel. A second torpedo went through the fiery waters to complete the destruction. A small patrol boat came from somewhere to search for us, but we easily evaded it....

...a departing bomber sent us a radio message. Ground fire had damaged one of the American planes in the squadron. It had crashed in our area. The radio message was sketchy. Apparently the crew bailed out; one chute did not open....We raced toward the spot where the plane was last seen....

On the same day, our lookouts spotted five of the crew. One was on a lifeboat dropped by another plane in the squadron. The other four were bobbing up and down in the ocean, held upright by the "Mae West" jackets....Reaching out to catch the exhausted men in bobbing life jackets posed a danger. They could crash against the boat and be injured. The solution was to lower our bow planes into a horizontal position. As we approached the men floating in the water, the flat surfaces gave them something sturdy to grasp. Our deck crew stood on the open bow planes and pulled the men aboard. All of the aviators were able to climb down the ladders to the Control room.

All night the "old man" stood on the bridge and occasionally shot green rocket flares into the air from our "Buck Rogers" gun. Hearing the shouts of survivors over the sound of the sea was difficult, but it was worth a try....The flares could give away our position; we were not far from a strong Japanese military installation on Yap Island....During the night we picked up two more men. One man was sighted floating about 100 yards from the boat. Lt. Neenan, a strong swimmer, took a rope and swam out to the floating airman. The men on deck pulled gently on the rope and eased the pair back to our boat. Both of the men rescued during the night were floating in their lifejackets. An empty "Mae West" was floating nearby; it was presumed the man was lost. The next day we rescued another fellow, and he was in good shape. Our deck crew did not see him until the airman released his package of green dye. A spot of the ocean suddenly changed color, and one lone man in a "Mae West" was sighted floating in the middle....

During the last run we discovered the danger of uncharted reefs. Our sound heads struck bottom when the boat went aground during an attack in Sarangani Strait; that memory did not make me feel relaxed and comfortable. Tizard Reef was a series of rocky ledges sticking above the level of the South China Sea. There were narrow openings between the ledges of protruding rock, but we did not know which one might be a channel into a protected anchorage. There were reasons to believe enemy merchantmen were hidden in those reefs. Navy Intelligence frequently provided us information about ship movements, and our course was suddenly shifted to these tiny specks of land. We stayed in the open sea and peered into the shallow water and protruding rock ledges. While moving slowly around the reef, the periscope watch searched the little inlets of water....

...the periscope watch spotted a tanker resting at anchor between two reefs in very shallow water. She was loaded and low in the water with very little freeboard. No visible escorts or naval vessels were protecting her. However, it was not prudent to attack on the surface; a destroyer might be around a rock protrusion waiting to strike us during an unprotected moment. The water depth was too shallow for us to get close to the vessel. She was sitting at an angle of about 165 degrees with the stern pointed toward us. From that angle it presented a very small target. The Captain used the periscope to estimate the distance, but finally surfaced enough to allow the SJ radar antenna to clear the water. The range was 3400 yards. It was a long shot, but it was the closest range we could safely find. The order was given to prepare Number 3 torpedo tube for firing. There was no rush or suspense; both our boat and the target were standing still. The Captain crisply said, "Fire three." The bow of the boat lurched slightly as the torpedo left the tube and started toward the target. Because of the distance, a long time delay was expected. Most of us were counting the seconds under our breath, and waiting; there was no explosion. The

Captain watched on the periscope for a time. Impatiently, he gave the order to surface and move closer. As the lookouts got to the bridge, they could see the ship through the darkness; we got a beautiful pip on the radar. Suddenly, the ship dropped out of sight. The lookouts saw her go and our pip on the radar faded and disappeared.

Apparently, our one torpedo hit directly on the stern and followed up the keel into the very bowels of the vessel. There was no explosion, fire, or noise. The 9000-ton tanker...just disappeared. A feeling of pride and excitement filled the boat; it was an excellent shot....

Two large tankers, escorted by two destroyers, passed us heading north, but we could not close on them. This route served as a lifeline for Japan; most of the oil and rubber for their war machine came from Java, Sumatra, Borneo and other southern islands. A very effective convoy procedure protected merchantmen moving precious commodities north along this route. The cargo ships stayed in the shallow water, only a few hundred feet from shore. The escorts, usually destroyers or destroyer escorts, stayed on the outboard side and formed a protective shield. An attack against the merchantmen could only come from the seaward side; the destroyers kept a vigilant watch seaward for submarines....

When a convoy was expected the little vessel pinged its sound gear almost continuously to locate possible American submarines. Staying out of range of the electronic pings was not difficult; our soundman notified the conning tower of any change in the patrol boat's direction. It was easy to follow them by the rhythmic sound of their screws pounding the water. The periscope watch checked occasionally to verify their location....The control room gang named the little sub-chaser Jojo; we almost developed a feeling of fellowship, as the game of hide and seek went on day after day.

...the Captain sighted two larger ships moving north. He called submerged battle stations. The crew waited, quietly and expectantly, hoping the convoy would not change course. Our boat was at periscope depth and almost dead in the water....

"Fire one, Fire two, Fire three!"

"B-O-O-M!"

The fish had barely left the tubes when a loud explosion vibrated our boat from end to end. An aerial bomb had dropped on us; the convoy was escorted by an airplane as well as the surface men-of-war. The bomb dropped below us and the explosion blew our boat toward the surface. The explosion and sudden vibration of our boat in the water startled most of us; for a moment the officers and crew were almost motionless.

The Captain did not want to give away our location. He made the attack without the use of radar....He had not seen the big bomber when making the final readings before the attack. When our torpedo left the tube, a trail of bubbles rose to the surface. The airplane followed the bubbles that led directly to our location. The bomb landed very close to us.

As soon as the third torpedo left the tube, the Captain raised the periscope to watch. The Japanese bomber was almost immediately overhead. His usual calm measured voice was a little high pitched as he almost shouted, "There is a plane! It's diving!"

It was at that moment the explosion occurred, and the submarine shuddered and bobbed in the water. The fury of the explosion shook the handles of the periscope out of the Captain's hands...."Down scope."

The boat was already under the water; the order was given to "Take her deep."...we went down at a sharp angle and hit bottom at 180 feet. A familiar scratching sound filled the boat; we slid along for a distance on the sand. At that moment, some of us heard a dull explosion in the distance; another of our torpedos hit the mark. The soundman reported a rumbling sound; our target was breaking up....

In less than a minute, our role was changed from the attacker to the attacked....The second ship in the convoy was a Japanese destroyer. The airplane had clearly identified our location; in moments the escort reached our diving position. A series of depth charges exploded as the destroyer ran our full length a hundred feet above us. The screw noise of the speeding destroyer was nearly deafening. After that flurry of activity, everything was quiet. Soon the depth charges and the noise of the attacker's screws disappeared....our Executive officer gave the order to ease up from the bottom and head toward the open sea....

In early afternoon, December 14, a big convoy of warships was sighted through the periscope....The Captain did not even call battle stations. He decided the convoy was more than we could handle and went deeper to avoid detection.

After waiting for the convoy to pass, the Captain prepared to surface; he wanted to report their course and location....The order was to raise the SD mast and give one quick pulse but not to leave it on. Excessive radar would reveal our location electronically to this giant naval force....we started to surface. Jack had a hunch and pulsed the SD again, though the Captain had given specific orders not to use it any more. There was a pip about an inch high. Jack yelled, "Contact SD." Instead of opening the hatch the order was given to go down again rapidly. The Officer of the Deck saw the plane through the scope before we dropped out of sight; it was a four-engine bomber. The Captain did not say a word to Jack for disobeying orders and taking another look. There are a lot of submariners alive because Jack had that hunch.

It was typhoon season in the South China Sea. In addition, the radio news reported earthquake activity somewhere near Japan. The combined action of the earthquake and violent winds created huge waves; they beat us constantly when we were on the surface. If our course was across the waves the boat would pitch fore and aft; if we dropped in a trough the rolling waves would rock us vigorously port to starboard. The spray from these tremendous waves splashed over the air induction vents; the water tumbled down into the engine room and the mess hall. The water splashing on the mess hall deck ran like rivulets across the linoleum, splashed over the low metal guards along the sides, and tumbled into the bilges. Very few of us were hungry, but the cook tried to serve a light meal of juice and finger food. One of the loaded mess hall tables suddenly collapsed. Pitchers of tomato juice fell to the deck and splashed in all directions; some of us sitting on the mess benches were saturated with it. Eventually, I joined others sitting on the floor; we minced at our juice and crackers and ignored the water that ran under our legs and soaked our cut-off shorts. The messboys broke out the bologna; they slapped slices of it on bread with artificial butter....The Captain tried to submerge to get away from the storm. When the boat was at the 60-foot periscope level the bow occasionally dropped into a trough caused by the enormous waves. This kind of weather contin-ued for several days; it was difficult to stay on the surface long enough to get a battery charge. Radio skeds reported a U.S.

destroyer escort, caught in the heavy waves, had cracked like an egg shell....The drenched men topside hung on to keep from being washed overboard....

Reprinted from *Pacific Patrol. A WW II Submarine Saga* with permission of Marion L. Shinn, author. 79

Guavina battle flag

• • •

DID YOU KNOW THAT...

Captain McVay of the Indianapolis was told only: ...Sometime tonight, a small but vital and top-secret cargo will be loaded aboard. You will sail tomorrow morning at high speed...to Tinian, where your cargo will be taken off by others. You will not be told what the cargo is, but it is to be guarded even after the life of your vessel. If she goes down, save the cargo at all costs, in a lifeboat, if necessary....The cargo will be accompanied en route by two army officers and will be guarded by your regular Marine detachment. No other persons must go near it. One small package must be kept as far from the crew as possible, preferably in officers' country, and the Army officers with it.

July 16...about 4:00A.M. two Army trucks came alongside, one of them containing a large crate. The other seemed empty, except for a small metal cylinder....A huge gantry crane waddled down the pier out of the night....took a work party ashore and quickly threw straps around the big crate. The towering gantry easily lifted it aboard and deposited it gently on the hangar deck amidships. Shipfitters quickly secured it to the deck, and a Marine guard surrounded it.

...The men paid little attention to the small cylinder in the other truck. Two sailors slipped a crowbar through a ring on the cylinder, put the bar on their shoulders and carried it up the gangway and into officers' country. A couple of Army officers...sauntered behind it....a couple of shipfitters...welded pad eyes to the deck in the center of the cabin and fitted them with steel straps on hinges. The strange cylinder was placed in the metal, the straps were closed over it. Major Furman secured them with a padlock and dropped the key into his pocket.

...Thursday, July 26, just 10 days and 5,000 miles out of San Francisco, the Indianapolis made landfall on Tinian....The Indianapolis eased in toward shore and dropped the hook about a thousand yards out. This was the moment all hands had been waiting for, and as many as possible crowded topside to see what would happen. They still hoped the secret of the strange cargo might be divulged.

An LCT, flat, low and ugly, waddled alongside....Shipfitters cut away the deck fittings, and the crate was lowered over the side into the LCT.

A plane bearing Captain Parsons touched down on one of the airstrips as the unloading was completed....Captain Parsons' most important job awaited him. It was he who went along on the Enola Gay, with Col. Tibbets at the controls....Captain Parsons...assembled the bomb while the plane was en route from Tinian to Hiroshima, and armed it before turning it over to the bombardier for the actual drop. The experts had decided against assembling the bomb before the B-29 took off, for fear it might crash at the end of the runway and blow Tinian right off the map. For the ship, a small part in history was over, and every man on board felt it. Nobody knew exactly what their mission had been, but they all felt they had accomplished it efficiently.

Reprinted from *Abandon Ship! Death of the USS Indianapolis*, with permission of the author, Richard F. Newcomb.[80]

D ★ LET US

U. S. WOMEN'S ARMY
AUXILIARY CORPS
(WAAC) 05-1942 BECAME WOMEN'S ARMY CORPS (WAC)
07-01-1943 150,000 ENLISTED 8000 SERVED IN EUROPE
5500 IN THE PACIFIC
BECAME PART OF REGULAR ARMY 10-20-1978

U. S. ARMY
NURSE CORPS
60,000+ SERVED IN EVERY THEATRE OF WAR
LANDED IN NORTH AFRICA & EUROPE
200+ LOST THEIR LIVES

One of ten panels on monument, Chicopee, MA.
Courtesy Delfo Barabani

DOROTHY AHLSWEDE BAKER

LUMBERTON, NC

Army Nurse Corps, 1st Lt., 1945-57
Basic Training: Camp McCoy, Wisconsin
Duty in Atlantic and Pacific

Our hospital ship, The Wisteria, took German POWs back to Germany and brought our patients home. One time, when almost at our pier in New York, a patient could see his house in Brooklyn and said, "I can swim faster than this old ship!" He jumped overboard and started swimming home. The skipper didn't take too kindly to that, had him rescued and brought back on the ship to wait his turn.

Dorothy Ahlswede Baker

On another trip, my friend, a nurse, and a doctor, fell in love on the ship and decided to get married in New York. Upon returning from a shopping trip in New York City for her wedding things, we found The Wisteria anchored in the middle of the harbor; we had to take a tender to it and climb up a rope ladder (called Jacob's Ladder). The bride lost her balance and fell into the water. The box with her wedding dress started floating away. One person grabbed her and another grabbed the box. After a good bath, all was well and we all attended the wedding in The Little Church Around the Corner in New York City the next day.

For six months I was a nurse on a train carrying war brides from the East Coast to the West Coast. We helped with the children and treated minor illnesses. A Red Cross worker or the bride's new family would meet us at each stop.

My Red-Letter Day was on a troopship, The Fred C. Ainsworth, in the Pacific, when I met a young surgeon who would later be my husband. We worked together in the hospital on this ship. Next year we will celebrate our 50th wedding anniversary!

• • •

DID YOU KNOW THAT...

In 1946, the Queen Mary made its first of 13 "Operation Diaper" trips. The ship carried more than 20,000 brides, as well as babies, from Southampton, England, to G.I. veterans in the U.S.81

DORIS GREGORY BECCIO

MARIPOSA, CALIFORNIA

Army Nurse Corps, 1st Lt., 1943-46
Basic Training: Camp Blanding, Florida
Duty in South Pacific

On Halloween night the 227th Station Hospital boarded a small ship which had seen better days as a Dutch freighter. This must be a joke, we thought. Could this little tub take us across the Pacific? It took 30 days, but it did get us to New Guinea, and we were actually sorry to leave it as it was our last tie to civilization.

Doris Gregory Beccio

New Guinea was a place most of us had never even heard of. It seemed hostile with its night-time jungle noises, steamy heat, bigger-than-life insects, snakes, lizards, and all manner of creepy-crawly things. There had been many fierce battles here, fought valiantly by the Americans and Australians against formidable Japanese forces. The enemy was finally vanquished and the Americans began their push north toward the Philippines. Our hospital remained there for a year, caring for patients who were suffering from malaria, jungle rot, and other tropical diseases.

Sam, our hospital sanitarian, was in charge of providing safe drinking water and preventing the spread of tropical diseases. He and his small cadre oil-sprayed every pot hole, rut, and rusting can containing stagnant water to kill the larvae of the Anopholes mosquito, which carried malaria. He checked to see that we took our daily dose of atabrine (malaria preventive). He lectured us on the importance of using mosquito nets on our cots, buttoning shirts at neck and wrists, tucking pants into boots after dusk. He became known affectionately as Sam, the Malaria Man. All of this paid off handsomely. Only one person in our outfit got malaria—Sam!

We worked long twelve-hour shifts, seven days a week, with only one day off a month. We lived in tents or grass shacks, used outdoor latrines, and took cold showers. Food was terrible. Our diet consisted of canned bully beef or mutton from Australia, tinned beet greens, dehydrated lumpy gray potatoes, powdered eggs, and coffee. Nothing fresh. I lost thirty pounds.

Living quarters, New Guinea

But there were good times, too. Occasionally we were invited aboard Navy ships for real food: steak, baked potatoes, apple pie ala-mode! But not often enough! My friend dated a well-known (at the time) singer who was a special service officer stationed nearby. He was responsible for escorting USO entertainers to various bases. Through his efforts some very popular Hollywood stars visited our hospital, including Gary Cooper, John Wayne, and Jack Benny. Our CO invited a group of us for dinner at his quarters while the Benny group was there. Jack Benny was seated next to me and kept asking, "Girlie, will you light my cigar?" Mrs. Douglas MacArthur also visited our hospital in New Guinea, and thanked us, on behalf of her husband, for the work we were doing.

In early January, 1945, our unit went to Leyte Island in the Philippines. Here we began treating many battle casualties. We also experienced nightly air raids. I was on night duty, and one night couldn't extinguish the Coleman lantern quickly enough when the air raid alert sounded. I threw a blanket over it, and it caught fire. Several patients jumped out of bed to put out the flames.

Doris Gregory Beccio — Manila, Philippines

Soon we were in Subic Bay on the island of Luzon. Lew Ayres, the film actor, was chaplain's assistant on my ward. He was wonderful with patients, spending hours talking with them and comforting them.

From there we went by truck across the Bataan Peninsula to Manila, where we witnessed close at hand the battle for that city. Our hospital soon overflowed with seriously wounded. For months there was no let-up. We worked round the clock. Finally, when the area was secured, we explored what was left of Manila. When the fighting wound down, we were assigned to care for some of the POWs who had been interned at Santo Tomas for three years. They were extremely weak, malnourished, and ill.

The war in the Pacific drew to a close and we were sent to Korea, along with the occupation forces. After three months we came home.

• • •

DID YOU KNOW THAT...

Girls sending kisses on their letters to boyfriends or husbands found them going by slower mail. The lipstick smeared and caused V-Mail equipment to be stopped and cleaned. V-Mail was light-weight letter paper designed to speed mail to the servicemen. Thirty-five million V-Mail letters were sent in 1943.[82]

JOHN CROSSMAN
GREENDALE, WISCONSIN

Army, 148th General Hospital Unit, Tech 4, 1941-45
Basic Training: Camp Shelby, Mississippi
Duty in Hawaii; Saipan

We were the largest hospital in the western Pacific area and were there prior to the invasion of the Philippines, Guam and other activities in the Central Pacific.

While on Saipan our patients were from the Army, Air Force, Navy, Marines, plus civilians and some liberated Prisoners of War. We had a number of patients and casualties from the Air Force, as Saipan was the base for the B-29 bombing flights to Japan; there were a certain number of accidents in the take-offs, landings and incidents enroute for the airmen.

We served as the principal hospital for the treatment of the wounded during the invasion of Iwo Jima and Okinawa, Guam and other Pacific Island invasions. Wounded were brought to our hospital by any means of transportation available, ships or planes. We then evacuated the patients back to Hawaii and San Francisco, by hospital ships or planes, for further treatment.

On October 7, 1942, at the Sixth Annual Reunion of the 148th General Hospital in Arlington, President George Bush wrote: "The record of the men and women who served in the Mariana Islands with the 148th General Hospital is a lasting testimony to the finest ideals of service and sacrifice. You used your life-saving skills to aid those who were injured in some of the toughest battles of the war—Tinian, Guam, Leyte, Peleliu, Angaur, Iwo Jima, and Okinawa. Having served in the Pacific Theatre during that time, I have a special appreciation of the dedication of those who worked under very difficult circumstances to treat those who were wounded while fighting to preserve our freedom. You can be proud of the significant contributions that the 148th made to the Allied victory.

"As our Nation pauses to commemorate the 50th Anniversary of World War II, I join with Americans across our land in expressing appreciation to each of you who answered our country's call to duty. We pay special tribute to those who made the ultimate sacrifice, knowing that many lives were spared because of medical units such as yours. On behalf of a grateful Nation, I salute you for your service to your fellow-man...."

• • •

DID YOU KNOW THAT...

Tokyo Rose, who made propaganda broadcasts for Japan and taunted GIs about home and girlfriends dating other men, was an American citizen, born and educated in the U.S. After the war she was charged with treason.[83]

ELAINE GOLDSBY
SHREVEPORT, LOUISIANA

Army Medical Corps, Captain, Nurse, 1943-45
Basic Training: Ft. Jackson, SC
Duty in Africa and Italy

I had some great and hectic experiences, many rewarding experiences, but what I saw so disillusioned me that it was years before I could think of anything good.

In Africa I saw soldiers lined up a half mile long waiting to go into a tent where an Arab was selling his daughter for sex. It made me sick, and the commanding officers did nothing to stop it.

In Italy I returned from detached duty with the 8th Army to my General Hospital to suddenly be called to the Chief Nurse's Office and falsely accused of hatched-up situations that were horrifying. I was given the option of taking a transfer or be court marshalled. The Adjutant who had been sent on to the post while I was gone told me to apply for transfer immediately, which I did. The Adjutant never spoke to me again until my transfer came through—it was when he brought me my orders that I found out that the Commanding Officer and Chief Nurse had confiscated silver and valuable objects of art and were living together as man and wife in a villa in Leghorn.

Because the Adjutant sat with me in the messhall and we talked, they thought he was telling me about them. I knew nothing.

It was not until years later that I was working at the V.A. Hospital in Shreveport, LA, that that same Adjutant General came there to work following a heart attack, that I learned the truth of the whole matter.

The Chief Nurse landed in Leavenworth for selling drugs (I had a card from her). The Commanding Officer took his life. Details of this whole story are unbelievable, which points up that our battle is between Good and Evil, regardless of where it is found.

· · ·

DID YOU KNOW THAT...

Fifty-four men died in WW II from mustard gas carried by an American ship. Fifteen more deaths were caused wholly or partly by exposure.

The John Harvey, secretly carrying one hundred tons of mustard to be stockpiled for retaliation in case Hitler used chemicals, was docked at Bari, Italy. German planes, with the harbor brightly lighted, made a night air strike.

Another ship, carrying ammunition and explosives, was hit, with the resulting explosion and fires blowing up the John Harvey. The mixture of mustard with the oil-covered water caused serious problems with men thrown or forced overboard.

During this disaster seventeen ships were sunk and eight others damaged. Over one thousand men were killed or missing. A conservative estimate of civilian casualties was over a thousand.

With the cargo of the John Harvey being very secretive and the hospital staff not being informed, the men were not treated for chemicals and many suffered extreme pain and died needlessly. But while care givers were kept in the dark, Axis Sally knew the situation and in each of her radio broadcasts taunted the Allies for killing their own men by poison gas.[84]

JEANNE H. LESSING

SIDNEY, OHIO

Army Nurse Corps, 2nd Lt., 1944-46
Basic Training: Camp Carson, Colorado
Duty in Pacific

Basic Training had everything the men did, except shooting guns and crawling under wires. We did have to climb rope netting, as if abandoning a ship. We had sit-ups before breakfast, went marching, had helmets and gas masks. We went to dances in field boots.

On the train to California I started feeling faint (hadn't eaten since breakfast and this was dinnertime), so I told my friend I was going to sit on the floor. She said, "You can't sit on the floor in your Class A uniform." So she got me back to a seat on the train, and all the fellows were laughing at me cause they thought I had a hangover.

From Camp Stoneman, California, we left on a Matsonian Luxury Liner, without the luxury. In San Francisco Bay we hit a storm and I was seasick; that seasickness continued for at least two of the four weeks it took to get to the Philippines. We were in a convoy to avoid the Japanese submarines, zigzagging all over the Pacific.

During a boat drill another girl and I, both of us still sick, were assisted with our lifejackets, but then we lay down on our bunks and decided it would be easier to go down with the ship. Our cabins had three layers of bunks, six to a cabin.

When arriving in the Philippines, I had pneumonia, probably from sleeping up on deck because of the heat. Every time we went under a cloud we'd get rained on. I was on a stretcher on a PT boat to go ashore. We were laid along a curb on a street, and while waiting to be carried into Santo Tomas, a University converted into a hospital, a soldier came up to me and asked if I was a battle casualty. Almost was, as the wardmen carrying me up a long flight of steps dropped the stretcher! I spent several weeks there but didn't miss anything, as our hospital wasn't built yet. It consisted of long barracks built on stilts, open to the air on the sides, and no doors or screens; wooden sidewalks connected buildings. Our living quarters were the same.

Our 312 General Hospital Unit was supposed to be the farthest from the front lines. Ordinarily there is a chain of hospitals, MASH, Field Hospital, and then the General Hospital. We discovered we were "it." One night we were out with a bunch of fellows, feeling sorry for them because they were going up to the front lines. The next night they were on our doorsteps; the front line was only a mile away.

In order to go overseas, my nearsighted friend and I had to find a colonel, who would cross out our eye exams. Did have to get our prescription lens in our gas masks, though.

Until our hospital, on the edge of Manila, was built, we were quartered in an abandoned Tuberculosis hospital. One night a gal got in bed and discovered a rat in with her; she had forgotten to tuck her mosquito netting in that morning. Also, we never put our boots on without turning them upside down first.

While waiting for the hospital to be finished, we spent our time going into Manila, either hitch-hiking or finding a fellow with a jeep. One night we went floating out in Manila Bay in some rubber boats, dodging the sunken Japanese ships which were only partially submerged.

As soon as we arrived, the fellows were on our doorstep for dates. Several of my friends and I became acquainted with the 11 Corps Artillery, who were "roughing" it in a Filipino doctor's house with a swimming pool. Nurses were officers, and as such, were not to go out with enlisted men; some did, however, but had to be careful not to be caught.

We wore tan pin-striped seersucker uniforms; also had cotton tan slacks and olive drab and tan dresses.

I had the post-op surgical ward. We took care of Americans mostly, but did have some Dutch escapees. They had converted their money to diamonds and swallowed them to escape with their money. One day we had a Filipino guerrilla who had been shot in the leg and stuffed the hole with tobacco. In admitting him, the plug came out and we had to scurry to get transfusions, etc. While in Manila, the nearby Filipino women did our laundry, washing them in a river on rocks. They did excellent ironing. We stood in mess lines to eat.

I met my husband to be, a major in the Field Artillery 11 Corps, on a blind date. His headquarters showed movies outside, and we took chairs out and watched, as the mosquitoes swarmed. We all had yellow complexions from the Atabrine, taken to prevent malaria.

We worked in Manila until the bomb was dropped in Japan. Then we flew to Japan in November, 1945, in suntans (typical army); Japan is like Minnesota in the winter! Our pilot was feeling no pain from partying, and we landed at Hiroshima, which was forbidden because the airstrip was thought to still be too soft. Our plane was a cargo plane, so we all sat lined up along the sides with our luggage piled in the middle. We were taken to an island off the coast of Japan, near Kyoto, called Eta Jima. We were there over Christmas. The building, gray concrete, was the former West Point of Japan. Not suited for women! We lived in large dorms with just a coal stove for heat. We had to bathe and wash our hair outside at large bin-type affairs, very spartan; had to tell each other when we were getting "blue." We slept in our sleeping bags on the beds.

In January we went to work in a Japanese hospital in Nagoya, turned over to the Americans. Had a few Japanese nurses helping. They had to be taught to use two sheets on a bed; they only used one on the bottom.

While in Hiroshima for a few days we went out in the rubble and looked for souvenirs. No one warned us about radioactivity!

My husband said that while they were in New Guinea and were going out on patrol, the Chaplain, a Catholic priest, wanted to go along. They outfitted him with a pistol for self-defense. Upon encountering a group of Japanese soldiers, the priest captured one and they took him back to headquarters.

• • •

DID YOU KNOW THAT...

Detonators for anti-tank mines were to be used for the first time with Patton in the invasion of Sicily. Americans planted them, but Germans came along with metal detectors and dug them up. Eight or ten hours later the Pentagon had a telegram saying to stop production.

Robert Frick, Sidney, Ohio, was working as Chief Engineer for Wald in Maysville, Kentucky, and helped to develop these detonators. A small brass pin controlled the ignition. Walking over it would not set it off, but 300 pounds or more would shear the pin, with contact and explosion resulting.

Wald engineers also designed the tooling for the rifle grenade, which was a cut-down version of the bazooka. The grenades would penetrate one-inch thick armor plate on a tank. In January, 1945, they made their 5th million shell.

They also made tracer inserts for a 40 mm shell, primarily used by the Navy for firing at aircraft. Every eighth shell was a tracer. When it was fired, there was a stream of fire so the men could see where it was going.

The company made at least a half million threaded sleeves that were used in bomb casings for the chemicals of a 100-lb. mustard bomb.

They were also working on a 20 mm shell that would shoot through the center of the propeller of a P-39.[85]

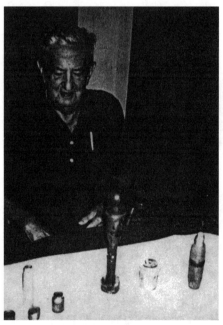

Robert Frick

MAHLON S. SHARP

E. LANSING, MICHIGAN; ST. PETERSBURG, FLORIDA

Medical Corps, 1st Lt.-Major; Unit Commander; 1941-45
Duty in Pacific

Arriving in North Australia in late August, 1944, we feared that we might stay there forever. We all were bored. With only one small town nearby, there was little activity except of our own making. On one several-hour march through the desolate North New Queensland, among scrub brush and stunted trees, several of us had stepped over a large fallen tree trunk when a man from the rural south, who was accustomed to using his eyes in wild wooded country, called out: "Captain, did you notice that tree is really a huge snake?" City boy me had, of course, not recognized it, which gave them all a good laugh, which everyone needed. A few of the men killed it and dragged it many miles back to camp. For years I had a photograph of it draped over the shoulders of ten men with it touching the ground on each side.

Mahlon S. Sharp

We got used to seeing these huge reptiles and were told by the natives that they were called Brown Snakes or Rug Snakes and were a specie of Boa Constrictor.

We had gotten used to the strange Kukabera bird, whose call was much like a mule braying. The first green lizard that ran on its hind legs through the camp was chased up a tree and finally captured and killed so that it could be examined closely.

Rumors started flying! We were going to leave! A stir of excitement ran through the company like electricity. Finally all was ready. Down the coast we boarded an old Dutch Ship that had previously engaged in coastal China trade, mostly hauling Chinese and Malaysian slave labor. The Dutch officers and Malaysian crew spoke no English. The crew cooked over an open fire on a sheet metal plate in the center of a smelly hold where we were to be quartered. I and my officers were assigned cabins from which we could see the cleanly dressed ship's officers on an upper deck drinking beer. I stayed with my men until we were under way and then we all went on deck and slept there. We ate our own rations which we had carried with us. We were moving north inside the great Barrier Reef.

We presumed that we were soon off shore of New Guinea and proceeding Northwest. The naval crew were as young and green as we were. However, they were friendly and realized that we were all on the same side in this war. Their charts were made from air photos and lacked much in the way of navigational information. We approached the shore and the big doors swung open; a few trucks went down the ramp to completely disappear under water. Their drivers fortunately escaped. We didn't lose any men, but the rumor was that there was enough artillery, ammunition, and equipment on this mucky shore, deep out of sight, to fight a small battle.

We sensibly moved on and nosed into an area with more substantial beach. Our company assembled and one platoon was instructed to follow and maintain contact with the Battalion Aid Station.

The Commander of our Division, General Irving, was there. Confusion was rampant. Gen. Irving was doing his best to establish order out of chaos. The great Gen. MacArthur came up to him as I stood there and said, "Irving, organize your ground!"

It was so dark that we were slipping and sliding on a mountain trail, and I decided to stop. It was beastly hot, and I noticed some of the heavier medical equipment was being abandoned along the trail. We (sort of) dug into the soft earth and tried to sleep with our helmets on and mosquito netting draped over our faces.

The Headquarters of both the Division and the Medical Battalion moved into a place near where we had located. Having arrived first, we felt we had the best spot. It was on the side of a shallow stream. Our vehicles and rear echelon had caught up with us. In one of our trucks was a work of carpentry that was a marvel to behold. It was an 8-hole latrine box, carefully and beautifully made, sanded smooth, and with hinged lids, quite the pride of the company. It had been made during the unwanted leisure back in Australia. I was happy to find that it hadn't been abandoned. A large pit was dug on the top of a small hill, not far from the company area. A kitchen fly (large canvas square) was strung over it and we had the fanciest latrine in the area.

Flies were a very severe problem. One could hardly open one's mouth without getting it full of the huge, black, buzzing insects. I suggested that we see if we could find some abandoned Japanese oil near the airfield. One fellow returned with a barrel of aviation gasoline. I presumed that it would suppress the breeding of the larvae effectively, and it seemed to.

Our clean little creek had turned into a milky white bubbly sewer from the hundreds of men bathing. We all desperately wanted to get wet. It occurred to me that, with all of the mountains around us, there might be a spring somewhere feeding our dirty stream, and one of our men located it. A small detachment was sent to cut large bamboo six or eight feet tall and maybe four or five inches in diameter. Starting with the spring, the bamboo was strung at decreasing height and with a gradual down slope; the clean water was brought to the bank of the stream and a long line of men stood waiting to get wet. Soon a large puddle of mud developed under the popular shower. We sidetracked the bamboo stream at night to prevent erosion of the stream bank.

The company's sergeant knew that the air corps unit nearby had cement. They were not forced to wear shirts as we were, and we resented that. Anyway, a "night-time requisition" got us a bag of cement, and a platform was built under the little six-foot bamboo waterfall; it continued to bathe a long line of hot, dusty, sweaty men.

Sometimes out in the field it is felt that higher echelons of command exist just to make the lives of lower echelons a bit miserable. The Medical Battalion had an Adjutant who fell into that category. He felt that something must be done to control the swarms of flies and went from company to company inspecting their latrines. He had developed the nasty trick of lighting a piece of toilet paper and dropping it into the pit. He did this to our pit, and boom went the aviation gas! The kitchen fly flew off like a hot air balloon! It was funny seeing the canvas square floating off into the jungle! The box was wrecked and the three men using the latrine were badly burned and had to be sent off to the hospital. Burns in this terribly hot, humid climate were not minor matters as infection was almost a certainty.

When we were first on our way into this area, litter bearers were bringing in a Japanese soldier whom they found at the airfield. I asked why they were carrying him; they said apparently he couldn't move. I pricked him slightly with my trench knife and he moved! Stood up! Headquarters had expressed a strong desire for a prisoner, so they took him there.

By now a highway had been constructed from Humbolt Bay (Hollandia) to the airfield and on to the beach where we had landed. Rumor was that "MacArthur has a castle up on top of that mountain!" The men that believed this were cancelling their war bonds wholesale! I found this out by censoring their mail. I hated to read other people's mail, but orders were orders. I took my First Sergeant and two members of the company with me in a jeep and went up the mountain. We drove through a camp very much like our own. Their latrine didn't seem in the class with ours. They did have a refrigerator that apparently functioned on gas. The men were satisfied and returned liking our own camp somewhat better. I read of no more war bond cancellations.

One man appeared with a tiny pig. During the night an infantry man had tossed a grenade at a commotion in the brush. It had killed the sow and part of her litter. The survivor became a company pet. The affection lavished on this little creature was what might have been directed to the children of these men were they in more normal situations. One night a large snake smelled the little pig. Sensing its danger, it squealed loudly as the open mouth sought to engulf it. The men were incensed! How could anything threaten their pet who was fattening on G.I. rations! The 15- to 18-ft. reptile ended up in many small sections as the men vented their righteous anger with their bowie knives.

Lt. Elmer Harris was badly wounded. He, with a small detachment of men, were maintaining contact with the advancing infantry Battalion Aid men. They had holed up in a foxhole, of sorts, after a shell made a gaping hole in his right knee. It also killed one of the men with him. I found him at day-break in the shallow depression with his foot in his lap and his knee buried in the sand. There had been a great deal of hem-orrhage and he was in shock. He opened his eyes to greet me as I was straightening out his leg, splinting it, and hauling him onto a litter. After treating the wound and bandaging it tightly, I sent him back to the beach where, fortunately, there was still an LST loading as a hospital ship. I sent eight men to take turns carrying the litter. When they returned, I found their hands bleeding, blistered, and almost raw. Testimony, I thought, to their sense of duty and their caring for this man.

I tried to send two of the NCOs to Officer Candidate School, which would have meant better pay and position. They refused to go, preferring to stay in the company where they were.

Just before leaving this area I was promoted to field grade (Major) and transferred to Co. D which was the unit most like a hospital, but still an intrinsic part of the infantry division. At this time I had been overseas long enough to be due for rotation back to the U.S. I gave up my turn for an officer that was falling apart and needed to go much more than I. It was a long time before I could tell my wife that I could have come home sooner. My inner turmoil was based on several things: How would I feel for the rest of my life to have almost, but not quite, faced the real thing. Second, I had gotten my outfit ready to function in combat, and I would feel that I had abandoned them. Further, back with civilians I would be uncomfortable after coming so close to seeing what it was all about. Writing this 50 years later, I'm glad I stayed. With D-Day on Leyte and Mindoro, I was given another chance—I grabbed it!

We left from Humbolt Bay, New Guinea, with all of the excitement of what we knew was going to be a major operation, and it was, indeed. All of the medical units were accustomed to their armaments and there was no accidental firing as there had been on the previous operation. Our mission was to establish a beach aid station. On leaving New Guinea, I thought that we must be the most enormous Armada ever to be assembled, only to be joined by one of equal size from the Admiralties, containing the first Cavalry Division. My Company D had been transported this far in a big Army Transport ship; previously we had always been on landing crafts; only in drill had we climbed down cargo nets from such a large ship.

As we neared Leyte Harbor our enormous fleet was joined by an equally large force from the Hawaiian Islands. The Navy had been pounding the beach long ahead of us, including the use of rockets that we hadn't seen before. All personnel had been cleared from the bow of the ship because of the possibility of mines in the harbor. We all had the treat of fresh water showers, customary before an assault landing. As we scrubbed our bodies in the luxury, we couldn't but think that this was a treat to perhaps lessen the probability of infection if wounds were soon to occur.

My company was preceded by infantry, but it was now our turn. Instead of the usual LCIs we were expecting, a bigger ramp-type boat arrived, loaded with wounded. They were being loaded as we climbed down in and, with a minimum of equipment, prepared to get our feet wet in going ashore.

One of the early casualties who walked in had been shot right between the eyes, with the wound of exit just behind his right ear. The right optic nerve obviously was severed. His right eye reflected the bright sunlight.

To return to our shore station we were immobilized with 30 to 50 litter cases and a good number of walking wounded, waiting for transportation back to the ship. A 2-1/2 ton truck appeared loaded with corpses stacked like firewood.

We moved on inland to establish a platoon in a schoolhouse in the village of San Juan. We fed the natives and evicted them. I was fortunate to have a man along who spoke fluent Tagalog. Here we set up ward tents and received casualties which were occurring from action at the edge of the little town, not more than a few hundred yards away. The action was so close that the morphine they received from the aid man where they fell had not been absorbed, especially if they were in shock, as many of them were. It took us a case or two to learn not to repeat it too soon.

The company had twelve MDs, one dentist, and two administrative officers. A number of the officers had more surgical training than I had. Three or four litters became operating tables. I was the only one that had any experience with Sodium Pentothal. It had been introduced at Mayos and was starting to be used at the hospital when I left. I became anesthetist as the teams started Control Bleeding and also closing lacerated guts; the debriding of minor wounds could wait until morning and daylight. The civilians crowded around outside as they had during the shelling before our landing. This was evident by the human feces outside near the building.

Sweat dripped copiously from us all. The first few cans of ether were gone before I could decant them. Obviously, the army had not planned for the tropics.

During that crazy, busy night, the portable surgical hospital had, on the other edge of town, been over-run by Japanese. A number of them were killed. A number of that unit joined us as we had more than we could do.

The other portable surgical hospital, I later learned, had been functioning on board an LST in a crowded small dispensary, caring for shipboard casualties. A shell fired from shore had penetrated the hull, killing or wounding enough of the unit so that it didn't function ashore at all, making our job that much greater. The surgical treatments went on all that night. We were filling two or three large tents and hoping that we could evacuate them soon.

During the night a Japanese prisoner had been admitted, badly wounded. When his bleeding was controlled, he had been put with our GIs; later he died.

I had found an unexploded grenade near one of our occupied tents, and it worried me. I was reluctant to handle it or ask any of my men to touch it. So I asked the expert for suggestions. He didn't hesitate; he asked one of my men to dig a deep hole, got in it and carefully placed the grenade in the bottom. Then we filled the hole in. I would have gladly given him a medal for that little job.

We leapfrogged across the Ormac Corridor, one platoon at a time. We were trying not to become immobilized and were lucky as the casualty rate was not great. Something bad seemed to happen everywhere we were, but it waited to happen until after we had left. Other units called us lucky; we didn't talk about it. Corps clearing was supposed to relieve us and, indeed they did replace our unit on the beach. A bulldozer had, in face of fire, buried a Jap concrete pillbox. When they dug themselves out, they over-ran the Corps Co. that had replaced us on the beach. Many were killed, including unarmed casualties helpless on litters or cots. This further burdened our units.

As in other times, the best laid plans often go astray. The Leyte operation had called for air evacuation of casualties on D-day plus one. This did not occur. We landed in hot dust that caked on our skin, only to have a heavy deluge of rains a few days later. P-38s (I think they were) were setting in the only landing field on Leyte in about a foot of water. That is the only landing place other than Tacloban. This had more far-reaching effects than building up masses of casualties. We didn't have the air cover that was planned. That made us more than ever dependent on the naval planes. We often were overjoyed to see these planes when we heard that things were not going well at the front.

The farthest that my whole company went was almost the western end of the Ormoc Corridor. We were located in a roofless church and had some ward tents set up when the storm hit. It took away all of our canvas, but fortunately, the poles had been anchored to the 2-1/2 ton truck bumpers and mostly remained standing. We were holding sick call on the natives and were popular because we had a very bright, energetic man that had been born in the Philippines who was fluent in Tagalog, even though he had lived in Chicago for most of his life. I asked him once what he had done before the army, and he told me that he had organized a union of the Filipinos in the area. He charged them all a yearly rate, for which they received an invitation to a party once a year and occasionally helped them with employment problems. He said that he made a good income from this activity and thoroughly enjoyed it.

One of our admissions was a woman who had been living with a Japanese officer and was pregnant by him. His farewell had been to stab her in the belly into the uterus. Having had the experience in my young life of doing a fair number of C

Sections, I couldn't believe that she hadn't hemorrhaged to death. I did a hysterectomy and closed her abdomen. No temperature, no distention, no vomiting. She did receive 1000 cc of fluid; when we figured that it was time for her to void, I watched her silently from a litter ten or twenty feet away in semi-darkness. The corpsman offered her a bedpan and when he finally made her understand what it was for, she pushed him to one side and, unaided, got up from the cot, walked outside the church, squatted, voided copiously, and came back in to lie down, as much as to say, "Why would anyone ever want to pee in a pan?" The next day or two she ate a full meal and we sent her home. It was here that a tragic incident occurred.

I was sleeping with one eye open and a number of headquarters personnel nearby. I heard a pistol shot very near and sat up wide-eyed. One of the company sergeants, a few feet from me, had awakened and saw a scantily clad figure climbing in the dimly illuminated window, shot and killed him. He was dead on the ground, a thin, poorly nourished Filipino that had been allowed to stay around for errands and his English. He had gone outside to the latrine and decided it was shorter to come back in by the window—fatal error! The NCO, who had fired the shot, was devastated. I reassured him that his quick alert action could well have saved our lives.

I stayed up most of a night with a 2nd Lt., 19th Infantry. Someone had found in his pocket a picture of his two small children and placed it on his chest where he could see it in his few moments of occasional consciousness. I had visited him while leaning on the rail of the A.P.A. as we approached the harbor. He noticed my Beta Theta Pi ring and announced that he was a brother.

With the flood of casualties that were so hungry and shockingly exposed for days to rain, lying part of the time in water, they were heroically cared for by a battalion surgeon by the name of Rosencranz, a Jew. He should have had some kind of award for working under the worst possible conditions and undoubtedly saving a number of lives. I pointed this out to some of my friends who were so critical of the two Jewish MDs but who had hung psychoneurosis tags on themselves and didn't come with us on the operation.

I received orders that one platoon was to report aboard the ship in the harbor that received a great deal of attention from the Japanese planes. I decided that I had to go with the platoon on this new operation, called The Western Vasayan Task Force, and chose six other officers by their previous surgical training. This included a captain who had recently had a refresher course in traumatic surgery under a "hot shot" in New York. He also was showing signs of coming down with the blahs. Some of the alcohol that we had landed with was disappearing, and I knew what was happening to it. It went splendidly with the "battery acid" that we all drank as our nearly only source of Vitamin C.

I don't remember exactly how we got back through the mud to the staging area, but we did and loaded half of the company supplies and personnel. Many had to go with our vehicles, but the two of us could go on either an LCI (Landing Craft Infantry), which was a very small target from the air, or an LST, which was 300 or more feet in length, carrying aviation gas and lots of ammo. We had practiced on both so that we knew their characteristics.

The LCI had scarcely room to lie down, even on the narrow decks, and when they poked their bow into the beach, they would run two narrow ramps, not unlike ladders, onto the sand or water, depending on how close it got to shore. We voted these down and decided to go for it, a bunk with possibly a sheet on it; solid comfort, not that sleeping on a litter was that bad, but come what may.

We knew that we were a big and desirable target from the air and also were very explosive, a quick way to go and less messy. We sat in the harbor for several days and found that we were one of thirty very similar LSTs. We really didn't mind as we were out of the mud and, if our premonitions were at all correct, something exciting was about to happen.

I think that we carried our own chow iron, meaning canned, and of course, had our canteens and mess kits on our web belts. Med officers also had side arms, as well as a modicum of medical equipment. I made rounds of my men and their vehicles; mostly they slept in their trucks, usually with some comfort articles stowed away. Having a big vehicle at times was a definite advantage.

At last we were signaled to get underway. A huge cruiser hove into sight and I was told by our young and inexperienced captain that it was to be our Flag Ship and all of the army and

Navy Brass involved in the operation was aboard her. When we moved out we were not unlike a mother duck followed by her little ones. Our ship was one of the bigger "little" ones. We watched the shoreline of Leyte go by and knew that the straits, a narrow, rather long passage between Leyte and the next more southern island, was just ahead of us.

Shortly after we had entered the most narrow area of the channel, two Kamikazes took off from the south of Cebu, the next island west of Leyte, and crashed the bridge of the cruiser. We later learned that many of the high command of both Navy and Army were killed. The whole flotilla stopped and the cruiser turned and left us; it was replaced by a destroyer. We passed Los Negros, after rounding Cebu, without further incident.

The day had passed and it became very dark. No navigational lights were shone; care was taken that no lights were on the open deck. Quite suddenly a very loud crashing boom was heard; other than the flash of a big gun, nothing was visible; we all held our breath. Shortly there was another similar crashing sound a long distance away on the horizon; a huge burst of flame appeared. A Naval officer told us that the destroyer had fired and exploded a Japanese ship, probably wooden, judging from the rapidity with which it burned.

We passed other islands and often there were lights ashore. We all knew, of course, that we were steadily getting closer to Manila and Luzon. We also knew that Luzon was heavily occupied with probably the largest force outside of Japan itself. Here also was Corregidor, once the great United States Naval Base, second only to Pearl Harbor.

Tensions increased as daylight dawned, and we could detect our approach to land. We had been briefed on this landing operation and presumed that this was the dry island of Mindoro. This whole operation had been to give us a usable land base where our planes could land and take off without encountering a field covered by water a foot deep. That was the reason we were carrying landing matting, the quick way to make a surface suitable for a plane to land. It was also the reason that we were heavily loaded with drums and drums of aviation gas and ammo. All of our guns on vehicles and on the ships were manned for the landing.

The LSTs were beaching in three columns of ten. We were the tenth in the middle column. Suddenly out of the rising sun came three Zeros, just slightly above the horizon. We stood open-mouthed as every gun of our forces opened up on them. They were, I think, a little tardy and so the best targets left were the last ships in each column. The plane headed for us, disintegrated, and we were showered with its fragments. The two ships on each side of us disappeared and their remains added to the debris coming down on us.

I had decided when we first boarded that there would be four thicknesses of bulkhead if I were at the foot of the ladder to the bridge. It was fortunate that I was there; almost at once there was a call to the bridge, so I climbed up to find the small housing awash with blood and the Helmsman lying in it. He was gushing from his femoral artery but still conscious. I immediately put a finger on the pumping vessel and quickly withdrew it as I contacted a piece of very hot steel. I put my finger back above the fragment and held it until someone brought me my aid pack. I clamped it and don't remember if I tied it or just left the clamp on. Anyway, he was soon going over the side in a basket; one of the LSTs had been designated Hospital. There were other casualties among the vehicles and their personnel on the top deck, but none below. One man raised his head, already with a cigarette in his mouth and a plasma unit running into his veins. He almost had a smile on his face.

We were soon set up on shore and the ships all left. Matting was rapidly being put down, and it wasn't long before we saw some of our own planes landing and taking off. Our casualties were not heavy and we growled about being on half rations. Not long after we set up, a big blonde Swede came in with some kind of minor injury. I don't know how I learned that he was a baker and knew how to make bread, but he started baking; we did have flour and yeast. The aroma spread and it was not long before men from other outfits came calling. We hung on to him as long as possible as we had a field range and plenty of flour and yeast.

We seldom were without attention from the Zeros, small bombers carrying small bombs. They flew day and night and except for the sound of our firing at them, there was no alarm or anti-aircraft sirens, which elsewhere we had accustomed ourselves to hearing as a signal to seek shelter. There always was a cold chill associated with the sound, be it on shipboard or land. In a few weeks we got so we didn't really pay enough attention to the usually solitary Jap planes.

A tanker came in and was hit by one of the Jap planes that buzzed about like mosquitos. It blazed mightily in the night sky. We noticed an increase in carrier-based planes and were very happy to see them as we were feeling rather naked and vulnerable. The word came from task force headquarters that we could expect bombardment by a Jap surface fleet almost any time and sure enough, shortly we could see the red anti-aircraft fire of surface ships a moderate distance off, close enough to make us dig our foxholes more than just a little deeper. Everyone complied with my order except for one officer, and he stayed on his cot and said, "What the hell!" He was depressed, and I had recommended that he be rotated back to the States. I chose not to make a big deal of it and took the attitude that if he wanted to take the chance, it was all right with me. Darned if I was going to ask an officer to dig his foxhole if he was too lazy to do it himself. If he had been enlisted, I would have ordered him to dig, but I left him above ground on a litter, which is what we lucky medics used for cots as long as they weren't all used for casualties.

Soon we all got interested enough to get out of our holes and stand up to look and saw the fire of some of our fleet. An air battle was going on. We couldn't have asked for a better Fourth of July fireworks demonstration to celebrate the Holy Day of Christmas. We soon recognized that the Japanese were not going to land, and so we stood easy and watched, our holes forgotten. Shortly, a destroyer pulled in close to shore and lobbed a shell into the burning tanker that was illuminating the entire area.

The ship was sunk in shallow water just off our near shore. I sent a small squad out to salvage some rations as we had been on half fare for a few weeks. They returned with the unbelievable story that there still was an officer on board, and he made them leave at gun point. I found it hard to believe that anyone in his right mind would not know that a ship with no power would soon lose all of its precious freezer stores and anyone who could use them should have been welcome to them. After all, the army and navy were supposed to be on the same side in this particular war.

The next day dawned bright and cheerful with none of the

enemy in sight. Between our little medical installation and the shore, where we had landed, there was a narrow gauge railroad. A small engine hove into sight pulling eight or ten flat cars. I supposed since there was nothing in sight on the island but sugar cane, the cars must have been intended for that purpose. They were loaded in huge piles with Navy dead; the total must have been in the hundreds.

• • •

DID YOU KNOW THAT...

On August 6, 1945, after eleven months of planning and practice, seven planes took off from Tinian to deliver "Little Boy." Whether it would go to Hiroshima, Kokura, or Nagasaki depended on reports from the three weather planes. Colonel Tibbets, carrying the atomic bomb in the Enola Gay, was accompanied by a plane with scientific instruments to measure the intensity of the blast; another to get pictures. A stand-by plane would land at Iwo Jima for use in case Enola Gay had mechanical problems.

Tibbets was given a cyanide capsule for each of the twelve-member crew "...because of the importance of this new weapon and the intensive questioning and possible torture they would have to endure if captured. Each carried a standard service pistol."

After dropping the bomb at Hiroshima, the plane was approximately nine miles away when the shock wave hit. One member of the crew said, "...it felt as if some giant had struck the plane with a telephone pole."

Tibbets reflected: "Awe and astonishment were my feelings as I viewed this scene. Although briefed in advance of the potential effect of this incredible new weapon, I was unprepared for what I saw."

Winston Churchill's quote in part was: "I am surprised that very worthy people, but people who in most cases had no intention of proceeding to the Japanese front themselves, should adopt the position that, rather than throw this bomb, we should have sacrificed a million American and a quarter million British lives in the desperate battles and massacres of an invasion of Japan."[86]

JUNE WANDREY
PORTAGE, MICHIGAN

Army Nurse Corps, 1st Lieutenant

Letter Describing Allach Inmates

June 4, 1945   Allach, Germany

Dearest Family,

I'm on night duty with a hundred corpse-like patients, wrecks of humanity...macerated skin drawn over their bones, eyes sunken in wide sockets, hair shaved off. Mostly Jewish, these tortured souls hardly resemble humans. Their bodies are riddled with diseases. Many have tuberculosis, typhus, enterocolitis, (constant diarrhea) and huge bed sores.

Many cough all night long, as their lungs are in such terrible condition. They break out in great beads of perspiration. Then there is the room of those who are incontinent and irrational. It sounds like the construction crew for the Tower of Babel....Poles, Czechs, Russians, Slavs, Bulgarians, Dutch, Hungarians, Germans. What makes it so difficult is that I understand only a few words. Their gratitude tears at my heart when I do something to make them more comfortable or give them a little food or smile at them....

The odor from the lack of sanitation over the years makes the whole place smell like rotten, rotten sewage. We wear masks constantly although they don't keep out the stench. There are commodes in the middle of the room. Patients wear just pajama shirts as they can't get the bottoms down fast enough to use the commodes. God, where are you?

Making rounds by flashlight is an eerie sensation. I'll hear calloused footsteps shuffling behind me and turn in time to see four semi-nude skeletons gliding toward the commodes. God, where were you?

You have to gently shake some of the patients to see if they are still alive. Their breathing is so shallow, pulse debatable. Many die in their sleep. I carry their bodies back to a storage room, they are very light, just the weight of their demineralized bones. Each time, I breathe a wee prayer for them. God, are you there?

...Our men sprayed the camp area to kill the insects that carried many of the diseases. We were told that the SS guards who controlled the camp used to bring a small pan of food into the ward, and throw it on the floor. When the stronger patients scrambled for it, like starving beasts, they were lashed with a long whip. It's a corner of hell. Too shocked and tired to write anymore.

Love,
June

Reprinted from *Bedpan Commando: The Story of a Combat Nurse During World War II*, pp. 204-6, with permission of 1st Lt. June Wandrey, Army Nurse Corps, WW II, author. Elmore Publishing Co., 348 Rice St., Elmore, OH. 43416-0286.87

MARIE BALANDIS

HOUSTON, TEXAS

WAC, Staff Sergeant
Basic Training: Daytona Beach, Florida
Duty in Pacific

When the Women's Army Auxiliary Corps was authorized by President Roosevelt, I was one of the first on line. After training in Daytona Beach, Florida, Scott Field, Illinois, and San Francisco, my unit sailed for 26 days on a troopship, thousands of us. There was no air conditioning in those days and port-holes had to be closed. We slept on bunks, nine inches of space between our bodies.

Marie Balandis

When landing at Hollandia, New Guinea, nothing was ready for us. Soldiers set up tents, a piece of canvas stretched across the center, which means our legs and upper torsos were exposed. We had only our class A uniforms, which were the clothes we wore in the U.S. We had nothing to wear in the jungles of New Guinea, so soldiers' pants were thrown at us as we got off the trucks taking us to our jungle home. We had to alter the pants with our sewing kits. In those days women were not wearing pants. We shed tears when the general said, "No skirts." Skirts were collected and we didn't see them again.

We had no belts. I used the strap from my shoulder bag; we didn't need a purse in the jungle. I wore a class A uniform dress shirt because the Army did not have anything for us to wear with the man's pants. The shoes were dress laced oxfords; we had no jungle shoes. When going to and from work in the jungle we put our winter galoshes over our dress shoes and sloshed through the jungle mud on the way to quonset huts that were headquarters.

Everyone asks, "What did you DO there?" I was a secretary. Among the 5,000 WACs in Hollandia, there were also truck drivers, telephone operators, cooks, typists. We worked from 7A.M. until 11A.M., went through the jungle back to our tents until 1P.M. Then back to work until 7P.M., seven days a week. We did manage to dance, however, danced our way through the war. There were thousands of soldiers to one WAC. If a soldier couldn't get a date with a WAC, he yelled, "Just wait until Manila!" meaning they would have Filipino girlfriends. That did happen.

Once a month the VA Hospital in my town has a lunch for female war veterans to show appreciation for what we did. Most people don't remember that thousands of servicewomen were sent into the jungles of New Guinea, Leyte, Manila. If you watched TV programs on the 50th anniversary of D Day, you saw what Americans went through for freedom. If you are acquainted with a veteran of WW II, thank him or her for leaving home to go off to suffer and WIN for freedom. We survived. We came home. And we would do it again.

• • •

DID YOU KNOW THAT...

"Sgt. Major Jacob Vouza...a famous scout for the Americans and Allies from the date of the initial landing (Guadalcanal)...was knighted by the King of England after the war for his distinguished service to the Allies." [89]

DOROTHY HINSON BRANDT
ALAMOSA, COLORADO

WAC, Acting Training Sgt.
Basic Training: Ft. Oglethorpe, Georgia
Duty in Europe

I stopped by to enlist after finishing an eight-hour graveyard shift at the local Defense Plant where I inspected tracer bullets. My family had a long history of military service, so enlisting seemed the only patriotic thing for me to do. My parents objected because I was much too young, and I was their only daughter. Although I was only sixteen, I convinced my neighbor to sign an affidavit stating I was really twenty-one years old. As gently as possible I broke the news to my parents.

At Ft. Oglethorpe recruits covered a wide range of age groups and occupations. Bunk mates consisted of a Powers model from New York, a woman logger from Oregon, a minister's daughter, a showgirl from Las Vegas, a set of twins, and a mother-daughter combo from Virginia.

Although I was assigned to interesting posts after Basic Training, I constantly requested overseas duty. Finally, I was ordered to join General Mark Clark's 15th Army Group in Verona, Italy. That would be temporary and the next step for me was Vienna, Austria.

My first glimpse of the destruction of war in Europe was when we arrived by ship at Le Havre, France. Since the French were our Allies, we could not understand the hostility shown towards us. Very quickly we learned that they held us responsible for bombing their town which had been occupied by the Germans.

In Verona we saw hungry children everywhere digging in garbage cans for food. After that I never ate the chocolate bars from my rations but passed them on to someone who needed them much more than I. It was here also that we got acquainted with our first foreign troops. A British Detachment was nearby and they invited us to tea every afternoon.

Vienna was a city struggling to survive after a long, hard war. The four powers (American, British, French, and Russian), each controlled a section of the city. Things were run differently in each sector. We were free to travel in all parts of the city, with a pass, except the Russian sector. That was absolutely forbidden. The Cold War had already begun, but at the time we had no idea what the words meant. Our only free contact with each other was on Sunday afternoons when we would gather in the Park by the Danube River and try to communicate with one another by singing and dancing.

Dorothy Hinson Brandt

I had one memorable encounter with a young Russian when I tried to take a picture of the only bridge left standing over the river. He ran towards me with his gun drawn and yelled, "Forbidden, Forbidden!" Under the circumstances I was quite frightened and, with a big smile, told him that I really had only wanted a picture of him, not the bridge. He smiled in return as we both stood in front of the bridge and smiled together for a photograph.

I had made friends with an Austrian lady who did our washing and ironing. Her son was still in a POW camp, she thought, but there had been no word since the war ended. One day she came running to me with a big smile across her tear-stained face, shouting that her son was coming home. She wanted me to join her for the occasion. Her husband had been killed early in the war and she had no other family near. I scrounged some C-rations to add to the boiled potatoes and we ended up with what we considered a real feast. Her son arrived pale and thin. None of that mattered then; he was home! He and I were both just eighteen.

Once I was allowed to fly on a military plane to Paris, where my brother was stationed. After that I also visited a few days in London. While there I was one of the fortunate few that were selected by the USO to have tea at Buckingham Palace, in the garden, while the King and Queen were present. I thought nothing could top that for the farm girl from North Carolina.

London had suffered horribly during the war but the British with "the stiff upper lip" had survived heroically. You could feel it everywhere. I visited an English family to bring them word from their daughter in Vienna and pictures of their grandchild whom they had never seen. Their only daughter had married an Austrian years before. After the war, with so many sad messages being delivered daily throughout Europe, I felt it a real honor to bring them some good news.

I had by now been overseas long enough to have accumulated 21 seniority points, which were enough for me to be sent home. It was then that I made the decision to inform my Company Commander of my correct age so that my future records would be in proper order. She advised against it because she was afraid I might possibly receive a dishonorable discharge and it might develop into a long, drawn-out, cumbersome process. It turned out to be good advice. After two years, I proudly returned home, with discharge in hand, and an education worth its weight in gold.

After a month's reunion with family and friends, I was approached by an Army Recruiting Sergeant. The Army was recruiting a company of ex-WACs for a one-year assignment to Heidelberg, Germany. All they had to do was issue orders and uniforms for us and we were on our way.

I celebrated my 19th birthday aboard ship on the way to Germany. My assignment was with the AG Records Section with the Third U.S. Army of Occupation.

The war was over and I felt it was time to create a dialog with the German people. I made friends with a young German girl, just my age, who had been a soldier. She had enlisted after her brother had lost both legs in the war. She was bitter in defeat because she had believed in her country and thought she knew what they were fighting for. We spent a lot of time discussing war and how it happened and why. We agreed war is hell, whether you win or lose, and through our friendship we both gained quite an insight into the lives of ordinary people and how war affected them.

We both hoped that it really was a war to end all wars but, sadly, even today wars still continue around the world. We understood that there would probably always have to be soldiers to fight and die, and yet, we could dream that someday we might get to know each other as human beings before the shooting started.

It was in that beautiful city I met another American soldier that was to become my partner for life. The city itself had not been bombed, and at times you could almost forget there had been a terrible war. We spent romantic evenings walking along the Neckar River and watching sunsets from the Heidelberg Castle high above the city. Romantic dreams sometimes do come true.

In April 1947, I left Heidelberg, was discharged and married in July. Sharing the Army experience has made our lives more compatible. After serving three and a half years, with two of them overseas, I was still not old enough to join up. The Army gave me an opportunity to serve my country and an education that money could not buy. Men and women served side by side to reach the common goal of winning the war. I learned to appreciate people I had known as the enemy. I gladly accepted authority and discipline which was necessary to bring a group of diverse recruits together to accomplish a task. Firsthand, I saw the results of following a leader blindly and how that could lead to devastation for a country and its people.

My husband and I are proud to have served our country and would do so again in a minute. I always hope civilians will remember that no one hates war more than a soldier who has seen it firsthand.

• • •

DID YOU KNOW THAT...

When General George S. Patton blazed triumphantly into Linz, Austria, as the end of the war seemed imminent, there was a handmade American flag hanging from a second-floor window where some GIs were housed. Gen. Patton saluted and then asked the GIs on the roadside: "Where in hell did you get that flag?"

Thinking that Patton would be coming and not being able to find a flag, with Yankee ingenuity, "They took the red stripes from a Nazi banner, dyed white cloth blue, and cut white stripes and 48 stars from an Austrian flag." Not being able to sew it themselves, they persuaded an Austrian tailor to do the job.

This handmade flag has been hanging near the portrait of Gen. Patton, "Old Blood and Guts," since 1984, in the U.S. Army Infantry Museum at Fort Benning, Georgia.[90]

DORATHEA ANN HENNINGSEN DAILY

MISHAWAKA, INDIANA

Army WAC, T/3, Clerk Typist, 1943-46
Basic Training: Ft. Des Moines, Iowa
Duty at Camp Shanks, New York

While in basic training, Eleanor Roosevelt visited us. There was a black detachment there at that time, and she came to see that they were treated well. She ate with all of us in the Mess Hall.

At first we were issued men's overcoats that were much too big for most of us and we looked lost in them. Later they traded them for ones that fit us better.

Dorothea Ann Henningsen Daily

When moving to Camp Shanks for duty, our supply sergeant brought a dog on the train as our mascot.

On the first weekend at Camp Shanks a group of paratroopers, slated for overseas, surrounded our barracks and tried to enter. We loved it, but they were quickly sent on their way. They went to Italy and, after parachuting, most were killed.

The first job I had was in the pharmacy at the Station Hospital. Later I was moved to the front office with others who worked for the Commandant of the hospital. Next I was sent to the Station Coordinator's office where they processed troops with shots, exams, etc., for overseas. We had to take turns doing 24-hour duty.

It was very difficult watching the GIs march down the road to the trains that transported them to ships on the Hudson River. One time it was on Christmas Eve and they were singing "I'll be Home for Christmas if Only in My Dreams." We had danced and talked with many of these men just days before at our Service Club.

As a Pfc. I had to take KP duty at the mess hall and also clean the latrines. I was glad when I received my corporal stripes for then I was excused.

New Year's Eve was a fun night; we went to Times Square and, packed in like sardines, waited for midnight. At 12:00A.M. everyone was kissing everyone else and wishing them Happy New Year.

We processed Prisoners of War returning to Germany. On one shipment there was a Russian that committed suicide on the train by hanging himself, as he knew that when he returned, he would be shot.

We also had many wounded Americans returning and they were so very glad to be back in the U.S. Some had no legs or arms, or heads were bandaged, but they could smile for they were so grateful to be back in the U.S. It made one proud to be a WAC, helping in the War.

. . .

DID YOU KNOW THAT...

Ploesti, the Nazis' rich oil region, covering 19 square miles, besides having anti-aircraft guns, was protected with 2,000 smoke generators and high blast walls. These walls, around every installation and refinery, were six feet thick at the bottom, twenty feet high, and two feet wide at the top.

At the end of May-July, 1944, when the Allies reached the climax of their all-out attack on Nazi oil producing centers, German production had dwindled to 20 percent of its minimum requirement. This left the Luftwaffe without enough gasoline to train pilots; Panzer divisions were stranded; and civilians were left with practically no gas or oil.[91]

HELEN O. ERSLEY

ESTERO, FLORIDA

WAAC, Sgt. T/4, Steno, 1942-43
Basic Training: Ft. Des Moines, Iowa
Duty in Algiers, N. Africa

S.O.S. SUSAN

"This is a heck of a time to learn the wireless" thought Rosie, as she scanned the machine.

"Dit-dit-dit" went the keyboard, as she hesitantly tapped out nessages. Not really like the PMGO (Provost Marshal General's Office).

From his station in the adjoining area, Slaybaugh grinned and winked as he said, "I'm glad they gave you this assignment. When things calm down, maybe we can practice our songs."

"Sure—I'll sing 'Only Forever' and the Captain will put us both on report."

Slaybaugh was a breezy, good-looking sailor and Rosie was a WAAC on the Susan B. Anthony which was on its way home to the U.S. from Algiers, N. Africa.

On the deck at night, when the smoking lamp was out, lots of the passengers gathered on deck to sing songs. It was a great relief from the tension.

Just then, their conversation was interrupted by the raucous G.Q. alarm. It sounded like a prehistoric monster.

Sailors were running everywhere, and Slaybaugh shouted as he flew by "Put on your Mae West and helmet!"

The small escort ships churned the water around the "Susan." They were the protectors and the Captain was shouting terse orders to zig-zag. Then it was over. Oil was surfacing where the depth charges had hit their mark.

"Thanks for staying in place," said the Captain. Now, sailor, take this WAAC to her quarters."

As he escorted her safely below, Slaybaugh's last remark was:

"See you on deck tonight. We'll be singing, 'Don't Get Around Much Any More'!"

Helen O. Ersley

• • •

DID YOU KNOW THAT...

The eruption of Mt. Vesuvius caused the loss of scores of Allied planes. The lava crested at fifty feet and flowed at nine hundred feet per hour.92

VIRGINIA KUCH
ST. PETERSBURG, FLORIDA

WAC, T/Sgt., Cryptographer-Secretary, 1942-45
Basic Training: Fort Des Moines, Iowa
Duty in Europe

The two years I spent in the European Theater will never be forgotten, under the command of OSS's General "Wild Bill" Donovan, the memories of friendships shared; unbelievable experiences.

Our first residence, a five-story townhouse in London, England, was close to Hyde Park. When the buzz bombs rained, our residence shook. I was in a room with two other WACs on the third floor. When those bombs came over during the night, we were ordered to the basement; each woman had with her a helmet and blanket. We stayed below until the all clear. This would occur two or three times during a night. Needless to say, we were suffering for sleep. Some of us asked, and were given the option to stay in our rooms. My two roommates decided to stay in our beds. Our windows were criss-crossed with tape; black curtains draped overall. But, we decided to open the windows and push back the curtains; thus we could see the white smoke as the bombs putt-putted in the sky. It was scary because we knew when the putt-putting stopped, the bomb would hit below. The morning after, if we had a chance, another friend and I would hop on our bikes to ride to where we thought damage had been done. I shiver now when I think how foolish we were.

I was in London for nine months when I was selected with three other non-commissioned officers to accompany our WAC Captain on the first lift to France, our first OSS Headquarters at St. Pair sur Mer. We crossed the English Channel on a ship, then transferred by rope ladder to a landing craft; we were dressed in unflattering fatigues. Once we were on land, the five of us huddled together for the night on our shelter halves. When we awoke at daybreak, we realized we were in the middle of a chicken yard.

Nearby was a company of GIs and we were invited to share our first French breakfast with them. We had to scoop out food from huge stainless steel pots into our messkits. Then we were provided transport to Cherbourg for the loan of a weapons carrier so we could continue our journey to the OSS Headquarters down the coast. GIs along our route thought at first that we were nurses, but when they realized we were female army "soldiers," they greeted us with shouts of, "What state are you from? Do you know my sister?" Etc., etc.

Virginia Kuch

Not too far in our travel we approached what had once been a large farm orchard. The field was full of tremendous craters, evidence of the bombings that had taken place. In one of the largest trees, which was bare of leaves, with branches widespread, we saw the body of a big cow being held in those top branches. She had been flung upwards by the force of the bombs. Our driver stopped our vehicle while we looked in amazement at the unbelievable sight before us.

The rest of our trip to Headquarters was uneventful. We were welcomed to our new home, thankful to have arrived safely. We almost immediately assumed our normal duties and stayed there until we left for Paris a week after it was liberated.

• • •

DID YOU KNOW THAT...

There were not enough uniforms for recruited men; some received second-hand ones; some received ones from WW I. Many had WW I helmets. But shoes were fit carefully, sometimes while the recruit was holding two buckets of sand.[93]

IRENE I. WARD
CLAREMORE, OKLAHOMA

WAC, Pfc., Message Center Clerk
Basic Training: Daytona Beach, Florida
Duty in N. Africa

After a few months of being a WAAC, we were told that the Women's Army Auxiliary Corps was to become the WAC (Women's Army Corps), be part of the regular army, and that the Articles of War would apply to us as it did to the men. Since women were not drafted, we did not have to join the WAC. Most of the girls got out, but I stayed.

I soon sailed for North Africa. With all the excitement I didn't notice until we were out in the harbor that a British flag flew overhead. We were on The Empress of Scotland, a converted British pleasure cruiser, formerly The Empress of Japan. Our company and 5000 paratroopers were on the top decks, plus a lot of GIs on the lower deck.

One night an American destroyer wanted our ship to identify itself, and, with no answer, it turned bright lights on us and we shot them out. They made us break radio silence, and to make sure we were safe from German U-boats, they followed us the rest of the way.

We landed in Casablanca and boarded a train for Algiers. Our new home was a large museum with several floors of cold hard marble, an elevator that didn't work and was never fixed. We were a communication company and I was assigned to work in the Message Center of AFHQ (Allied Force Headquarters). General Eisenhower came in and out on the day shift. We rotated three shifts around the clock.

The U.S. Army took over the St. George Hotel and British soldiers and WACs worked one each to a desk. We sat through lecture after lecture on security and what top-secret meant, every day before every shift. I soon learned the importance of my work as I logged in messages from the frontline, listing all our men killed or missing in action each day, airplanes lost, etc. Before I left N. Africa, besides Personnel Clerk, my discharge had three more Army specialty classifications: Clerk Typist, Medical Attendant, and Message Center Clerk.

Irene I. Ward

Time flew by for I liked my work and knew I was doing something important for my country. As for our living conditions, we slept on a double bunk nailed together out of boards. The spring was a flat chicken wire stretched across the corrugated mattress which was stuffed with straw; and two wool blankets issued. When it was cold enough to freeze ice we slept in our flannel pajamas and used the extra one for a pillow. When it was hot as Hades we used the cotton seersucker pajamas. That's when the giant mosquitoes were in season and we had to sleep under an olive-drab tent of netting. But no one wanted to get malaria from those "dive-bombers," and we took our "yellow pills" regularly to help prevent malaria.

A few days after Thanksgiving my husband surprised us all when he showed up in my CO's office. Captain Buetell was very happy for me and wrote out three one-day passes. We were the only couple in NATO (North African Theater of Operation) that was married before we were sent overseas. Amos hitch-hiked on a cargo plane and when he got back to his company, the *Stars and Stripes* wrote an article about his visiting his wife.

From my work I kept up with Amos's Company as they fought their way through Italy.

• • •

DID YOU KNOW THAT...

In a suburb of Luxembourg City (Luxembourg being between Belgium, France, and Germany) there is a military cemetery where 5,076 U.S. troops are buried. Most were killed during the Battle of the Bulge, 1944-45. General George S. Patton is also buried there. The graves are marked with white crosses and Stars of David.94

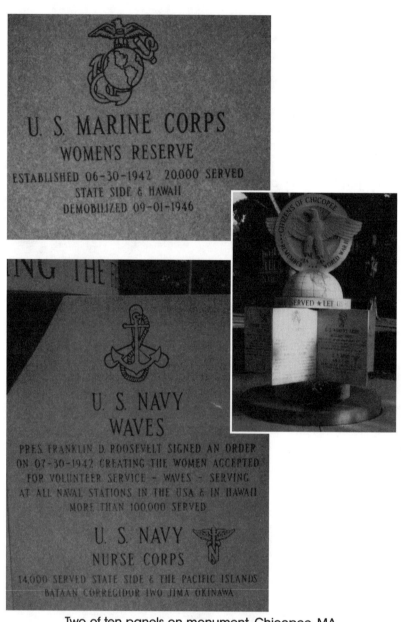

Two of ten panels on monument, Chicopee, MA.
Courtesy Delfo Barabani

Two of ten panels on monument, Chicopee, MA.
Courtesy Delfo Barabani

• • •

DID YOU KNOW THAT...

There were more than 140,000 WACs (Army); 100,000 WAVEs (Navy); 13,000 SPARs (Coast Guard); 23,000 Marine Corps Women's Reserve; 76,000 Army and Navy Nurse Corps; 1,000 Air Force Service Pilots; 50,000 Red Cross.[88]

Women's Bell Tower, dedicated in 1967, as the first memorial to America's female war dead — courtesy Jed Brummer, Cathedral of the Pines, NH

EPILOGUE

On the 50th anniversary of D-Day, as the world was celebrating and honoring World War II veterans, President Clinton said: "...WHEN THEY WERE YOUNG, THEY SAVED THE WORLD."

NAS Museum, Pensacola, FL

Barrancas National Cemetery, Pensacola, FL

FOOTNOTE REFERENCES

1   Charles L. Phillips, Jr., RAIN OF FIRE; B-29s OVER JAPAN, 1945. (Moreno Valley, CA: B-Nijuku Publishing, 1995).

2   Lee Kennett, GI, THE AMERICAN SOLDIER IN WORLD WAR II. (New York: Warner Books, Inc., 1987), p. 184.

3   Ian Traynor, "Unexploded Arms Lurk in Berlin Building Sites," DAYTON DAILY NEWS, March 16, 1997, p. 19A.

4   Naval Air Station Museum, "The American Volunteer Group, The Flying Tigers," Pensacola, Florida.

5   WORLD WAR II CHRONICLES, Vol. 10, No. 2, p. 13, 17; Vol. 9, No. 3, p. 14-5.

6   WORLD WAR II CHRONICLES, Vol. 9, No. 3, p. 16, 18.

7   Hiroo Onoda, NO SURRENDER. MY 30-YEAR WAR. (San Francisco: Kodansha International Ltd., 1974); Richard K. Kolb, "World War II Didn't End in 1945," *VFW*, December, 1995, p. 18.

8   Chris Schneider, "Pushbutton Warfare," WORLD WAR II CHRONICLES, Vol. 9, No. 3, p. 10.

9   Thomas Fleming, "Deliver Us from Evil," READER'S DIGEST, August, 1991, p. 115.

10 Wanda Briggs and John Stang, "A blinding flash of light filled the sky," TRI-CITY HERALD, Tri-Cities, WA, Sunday, August 6, 1995, p. G-6.

11 Wanda Briggs and John Stang, "America was right, says Korean slave in Nagasaki," TRI-CITY HERALD, Tri-Cities, WA, Sunday, August 6, 1995, p. G-8.

12 Wanda Briggs and John Stang, "POW says Nagasaki bomb saved his life," TRI-CITY HERALD, Tri-Cities, WA, Sunday, August 6, 1995, p. G-9.

13 Wanda Briggs and John Stang, "Destroyed city rises from ashes," TRI-CITY HERALD, Tri-Cities, WA, Sunday, August 6, 1995, p. G-12.

14 WORLD WAR II CHRONICLES, Vol. 8, No. 3, p. 18.

15 Ralph G. Martin, THE GI WAR. 1941-45. (Boston: Little, Brown and Company, 1967), p. 71.

16 WORLD WAR II CHRONICLES, Vol. 9, No. 4, p. 18.

17 Matt Hempel, "Requiem for Heroes," THE AMERICAN LEGION MAGAZINE, January, 1997, p. 69; NBC Today Show, April 29, 1996.

18 "The A. J. Miller Company History," THE DAILY EXAMINER, Bellefontaine, Ohio, August 4, 1944; June 8, 1945; June 9, 1953.

19 Benita Saplala Yap, OUR LIVES. (Angeles City, Philippines: Esline Printing Mechanism, 1996).

20 Whayland H. Greene, GRATEFUL SOLDIERS…NOT GREAT SOLDIERS. (Vivian, LA: Whitecotton Printing Co., 1996).

21 "National Cemetery Trivia," VFW AUXILIARY, November, 1996, p. 8.

22 Stanley Sandler, SEGREGATED SKIES. ALL-BLACK COMBAT SQUADRONS OF WORLD WAR II. (Washington, D.C: Smithsonian Institution Press, 1992), p. 159.

23 *Ibid.*, p. 40.

24 "Proudly We Served. The Men of the USS Mason." Video compiled by Mary Pat Kelly, narrated by Ossie Davis. Patriots Point Naval and Maritime Museum. DESA NEWS, May-June, 1996, p. 13.

25 Shelby L. Stanton, ORDER OF BATTLE, U.S. ARMY, WORLD WAR II. (Novato, CA: Presidio Press, 1984), p. 88-89.

26 "The WACO Word," Vol. 17, No. 3, WACO Historical Society, Troy, Ohio, August, 1996.

27 Judy Barrett Litoff and David C. Smith, WE'RE IN THIS WAR, TOO. WORLD WAR II LETTERS FROM AMERICAN WOMEN IN UNIFORM. (New York: Oxford University Press, 1994).

28 Rich Wallace, "Monarch Machine Tool aided war effort; difficult times were destined to follow," THE SIDNEY DAILY NEWS, July 18, 1997, p. 4B.

29 Stephen J. Ackerman, "Sweet Retreat," THE AMERICAN LEGION MAGAZINE, February, 1997, p. 26-8.

30 Eric Hirsimaki, "Ploughshares and Swords," LIMA THE HISTORY, 1986.

31 Richard Osborne, "Bringing the War Back Home," WORLD WAR II CHRONICLES, Vol. 7, No. 6, p. 9.

32 *Ibid.*, p. 8.

33 Eugene Rachlis, THEY CAME TO KILL. (New York: Random House, 1961).

34 E. Bartlett Kerr, SURRENDER AND SURVIVAL. THE EXPERIENCE OF AMERICAN POWs IN THE PACIFIC 1941-45. (New York: William Morrow and Company, Inc., 1985).

35 Sandler, *Op.cit.*, p. 18.

36 WORLD WAR II CHRONICLES, Vol. 8, No. 3, p. 18.

37 Stan Cohen, THE FORGOTTEN WAR. (Misssoula, Montana: Pictorial Histories Publishing Company, 1981), p. 2.

38 Brian Garfield, THE THOUSAND-MILE WAR. WORLD WAR II IN ALASKA AND
      THE ALEUTIANS. (Garden City, New York: Doubleday and Company,
      Inc., 1969), p. 135.

39 *Ibid.*, p. 17.

40 Garfield, *Op.cit.*, p. 44.

41 Naval Historical Center, THE ALEUTIANS CAMPAIGN. JUNE 1942- AUGUST
      1943. (Washington: Department of the Navy, 1993. Originally pub-
      lished: Washington Publications Branch, Office of Naval Intelligence,
      U.S. Navy, 1945), p. 19.

42 Dean Kohlhoff, WHEN THE WIND WAS A RIVER. ALEUT EVACUATION IN
      WORLD WAR II. (Seattle, Washington: University of Washington Press
      (in association with Aleutian/Pribilof Islands Assoc., Anchorage,
      1995), p. 45.

43 Garfield, *Op.cit.*, p. 111.

44 Garfield, *Op.cit.*, p. 69.

45 Heath Twichell, NORTHWEST EPIC. THE BUILDING OF THE ALASKA
      HIGHWAY. (New York: St. Martin's Press, 1992), p. 283.

46 Garfield, *Op.cit.*, p. 209.

47 Garfield, *Op.cit.*, p. 247.

48 Garfield, *Op.cit.*, p. 262.

49 Garfield, *Op.cit.*, p. 265.

50 Naval Historical Center, *Op.cit.*, p. 117.

51 Naval Historical Center, *Op.cit.*, p. 123.

52 Garfield, *Op.cit.*, p. 308.

53 Kohlhoff, *Op.cit.*, p. 116.

54 Marilyn George, SENIOR VOICE, November, 1990, p. B-15-19.

55 Kohlhoff, *Op.cit.*, p. 167-8.

56 George, *Op.cit.*, p. B-19.

57 Kohlhoff, *Op.cit.*, p. 170.

58 Muktuk Marston, MEN OF THE TUNDRA. ESKIMOS AT WAR.
      (New York: October House Inc., 1969), p. 42.

59 Marston, *Op.cit.*, p. 43.

60 Marston, *Op.cit.*, p. 36.

61 Marston, *Op.cit.*, p. 186.

62 Stan Cohen, THE FORGOTTEN WAR, Vol. 2. (Missoula, Montana: Pictorial Histories Publishing Company, 1988), p. 3.

63 *Ibid.*, p. 3.

64 Naval Air Station, Pensacola, Florida.

65 Ray Davis, THE STORY OF RAY DAVIS. (Varina, NC: Research Triangle Publishing in association with Korean War Veterans Memorial Dedication Foundation, Inc., 1995).

66 WORLD WAR II CHRONICLES, Vol. 8, No. 6, p. 22-23.

67 WORLD WAR II CHRONICLES, Vol. 9, No. 3, p. 20.

68 Harry Smith, CBS NEWS, January 31, 1997.

69 Norm Hatch, LEATHERNECK, February, 1995.

70 "K-Ships," Naval Air Station, Pensacola, Florida. Dorothy Burns Peterson, "Discovering Our History, Hitchcock, The U.S. Naval Air Station," BAY WATCHER, Vol. 1, No. 12, August 11, 1994. Bill Parks, "Guardian Angels of the Seas," THE AMERICAN LEGION MAGAZINE, January, 1997, p. 46-7.

71 FRANKLIN CHRONICLE, Franklin, Ohio, October 16, 1990. Eric Hammel, "GUADALCANAL. THE CARRIER BATTLES. CARRIER OPERATIONS IN THE SOLOMONS AUGUST-OCTOBER, 1942." (New York: Crown Publishers, Inc., 1987).

72 Marion L. Shinn (from diary of Gail Diamond), "The First Patrol of the Scorpion (SS-278)," POLARIS, Vol. 40, No. 3, June, 1996, p. 14-17.

73 Steve Kluger, YANK, THE ARMY WEEKLY. (New York: St. Martin's Press, 1991), p. 16.

74 "Copeland—Hands on Today, Vision for tomorrow, 1921-1996." "Helping 'Cool Off' the Axis," Copeland Refrigeration Corporation, Sidney, Ohio.

75 Melanie Wiggins, TORPEDOES IN THE GULF: GALVESTON AND THE U-BOATS. (College Station, Texas: Texas A & M University Press, 1995). WORLD WAR II CHRONICLES, Vol. 8, No. 6; Vol. 10, No. 2.

76 Kennett, *Op.cit.*, p. 116.

77 Warner Olivier and J. V. Harris, "Sidney's Answer to the Manpower Problem," THE SATURDAY EVENING POST, March 27, 1943, p. 28.

78 VFW, December, 1996, p. 36.

79 Marion L. Shinn, PACIFIC PATROL, A WW II SUBMARINE SAGA. (Lewiston, Idaho: Triad Publishing Company, 1993).

80 Richard F. Newcomb, ABANDON SHIP! DEATH OF THE USS INDIANAPOLIS. (New York: Henry Holt & Co., Inc., 1958), p. 28-44.

81 "Bride and Baby Brigade Sets Sail," VFW AUXILIARY, July- August, 1996, p. 22-23.

82 WORLD WAR II CHRONICLES, Vol. 8, No. 5, p. 23.

83 WORLD WAR II CHRONICLES, Vol. 10, No. 2, p. 12.

84 Glen Infield, DISASTER AT BARI. (New York: Bantam Books, 1988— Macmillan Edition, 1971).

85 Robert Frick, Sidney, Ohio. Interview.

86 Paul W. Tibbets, FLIGHT OF THE ENOLA GAY. (Reynoldsburg, Ohio: Buckeye Aviation Book Co., , 1989), p. 207, 227, 6, 303.

87 June Wandrey, BEDPAN COMMANDO: THE STORY OF A COMBAT NURSE DURING WORLD WAR II. (Elmore, OH: Elmore Publishing Co., 1989), p. 204-6.

88 Litoff and Smith, Op.cit., p. 29-30.

89 William Chaney, "The Guadalcanal Campaign," WORLD WAR II CHRONICLES, Vol. 8, No. 3, p. 9.

90 Valerie A. Zehl, "Rollie Noble's Flag," THE AMERICAN LEGION MAGAZINE, p. 20.

91 Charles E. Francis, TUSKEGEE AIRMEN. (Boston: Bruce Humphries, Inc., 1955), p. 95-100.

92 Sandler, Op.cit., p. 59.

93 Kennett, Op.cit., p. 27-33.

94 Tom Bross, "Little Luxembourg's Big Appeal," AAA TODAY, Vol. 9, No. 5, Shelby Co. Motor Club (Ohio), September/October, 1996, p. 13-15.

ADDITIONAL BIBLIOGRAPHY

ALASKA GEOGRAPHIC. UNALASKA/DUTCH HARBOR. The Quarterly, Vol. 18, No. 4. Anchorage, AK: The Alaska Geographic Society, 1991.

Armament Museum, Niceville, FL.

Beyerlein, Tom. "'Thank you, America.'" DAYTON DAILY NEWS, October 6, 1996.

Blum, Howard. WANTED! THE SEARCH FOR NAZIS IN AMERICA. Greenwich, CT: Fawcett Crest Books, 1977.

Brady, Patrick H. "Where Cynics Fail, Patriots Prevail. THE AMERICAN LEGION MAGAZINE, January, 1998.

Breuer, William. DEVIL BOATS, THE PT WAR AGAINST JAPAN. Novato, CA: Presidio Press, 1987.

"Capacity crowds visit campus for Schwartz series on the Holocaust." MUSKINGUM COLLEGE BULLETIN, Summer, 1995.

Cohen, Stan. THE FORGOTTEN WAR, A PICTORIAL HISTORY OF WORLD WAR II IN ALASKA AND NORTHWESTERN CANADA, Vol 2. Missoula, MT: Pictorial Histories Publishing Company, 1988.

Cohen, Stan. THE FORGOTTEN WAR, A PICTORIAL HISTORY OF WORLD WAR II IN ALASKA AND NORTHWESTERN CANADA, Vol. 3. Missoula, MT: Pictorial Histories Publishing Company, 1992.

Collins, Larry and Dominique Lapierre. IS PARIS BURNING? New York: Pocket Books, Inc., 1965.

Cutler, Don. "Patton." HIGHWAYS, June, 1997.

"Dedicated to all women veterans past, present, future." OHIO LEGION NEWS, August/September, 1997.

Epstein, Ron. "War Heroes." HIGHWAYS, April, 1996.

Fahey, James J. PACIFIC WAR DIARY. New York: Kensington Publishing Corporation, 1963.

Flake, Carol. "Atomic War Fare." TEXAS MONTHLY, Vol. 23, Issue 4, April, 1995.

"Four Faiths, One Mission." THE AMERICAN LEGION MAGAZINE, February, 1997.

Frank, Pat and Joseph D. Harrington. RENDEZVOUS AT MIDWAY. USS YORKTOWN AND THE JAPANESE CARRIER FLEET. New York: Warner Books, Inc., 1968.

Freeman, Elmer A. THOSE NAVY GUYS AND THEIR PBYs. THE ALEUTIAN SOLUTION. Spokane, WA: Kedging Publishing Company, 1991.

Gasior, Anne. "War brides en route...again." DAYTON DAILY NEWS, May 5, 1996.

Gavin, Gen. James M. ON TO BERLIN. BATTLES OF AN AIRBORNE COMMANDER 1943-1946. New York: Bantam Books, 1979.

Glasheen, Leah K. "U.S. military women to be honored—finally." NRTA BULLETIN, Vol. 38, No. 5, May, 1997.

Graham, John. "Houston students learn of war from veterans." THE SIDNEY DAILY NEWS (OH), December 4, 1997.

Glover, Charles E. "'Vinegar Joe' too tart for Chiang." DAYTON DAILY NEWS, October 30, 1994.

Gross, Linden. "Steven Spielberg's Close Encounter With the Past." READER'S DIGEST, April, 1996.

Guggenheim, Charles. "D-Day," THE AMERICAN EXPERIENCE. Idaho PBS, May 19, 1996.

Harrington, Herman G. "History Upheld." THE AMERICAN LEGION, August, 1995.

Huffman, Dale. "'Couldn't stop the tears.'" DAYTON DAILY NEWS, October 20, 1996.

Kessler, Ronald. MOSCOW STATION. New York: Pocket Books, 1989.

Knappe, Siegfried with Ted Brusaw. SOLDAT. REFLECTIONS OF A GERMAN SOLDIER, 1936-1949. New York: Dell Publishing, 1992.

Markovna, Nina. "Nina's Journey" (condensed). READER'S DIGEST, September, 1990.

Mitchell, Robert, Collector. THE CAPTURE OF ATTU. TALES OF WORLD WAR II IN ALASKA. Anchorage, AK: Alaska Northwest Publishing Company, 1984. (Originally published in Adak by Intelligence Section Field Force Headquarters).

Murphy, Audie. TO HELL AND BACK. New York: Bantam Books, 1979.

"Navy commissions ship named for slain Sullivans." DAYTON DAILY NEWS, April 20, 1997.

"Operation Commemoration." OHIO LEGION NEWS, January/February, 1996.

"POW/MIAs are not forgotten." VFW AUXILIARY, April/May, 1997.

Rearden, Jim. "Aleutian Change." ALASKA, September, 1996.

Ryan, Cornelius. JUNE 6, 1944. THE LONGEST DAY. New York: Pocket Books, 1967.

Schultz, Duane. THE MAVERICK WAR. CHENNAULT AND THE FLYING TIGERS. New York: St. Martin's Press, 1987.

"Security Specialists Score World Hot Spots." OHIO VFW NEWS, March/April, 1996.

Shoemaker, Lloyd R. THE ESCAPE FACTORY. THE STORY OF MIS X. New York: St. Martin's Press, 1990.

Stilwell, Joseph W. THE STILWELL PAPERS. New York: MacFadden- Bartell Corporation, 1948.

Simon, Mayo. "No Medals for Joe." READER'S DIGEST, December, 1990.

"Tug of War." THE AMERICAN LEGION MAGAZINE, December, 1996.

Ullmer, Katherine. "Inventor, pilot meet after 51 years." DAYTON DAILY NEWS, July 21, 1996.

"The United States Flag." OHIO VFW NEWS, May, 1997.

Vance-Watkins, Lequita and Aratani Mariko, Editors and translators. WHITE FLASH/BLACK RAIN, WOMEN OF JAPAN RELIVE THE BOMB. Minneapolis, MN: Milkweed Editions, 1995.

Verges, Marianne. ON SILVER WINGS. THE WOMEN AIRFORCE SERVICE PILOTS OF WORLD WAR II, 1942-44. New York: Ballantine Books, 1991.

Wadsworth, Kent. "Tin Can Odyssey." THE AMERICAN LEGION MAGAZINE, December, 1996.

"War History of The USS Horace A. Bass (APD-124). DESA NEWS, May-June, 1996.

Wright-Patterson Air Force Museum, Dayton, OH.